THEORETICAL AND PRACTICAL PEDAGOGY OF MATHEMATICAL MUSIC THEORY

Music for Mathematics and Mathematics for Music, From School to Postgraduate Levels

THEORETICAL AND PRACTICAL PEDAGOGY OF MATHEMATICAL MUSIC THEORY

Music for Mathematics and Mathematics for Music, From School to Postgraduate Levels

Editors

Mariana Montiel
Georgia State University, USA

Francisco Gómez
Universidad Politécnica de Madrid, Spain

World Scientific

NEW JERSEY • LONDON • SINGAPORE • BEIJING • SHANGHAI • HONG KONG • TAIPEI • CHENNAI • TOKYO

Published by

World Scientific Publishing Co. Pte. Ltd.
5 Toh Tuck Link, Singapore 596224
USA office: 27 Warren Street, Suite 401-402, Hackensack, NJ 07601
UK office: 57 Shelton Street, Covent Garden, London WC2H 9HE

Library of Congress Cataloging-in-Publication Data
Names: Montiel, Mariana. | Gómez, Francisco, 1965–
Title: Theoretical and practical pedagogy of mathematical music theory :
music for mathematics and mathematics for music, from school to postgraduate levels /
edited by: Mariana Montiel (Georgia State University, USA) and
Francisco Gómez (Universidad Politécnica de Madrid, Spain).
Description: New Jersey : World Scientific, [2018]
Identifiers: LCCN 2018016233 | ISBN 9789813228344 (hc : alk. paper)
Subjects: LCSH: Music--Mathematics. | Music theory--Mathematics.
Classification: LCC ML3800 .T447 2018 | DDC 781.01/51--dc23
LC record available at https://lccn.loc.gov/2018016233

British Library Cataloguing-in-Publication Data
A catalogue record for this book is available from the British Library.

Cover image: Dr. Maria Mannone

For any available supplementary material, please visit
https://www.worldscientific.com/worldscibooks/10.1142/10665#t=suppl

Desk Editors: V. Vishnu Mohan/Tan Rok Ting

Typeset by Stallion Press
Email: enquiries@stallionpress.com

Printed in Singapore

Introduction

Mathematical Music Theory has a trajectory both as an area of scientific research and as a pedagogical endeavor. As in any specialized subject, there are aspects that lend themselves to rapid comprehension and can be transmitted without needing sophisticated knowledge, whereas other concepts require previous preparation in either or both disciplines. In particular, there is a gamut of relevant mathematics that intersects with different musicological perspectives; in addition, there is no unequivocal separation between mathematics and music, as there is not in areas such as computer science and physics.

During the past 40 years, mathematical music theory arose in music and mathematics departments. In music pedagogy, the need to analyze patterns of modern composition produced Musical Set Theory, and the use of Group Theory and other modern mathematical structures became as common as the application of mathematics in engineering or chemistry departments. Mathematicians found stimulating ideas when exploring applications to established musical relations. Mathematics students have seen, in these courses, how their accumulated knowledge of abstract ideas can be applied to an important human activity while reinforcing their dexterity in mathematics. Similarly, general education courses for those without a sophisticated background in either subject have been developed at the university level, and for high school and popular audiences.

Courses for high school teachers and students of mathematics educations have also played a role in these pedagogical endeavors. The courses illustrated in this volume, together with the projects and materials that have been developed for them, were implemented in the USA, China, Ireland, Spain, France, and Australia. Our objective is to expose the motivation and content of some of these courses while contributing concrete materials to those interested readers.

We insist that this volume could have been organized in many ways and we ask the reader for benevolence if he thinks that the presentation should have been carried out differently or that another sequence would have been better. This said, the organization of this book and its chapters will be as follows.

Section I is dedicated to interdisciplinary courses carried out in liberal arts colleges in the USA. In this case, the participants are usually not mathematics or music majors and the objective of this kind of course is to approximate the student to both disciplines in the context of general culture, an important aspect of the liberal arts educational style. (Hall, Johnson, Hughes, Kochavi). Section II groups courses specifically designed for students of mathematics and music that have been carried out in the USA, Australia, and China (Montiel, Cohn). Section III is focused on pre-university education and on material designed both for children and for teacher courses, in Australia, Spain, and France. In this section, there are also two chapters on popularization work, one which reports on activities carried out during the annual *Maths Week* in Ireland and the other that addresses the importance of *concerférences* (shows with both a taste of mathematics and music) and contributes ideas and materials for their development (Gómez, Amiot, Hilton, Calilhanna and Milne, Wilhelmi and Montiel). Section IV picks up again the subject of non-specialized students in the first years of university (Mannone).

In the first chapter of Section I, Hall describes material that she uses in her university-level, general education mathematics course "Sounding Number: Music and Mathematics from Ancient to Modern Times". Topics covered in the course include musical combinatorial problems from Ancient India, rhythm patterns and their transformations, the physical properties of musical sound, consonant intervals and scale construction, spectral analysis, and musical form and composition.

The course is designed for students from a variety of backgrounds and majors. There is no prerequisite, and the course satisfies the university's math requirement for some majors. The typical student in the class has limited math skills and has not taken calculus. Some students have experience in music or audio recording, while others have no musical background. The ability to read music is neither required nor taught.

In her chapter, Hall presents an excerpt from the text that she is writing for this class. Mathematical topics covered include modular congruence, equivalence classes, and actions on a set. Musical topics include meter, rhythm patterns, and transformations. This material may be covered in three or four weeks. She introduces rhythm before pitch because she has found that rhythm is easier for non-musicians to grasp. Modular congruence and transformations are also applicable to pitch, and when the subject of pitch classes and transposition is taught later on in the course, this section is revisited.

In Chapter 2 of Section I, Johnson addresses the following situation. Although mathematical music theory provides a rich environment for interdisciplinary courses for non-music majors, discrepancies between the inevitably and widely varied musical backgrounds and experiences of students can be a difficult obstacle to overcome. Some students attracted to such a course may have strong musical backgrounds developed through instrumental or vocal lessons, traditional ensemble experiences, participation in popular music groups of diverse styles and shapes, and even formal instruction in music theory. Other students, on the other hand, may have little to no prior musical experience on which to draw, yet become attracted to a course of this kind because of their mathematical interests or backgrounds, or due to their love of music. The result is a diverse collection of students, some of whom already know intervals, scales, and chords, and others of whom cannot name a note. Some students can relate course activities to their experiences on an instrument, while others are not personally familiar with any instrument. Although non-music major courses in mathematical music theory also contain students with a wide range of experiences in mathematics, this diversity in mathematical backgrounds seems easier to overcome than the musical disparity because the range of differences is less acute and often can be overcome relatively easily as the course progresses due to the nature of the mathematical material or the pacing of the introduction of new concepts.

Johnson, widely known among those who have carried out pedagogy in the context of mathematical music theory for his text *Foundations of Diatonic Theory: A Mathematically Based Approach to Music Fundamentals*, takes his educational efforts one step further by considering the aspects mentioned above. The chapter contains examples and exercises that will be useful for those who are thinking about carrying out a similar endeavor.

In Chapter 3 of Section I, Hughes explains that every two years since 2009, he has offered an undergraduate course entitled *Mathematics in Music*. The main impetus for the course was a desire to introduce students to some of the principal ways mathematics is currently being used in the creation and study of music. In designing the course, he placed a high priority on interdisciplinary authenticity, focusing on clear and effective application of mathematical approaches and tools to problems of mainstream interest to music practitioners. He also sought to present the course at a level midway between the popular level (which assumes no prerequisite knowledge of either discipline) and the research level (which assumes graduate-level familiarity with both disciplines). A constant guiding principle of approach was the facilitation of connections between students' actual experience of music with mainstream use of mathematics in musical research. His own review of contemporary scholarly literature on connections between mathematics and music eventually led him to design the course around six main units: Fundamentals, Acoustics, Tuning, Theory and Analysis, Composition, and Education.

In Chapter 4 of Section I, Kochavi explains that in the math–music course he teaches at Swarthmore College, the focus is on the intersection of the two disciplines as examples of lines of intellectual inquiry, modes of understanding and organizing the world, and foundational approaches to conceptualizing and contextualizing thought and knowledge. That is, the course is designed as an introduction to studies in the liberal arts tradition, using music and mathematics as a rich playing field for relatively straightforward questions prompting discussions, if not always answers. The population of students in the course generally falls into two (not necessarily discrete) categories: (1) music students who are interested in finding out more about the connections between mathematics and the art form they practice, and (2) math and science students who are interested in applying their knowledge to a field that they are connected to informally (though often passionately).

Kochavi's interdisciplinary course aims to broaden the scope of inquiry far beyond the boundaries of both math and music, and his chapter focuses on his classroom treatment of concept of loudness as a case study. Loudness is a perceptual phenomenon that is only loosely associated with the physics of sound. Using the epistemological frame of phenomenology, Kochavi argues that we can "bracket" the physics of sound intensity to uncover the experiential concept of loudness (which is what we as musicians and music lovers care most about), itself a moving target in the wide range of human perceptual experience. The methods we use to "freeze" that target (involving phons and sones) exclude and implicitly reject the validity of the experience of the non-normative listener. What does it say that we use these idealized measures to officially represent the "truths" of human hearing? Are there other realms in which we equate the "normal" with the "human"? Getting at these profound questions in the classroom requires a thorough understanding of the math and the music, so this type of course is ideally situated to frame discussions delving into topics seemingly far afield, emerging from the intersecting fields of philosophy, neuroscience, psychology, and disability studies among others.

In Chapter 5 of Section II, Montiel describes two university courses that integrated mathematics and music. One took place at the East Chinese University of Science and Technology (ECUST) and included mathematics and music students from China and the United States. The other was a pilot course that arose in the context of a course pairing experiment, and consisted in a collaboration between the *Postonal Analysis* course corresponding to the School of Music and the *Mathematical Music Theory* course offered at the Mathematics and Statistics Department, both at Georgia State University (GSU). This pilot experiment was the result of a selection process in a call for proposals related to interdisciplinary course pairing. This chapter consists in an explanation of the genesis of both courses, a presentation of their antecedents and objectives, a description of the contents, examples of work done by the participants, and concrete examples of materials that can be implemented. Precise characteristics that are needed for the collaboration to be successful and enhance the learning process in both disciplines are identified.

The subjects are clustered under the categories of *symmetries and transformations, groups and transformational theory, signature transformations and spelled heptachords*, as well as a section dedicated to aspects of *mathematical analysis of postonal styles.* Each section is accompanied by abundant examples, diagrams, and exercises directed at students of both disciplines. Indeed, a fair amount of the examples were created by the students themselves in the process of the courses, and the author wishes to give them their well deserved credit in the acknowledgements.

In Chapter 6 of Section II, Cohn presents a novel approach to traditional atonal theory and advances a pedagogical program that models small cyclic systems before teaching the usual 12-element chromatic system. The central properties, relations, and protocols of atonal theory (complementation, inclusion, invariance, transpositional equivalence, set classification and labeling, maximal evenness) are introduced in the smallest cyclic system to which they apply. All cyclic systems of 2–9 elements have at least one familiar musical application, modeling beat-class (rhythmic) cycle, pentatonic and diatonic scales. By the time students have scaled up to a 12-element universe, they are technically prepared to explore it, and to appreciate its special properties. Along the way, they have learned a model of meter, an otherwise under-theorized aspect of music pedagogy. Cohn presents abundant examples that, while logically arising from real music constructions, have not been used to illustrate the ideas of atonal theory that habitually uses the 12-tone chromatic scale as a starting point, not results of previous initiation. Included is a section of exercises specific to this novel pedagogical concept in the teaching of atonal analysis.

In Chapter 7 of Section III, Gómez presents a mixture of mathematical theory of divisibility and musical theory of rhythm blended in such a way that it can be used for both mathematics teachers seeking to illustrate mathematical concepts through musical ideas and music teachers seeking to illustrate musical concepts through mathematical ideas. The lessons originated in a show presented by the author of this chapter and colleagues at the math-appreciation event *Maths Week Ireland*. The show is divided into three sections; in the first section, concepts on divisibility (exact division, division with remainder, greatest common divisor, Euclid algorithm) are developed; in the second section, basic concepts such as time span, pulse, rhythm, and timeline are presented to the audience; in the third section, the *matherhythm* section, the evenness principle is used to compose rhythms that all together will make up a musical piece. The lessons describe here are suited to high school and college audiences. Exercises for each section are provided.

In Section III, Chapter 8, Amiot claims that the discipline of mathematical music theory often suffers from ignorance or, worse, misknowledge. A good way, he argues, to get the message through about the importance of the relationship between math and music is to put on a "concerférence", a French term coined to designate anything between a talk-cum-music and a concert cum fairly detailed scientific explanations. This format of exposition is quite versatile, and the content can be adapted to a wide range of publics. In the chapter, Amiot relates a choice of such experiences in order to exemplify which selected topics can be fruitfully exposed to whom, with an eye on helping would-be *concerférencers* (or mathemusic speakers in general) in developing their own endeavors. The topics of Hamiltonian cycles in the Tonnetz and rhythmic tiling are presented in some detail.

In Chapter 9 of Section III, Hilton and Milne discuss what software applications offer to the practice of mathematical music theory and, more broadly, to music education. Traditionally, mathematical music theory uses the formalism of mathematics (such as equations and graphs) to represent and produce models of musical phenomena that serve explanatory, predictive, or generative purposes. By contrast, computer-based models use interactive elements to represent and model musical phenomena within a software environment.

These two approaches support quite distinct ways of working, thinking, and learning. The former entails a slow analytic process, constrained by step-wise workings and calculations, and the latter allows for faster and more intuitive experimentation and hypothesis testing. While for most learners, learning to model musical phenomena in purely mathematical terms is cumbersome and challenging, well-designed software may enable such model-based learning to become more accessible and fluent. By describing relevant mathematical music theory concepts and their software representations, Milne and Hilton argue that software can uniquely contribute to the visualization and sonification of challenging concepts in mathematical music theory, helping students learn them more intuitively, and in ways that are more likely to support transfer to real musical situations.

In this same chapter, Andrea Calilhanna — a practicing music teacher — gives a qualitative account of how introducing software based on mathematical representations positively influenced her teaching practice and her students' learning. In these case studies, the population consists of middle-level piano students, and it is a novelty to see how computer programs based on notions from mathematical music theory are incorporated into the piano teacher's practice so successfully. In this chapter as well, concrete exercises used to illustrate the process are available to the readers of this volume.

In Chapter 10 of Section III, Wilhelmi and Montiel explain that the search for novel ways to convey mathematical concepts is a constant for pedagogues at all educational levels. They find that interdisciplinarity in the context of mathematics education is referred to more and more as a way of reinforcing mathematical content. The use of music, in particular, as a context for mathematics education at different school and university levels has been reported upon, but little can be found in the context of preservice teacher training.

The chapter is a report on various study sessions concerning Euclidean rhythms and permutations for future mathematics teachers at the secondary level in Spain (FDMS) with a solid technical-scientific background but very little or no background in music. The training sessions relied on the musical intuition of the FDMS, and the objective was to model this informal intuition by using concepts, processes, and meanings in agreement with the official school standards that teachers need to comply with.

In the first section, they explain the musical and mathematical content of the sessions, as well as their interrelations. The second section describes the theoretical and methodological frameworks used. In the third section, all aspects of the experiment are described, including the sample, the instruments employed, and the explicit objectives; in the fourth section, the results are presented and discussed. Finally, specific conclusions are established and some implications for teaching are offered. In the first and third sections, specific exercises are described in detail, with the hope that they can serve as didactical material in future courses, as well as tools that will permit the repetition of the experiment, contributing to the establishment of mathemusical content in the training of future secondary level teachers.

In Chapter 11 of Section IV, Mannone proposes an effective approach to teaching mathematical music theory to upper-level high school or freshmen and sophomore university-level students, where it is important to take into account the motivations of the learner and profit from the professionalism and empathy of the teacher. In fact, the teacher, according to Mannone, needs to be able to catch and solve difficulties, even unvoiced, of the student and remove prejudices related to the two fields, math and music, fields in themselves that are often attractive but feared. The duties of the teacher, according to this author, include the facilitation and improvement of the specific languages by introducing and using a connecting language between the two fields. Moreover, the successful teacher will show students some examples and applications by accurately choosing the degree of difficulty, and not creating discrepancies and discomfort between the acquired knowledge and the newly proposed concepts. Indeed, cognitive discomfort reduces the probability of success.

Mannone considers two case studies to show how abstract ideas can stimulate thinking and creativity and, at the same time, can be fun. The examples relate music theory and music composition to combinatorics and category theory through the Rubik's cube and the *scales* of the armor of an endangered species, the pangolin.

Finally, we want to reiterate our heartfelt appreciation to all the authors that have brought this project to fruition. Each one of them, apart from being pedagogues with vast experience (given that the chapters are based on their concrete experiences and that they contribute with the corresponding didactic materials) are top-level researchers in such varied fields as music theory, music cognition, software development, pure and applied mathematics, and mathematics education. We hope that this volume will be very useful to all teachers and professors who are convinced of the importance of this interdisciplinary endeavor and that wish to implement a session, a unit, or an entire course.

Mariana Montiel
Francisco Gómez

About the Editors

Mariana Montiel is Associate Professor at Georgia State University. Her research revolves around Mathematical Music Theory and frequently she carries out interdisciplinary work with music theorists and computer scientists. Simultaneously she cultivates an interest in pedagogical aspects and, in particular, in the use of abstract and symbolic representations, common to both disciplines, mathematics and music.

Francisco Gómez is a Mathematics Professor at Technical University of Madrid (Universidad Politécnica de Madrid). He teaches mathematics for computer scientists. He does research on Mathematical Music Theory with an emphasis on rhythm, emotions and improvisation. He is also involved in the popularization of this field.

Contents

Section I

Chapter 1

Rhythm and Transformation

Rachel Hall

Department of Mathematics, Saint Joseph's University,
5600 City Avenue, Philadelphia, PA 19131, USA
rhall@sju.edu

1.1. In the Beginning Was the Beat

Rhythm is part of the human experience. Even before birth, we hear the regular pulse of our mothers' heartbeats. The rhythms of nature cause us to experience time as simultaneously linear (progressing forward) and cyclic (repeating, as on a clock). This dual sense of linear and cyclic time is fundamental to most music.

Musical rhythm operates on multiple levels. A *rhythm* is an audible pattern of drum hits or note onsets, while a *meter* is a framework in which musical "events" — sounds and silences — occur. In traditional and popular music, a rhythmic pattern, or *timeline*, that is repeated throughout a piece is intermediate between a rhythm and a meter. This chapter also covers transformations used by composers to vary rhythms and create new ones.

1.2. Metered Time

Meter is similar to the system of hours, minutes, and seconds in that it determines a hierarchy among divisions of time. Although Western classical musicians associate meter with time signature, meter, in its broadest sense, is a psychological construction that reflects our perception of and engagement with rhythmic organization [4]. This concept of meter applies cross-culturally to forms of music with a regular pulse.

Meter is indicated by visual cues in some forms of music. Watch the video "16 beat tala — Indian Rhythms" [5]. In this video, the performer's repeated hand gestures indicate the tāla, or meter. These same gestures accompany any piece using this tāla. The gestures used in Western classical conducting also help performers to synchronize, or *entrain*, their perceptions of rhythmic structure.

Underlying meter is a steady pulse, or *tactus*, marking the times when someone would naturally tap their foot. When tapping along with a piece of music, we expect some musical "event" to happen at every tap. Normally, this event is something we can hear (a drum hit or the beginning of a note, for example), but sometimes there is a silence — a *rest*.

The tactus acts as a ruler that measures musical time. Unlike seconds or minutes, the length of the fundamental unit of time, or *beat*, is chosen relative to a particular piece of music, so that the time between the beginnings (*onsets*) of successive pulses in the tactus has a duration of one beat or some fixed whole number of beats. The *tempo*, or speed, of the tactus is measured in beats per minute. Tempos of about 120 beats per minute are typical for pop songs, while a comfortable walking tempo is around 100 beats per minute.

Beats are grouped into units of time called *measures*, or *bars*, just as seconds are grouped into minutes. Musicians normally count beats by their position in the measure and use a vertical line to mark the beginning of each measure. Figure 1.1 represents counting in four beats per measure, which is the most common grouping used in Western music.

Beats may also be subdivided. Divisions into two, three, or four equal parts are common. Figure 1.2 shows a 4-beat measure with each numbered count subdivided into two parts (second line) or four parts (third line), while Fig. 1.3 shows division of the beat into three parts

| 1 2 3 4 | 1 2 3 4 | 1 2 3 4 |

Fig. 1.1. Counting in four beats per measure.

1				2				3				4			
1		&		2		&		3		&		4		&	
1	e	&	a	2	e	&	a	3	e	&	a	4	e	&	a

Fig. 1.2. A 4-beat measure (first line) with duple (second line) and quadruple (third line) subdivisions.

1			2			3			4		
1	e	a	2	e	a	3	e	a	4	e	a

Fig. 1.3. Triple subdivisions of a 4-beat measure.

(triplets). Practice clapping on the numbered beats at a constant rate and speak each line of the drill along with your claps ("&" should be read as "and"). Then practice 3-beat measures, using the patterns 123, 1&2&3&, and 1e&a2e&a3e&a.

In some meters, there are intermediate levels of grouping between the measure and the tactus and, in addition, higher-level groupings of measures. In Western musical notation, some time signatures indicate levels of division of the measure. For example, the time signature 12/8 is normally interpreted as four counts per measure, each subdivided into three parts.

Exercise 1. Practice clapping to three songs: "Respect", by Otis Redding (1965; made famous by Aretha Franklin), the Beatles' "Norwegian Wood" (1965), and Sister Rosetta Tharpe's "That's All" (1939). First, find the tactus. It should be where you naturally step when you're dancing. Use a metronome (available online) to estimate the tempo in beats per minute. Are beats in the tactus grouped any particular way, such as into groups of two, three, or four? Can those groups be grouped into larger groups? Are the beats in the tactus subdivided, and, if so, into how many parts? Describe the rhythmic structure of the piece.

1.3. Rhythms

Unlike meter, rhythms are patterns that we can hear. *Drum tablature*, or drum tab, is a common way to notate rhythms. Sequences of drum hits can be written with `x`'s, indicating hits, and `.`'s (periods), or rests, indicating that the drum is not sounded. Each symbol occupies the same amount of time, a pulse in either the tactus or some regular subdivision of the tactus. For example, the notation `x..x..x.` means "hit rest rest hit rest rest hit rest". This is a common pattern in music with four counts to a measure, subdivided once. Practice clapping the pattern while you speak the names of the counts:

```
Count: 1 & 2 & 3 & 4 &
Clap:  x . . x . . x .
```

Exercise 2. Write the drum tab for a 4-beat measure, with hits (a) on the first beat only, and (b) on beats two and four. Each `x` or `.` occupies one beat.

Steve Reich's "Clapping Music". We can use drum tab to visualize Steve Reich's "Clapping Music". Player A claps the rhythm `xxx.xx.x.xx.` over and over until the piece ends. Player B progresses through a number of patterns, playing each one eight times. The first pattern is the same as Player A's, then the pattern is repeatedly shifted by one beat, so that, for example, `xx.xx.x.xx.x` is the next pattern.

When two drum patterns are played simultaneously, a third rhythm is heard, called the *resultant rhythm.* It is the rhythm that has rests whenever both of the original drum patterns had a rest and drum hits otherwise.

Drum tab is convenient for finding resultant rhythms. Any beat that has an `x` for either player A or player B (or both) has an `x` in the resultant rhythm. Here are patterns A and B in the previous example, plus the resultant rhythm. The seventh beat is the only rest in the resultant rhythm.

```
Player A:     x x x . x x . x . x x .
Player B:     x . x x . x . x x . x x
resultant:    x x x x x x . x x x x x
```

Led Zeppelin's "Kashmir". Here is the rhythm of the lead guitar. The drums are hit on the numbered beats and establish the meter.

```
Count:   1 & 2 & 3 & 4 & |1 & 2 & 3 & 4 & |1 & 2 & 3 & 4 & |1 &  etc.
Guitar:  xxx...xxx...xxx.|..xxx...xxx...xx|x...xxx...xxx...|xxx. etc.
```

Exercise 3. Describe the rhythmic organization of "Kashmir" mathematically. How would the pattern continue?

1.4. Timelines and Groove

Somewhere between a meter and a rhythm is a *groove.* Grooves are repeating rhythm patterns and accents that characterize different styles of music, such as salsa, reggae, and Irish jigs. Such repeated rhythm patterns are called *timelines* [6]. Grooves are particularly important in dance music. They may be highly complex, with several musicians playing interlocking rhythms, each with different accent patterns. We can study both the pattern that each instrument plays and the combination of all these patterns.

The most basic grooves in Western pop music use 4-beat measures. The first beat in every measure is called the *downbeat* and the last beat is called the *upbeat,* because it comes right before the downbeat of the next measure. Beats one and three are called the *on-beats* and beats two and four are the *off-beats*. "Backbeat" grooves, popular in blues and R&B, emphasize the off-beats, while downbeat-oriented grooves have a primary accent on the downbeat and a secondary accent on count three.

In some grooves, musicians intentionally play a little ahead or behind the beat. This kind of variation is called *microtiming* or *swing*. Although microtiming is an important feature of dance music grooves, it is difficult to write down in music notation. Musicians normally learn it by ear.

Exercise 4. In a 2005 interview, James Brown, "The Godfather of Soul", discussed grooves in his music [2]. He compared two versions of the "I Got You" groove and described how his groove changed with his 1965 song "Papa's Got A Brand New Bag", which was his first song to give a strong emphasis to the downbeat. Practice both on-beat and off-beat clapping to each song. Do you prefer to clap on the on-beats, or on the off-beats? Find a piece of popular music in four beats per measure that clearly emphasizes the on-beats and another piece that clearly emphasizes the off-beats.

Exercise 5. Write the drum tab for a 4-beat measure, with hits (a) on the downbeat only, (b) on the off-beats, (c) on the upbeat, and (d) on the on-beats. Each **x** or **.** occupies one beat.

1.5. The Beat Class Circle and Modulus

Since the tactus is often subdivided, using the tactus as a "ruler" to measure time would mean using a lot of fractions. To avoid this, let's measure time using the smallest level of subdivision, called the *tatum*. (In music notation, the tatum might be a pulse of eighth or sixteenth notes.) I will call the length of time between successive pulses in the tatum a *beat*. Each pulse in the tactus lasts a whole number of beats.

The fact that a beat, like an hour or a minute, is a measure of time — not a specific point in time — means that we ought to measure musical time starting at zero, just like a ruler starts at zero, so that "beat 0" refers to the beginning of the first measure and "beat a" refers to the time a beats later. The first beat is the time between beat 0 and beat 1, the fourth beat is the time between beat 3 and beat 4, and, in general, the nth beat is the time between beat $(n-1)$ and beat n.[a]

Any pattern of hits corresponds to a pattern of time intervals (durations) that measure the time from the beginning of one hit to the next. For example, the pattern `x..x..x.x..x..x.` is described as "3+3+2+3+3+2" and shown in Fig. 1.4. The onsets in the pattern

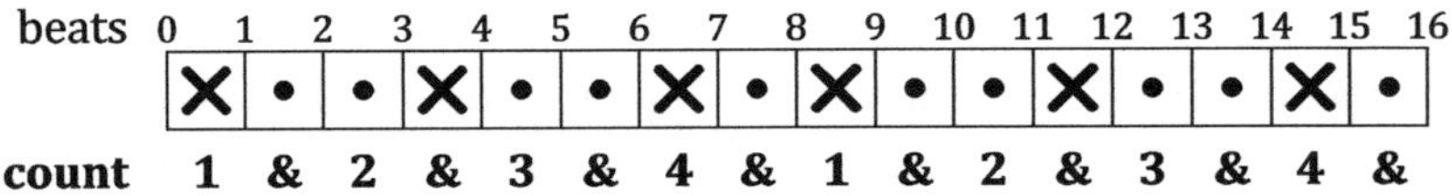

Fig. 1.4. Two repeats of the pattern `x..x..x.`

[a] An analogy is that the third year of your life is the year between your second and third birthdays.

fall on beats 0, 3, 6, 8, 11, and 14. The multiple levels of counting in Fig. 1.4 give some idea of the complexity of musical time. The tatum is, here, twice as fast as the tactus.

When we translate between the tactus and the measure, certain points in time are associated with one another. Just as a clock represents the organization of time within a day, the *beat class circle* represents beats in a musical measure. Since the rhythm patterns in a timeline repeat, we often depict timelines on a circle. The downbeat begins at the top and the other beats proceed clockwise. Dots show the onsets of drum hits.

Figure 1.5 shows the timeline `x..x..x.` on a beat class circle with eight beats. The dark circles indicate where the hits begin.

Exercise 6. Write the timelines in Fig. 1.6 in drum tab and circular notation. The durations of beat groupings correspond to the difference between onsets of drum hits, so that a duration of one is written "x"; two is written "`x.`", and three is written "`x..`".

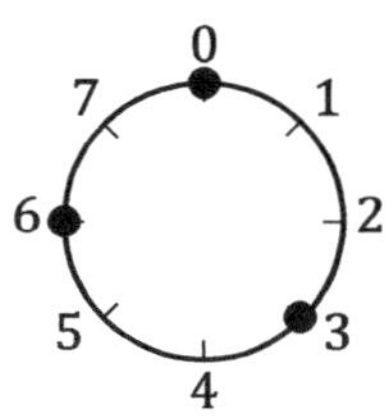

Fig. 1.5. The timeline `x..x..x.` represented on the beat class circle.

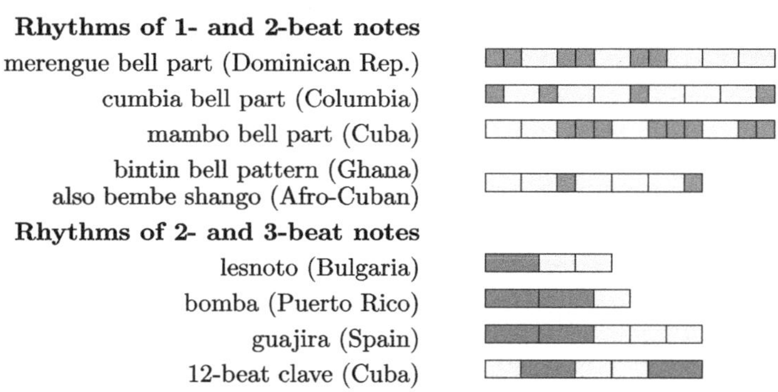

Fig. 1.6. Rhythms from around the world.

Definition 1.1 (Beat class). Let beat a be the time a beats after the beginning of the first measure of a piece. The *beat class* (bc) of beat a is its position in the measure, calculated from the beginning of the measure.

A measure with n beats has n beat classes,

$$0, 1, 2, \ldots, n-1$$

The *downbeat* is the first beat in the measure. Every downbeat starts at bc 0.

Suppose a piece has 12 beats per measure and you start at the beginning of a measure. After 54 beats, what is the beat class? Since moving backward 12 beats has no effect on the position in the measure, we start by subtracting as many multiples of 12 as we can, then look at what's left. Since $54-12-12-12-12 = 6$, beat 54 is in bc 6. It occurs six beats after the beginning of a measure. We can do this more efficiently using remainders: 6 is the remainder when 54 is divided by 12.

In general, suppose there are n beats in a measure. Beat a falls in beat class R, where R is the remainder when a is divided by n. Mathematicians call this remainder the *modulus*.

Definition 1.2 (Modulus). If a is an integer and n is a positive integer, then the *modulus* of a relative to n is the remainder when a is divided by n. If R is the remainder, we write

$$a \bmod n = R$$

Two beats have the same beat class if and only if they are in the same position in the measure. Mathematicians call this relationship *modular congruence*.

Definition 1.3 (Modular congruence). Two integers a and b are congruent modulo a positive integer n if $a \bmod n = b \bmod n$. We write $a \equiv b \pmod{n}$.

The triple equals sign $\equiv$ is read as "is congruent to". For example $23 \equiv 51 \pmod 7$ because the remainder when either 23 or 51 is divided by 7 equals 2. That is, $23 \bmod 7 = 51 \bmod 7$.

Belonging to the same beat class is the same thing as being separated by a whole number of measures. Therefore, beat a and beat b belong to the same beat class if and only if the distance between them, $a - b$, is divisible by n. (In general, an integer m is *divisible* by an integer n if m/n is an integer.)

Theorem 1.1 (Modular Congruence Theorem). *Two integers a and b are congruent modulo a positive integer n (that is, $a \equiv b \pmod n$) if and only if $(a - b)$ is divisible by n.*

For example, $23 \equiv 51 \pmod 7$ because $(23 - 51)/7 = -28/7 = -4$, which is an integer. Notice that $(51-23)/7 = 4$ is also an integer, and, in general, either $(a-b)/n$ or $(b-a)/n$ may be used to determine congruence.

Corollary 1.1 (The beat class formulas). *If there are n beats per measure, then beat a falls in beat class $(a \bmod n)$ and beats a and b lie in the same beat class if and only if $a \equiv b \pmod n$.*

For example, suppose there are seven beats to a measure. Then:

- The downbeats start on bc 0; that is, on beats $0, 7, 14, 21, \ldots$.
- Beat 100 falls on beat class 2 because $100 \div 7 = 14\,r.2$. Therefore, the 101st beat *starts* on bc 2.
- Beat 28 falls on beat class 0 because 28 is divisible by 7 ($28 \div 7 = 4\,r.0$). Therefore, beat 28 is the onset of a downbeat.
- Beats 100 and 849 belong to the same beat class because they are separated by $849 - 100 = 749$ beats, which equals exactly 107 measures. Equivalently, use modular congruence and the beat class theorem: $100 \equiv 849 \pmod 7$ because $(100 - 849)/7$ is an integer. Another way to solve the problem is to use modulus. Beat 100 belongs to bc 2 (see above) and, since $849 \div 7 = 121\,r.2$, beat 849 is also in bc 2.

Exercise 7. Evaluate (a) 144 mod 13 and (b) 169 mod 13. Determine whether the statements are correct: (c) $25 \equiv 61 \pmod 6$ and (d) $-4 \equiv 4 \pmod 3$.

Exercise 8. Suppose there are six beats to the measure. Which beats mark the onsets of downbeats? To which beat class does beat 50 belong? Beat 90? Are beats 36 and 63 in the same beat class?

Exercise 9. Suppose there are four beats per measure and you clap on every third beat, starting at beat 0. Find the sequence of beat classes on which your claps begin. Practice counting in four and clapping every third beat.

1.6. Application of the Modulus: Polyrhythm

What happens when two musicians repeat patterns of different lengths? What happens when a musician plays a repeating pattern whose length is not a divisor of the number of beats in a measure? The rhythms produced are called polyrhythms and can be described mathematically.

Definition 1.4. Suppose p and n are positive integers. A *p-against-n polyrhythm* is the result of repeating a pattern of length p beats and a pattern of length n beats simultaneously or repeating a pattern of length p beats in a meter with n beats per measure.

Example: Led Zeppelin's "Kashmir". See p. 6. The guitar pattern has six beats ($p = 6$), while there are sixteen beats per measure ($n = 16$). Note that eight repeats of the guitar pattern equal 48 beats and fill three measures, because $(6 \cdot 8) \bmod 16 = 0$. This rhythm is a 6-against-16 polyrhythm.

Example: Taylor Swift's "22". Taylor Swift's 2012 hit "22", written by Swift, Max Martin, and Shellback, embeds a three-against-four polyrhythm in the line "We're happy, free, confused, and lonely at the same time". The tatum has sixteen beats per measure, and four beats (of the tatum) make up a pulse in the tactus.

```
& a|1 e & a 2 e & a 3 e & a 4 e & a|1 e &
x .|x . x x . x x . x x . x x . x x|. . x
```

Fig. 1.7. The rhythm of "happy, free, confused, and lonely" in Taylor Swift's "22".

The overall meter is four beats (of the tactus) per measure. Swift squeezes four repeats of the pattern `x.x` into the first three counts of the tactus, corresponding to the lyrics "happy, free, confused, and lonely" before breaking out of the polyrhythm, as shown in Fig. 1.7. This phrase takes $4 \cdot 3 = 12$ beats, which equals three counts of the tactus. At 1:29 in her video, she counts to four on her fingers, as if to highlight the polyrhythm.

In general, repeating a pattern whose duration is p beats r times takes rp beats. This equals a whole number of n-beat patterns or measures if and only if $rp \bmod n = 0$, which occurs when rp is a multiple of n. Since rp is also a multiple of p, we have the following theorem. The least common multiple of p and n is written $\text{lcm}(p, n)$.

Theorem 1.2. *Suppose n and p are positive integers. The smallest positive integer value of r for which $rp \bmod n = 0$ is $r = \text{lcm}(p, n)/p$.*

Corollary 1.2. *An n-against-p polyrhythm repeats after every $\text{lcm}(p, n)$ beats. The n-beat rhythm is repeated $\text{lcm}(p, n)/n$ times and the p-beat rhythm is repeated $\text{lcm}(p, n)/p$ times.*

For example, the "Kashmir" polyrhythm features a pattern of length 6 beats played in a 16-beat measure. Since $\text{lcm}(6, 16) = 48$, the resulting polyrhythm is repeated every 48 beats — that is, when the 6-beat rhythm is repeated $48/6 = 8$ times, while the 16-beat measure is repeated $48/16 = 3$ times.

Exercise 10. Explain why $np \bmod n = 0$ for any positive integer values of p and n. What musical fact does this reflect?

Exercise 11. Suppose you choose a value of p and clap the p-beat pattern of one clap followed by $p - 1$ rests (like `x....` or `x..`). If there are n beats per measure, the beat classes on which you clap are 0, $p \bmod n$, $2p \bmod n$, $3p \bmod n$, $4p \bmod n$, etc. Some interesting effects happen when p is either one more or one less than n. In these cases, p and n can have no common factors, so $\text{lcm}(p, n) = np$. If

$p = n + 1$, then $p \bmod n = 1$, and so the sequence of beat classes on which you clap is bc $0, 1, 2, 3, \ldots, n-1, 0$, etc. In a 4-count measure, the rhythm might look something like this (the **x**'s are replaced by the count).

```
1 . . .|. 2 . .|. . 3 .|. . . 4|. . . .|1
```

What is the corresponding sequence of beat classes when $p = n - 1$? Illustrate your answer in a 4-count measure.

Exercise 12. George and Ira Gershwin's 1924 song "Fascinating Rhythm" features the catchy rhythm shown below. The song is performed in "swing eighths", meaning that the "&'s" happen later than the midpoint between the numbered counts.

```
1  &  2  &  3  &  4  & |1  &  2  &  3  &  4  & |1  &  2  &  3  &  4  & |1  &
x  x  x  x  x  x  .  x |x  x  x  x  x  .  x  x |x  x  x  x  .  x  x  x |x  x
fascinating rhythm, you've got me on the go, fascinating rhythm, I'm all a-quiver
```

The first three phrases ("Fascinating rhythm, you've got me on the go, fascinating rhythm") are the beginning of a polyrhythm, though the pattern is broken in the fourth phrase. Which polyrhythm? How long would the pattern have to continue to complete a whole number of measures?

1.7. Application of the Modulus: Tihai Endings

In classical Indian Carnatic music, a *tihai* often ends a piece or a solo [1, 172]. A tihai consists of a rhythmic pattern that starts and ends on a hit and repeats three times, with some fixed number of beats between the repeats. A tihai starts on the beginning of a downbeat (bc 0) and ends on the *end* of another downbeat (bc 1), so its total duration equals some number of whole measures plus one beat. The pattern `xxxxx.xxxxx.xxxxx` is a tihai with eight beats per measure. In this case, the pattern is `xxxxx` and the gap is one beat, so the total number of beats is seventeen — that is, one more than a multiple of eight. Here's a different tihai with eight beats per measure, using the pattern `xxx.x` and a gap of five beats.

```
Count:   1 & 2 & 3 & 4 &|1 & 2 & 3 & 4 &|1 & 2 & 3 & 4 &|1
Play:    x x x . x . . .|. . x x x . x .|. . . . x x x .|x
```

If n is the number of beats in a measure, p is the length of the pattern, and g is the length of the gap, then the tihai's length is $(p + g + p + g + p)$ and satisfies the *tihai equation*

$$(3p + 2g) \bmod n = 1$$

The tihai equation is an example of a *Diophantine equation* — that is, an equation whose solutions are required to be integers (remember that we are measuring beats at the tatum level, so p and q can't be fractions). Finding integer values of p and g that work for a given n is not always straightforward. For example, if p is an even number, $(3p + 2g)$ is even and therefore $(3p + 2g \bmod 8)$ is even, so the tihai equation cannot be solved in this case.

Exercise 13. Verify that, in a 6-beat measure, a 3-beat pattern and a 5-beat gap works for a tihai ending. Write a tihai of this type in drum tab. Explain why it is impossible to use a 4-beat pattern when there are six beats per measure. Is it possible to have a 3-beat gap in a 6-beat measure?

Exercise 14. Find all possible p, g combinations for an 8-beat measure where p and g are less than 8.

1.8. Transformations of Rhythms

A transformation is a process that composers use to alter a melody, rhythm, or chord in order to create new musical material. We will study three transformations of a rhythm pattern: its shift, retrograde, and complement. Rhythms that are related by transformations have many similar features, and this will allow us to classify them.

Watch the video of Steve Reich's "Clapping Music". "Clapping Music" uses a single repeated rhythm pattern. The two players start by clapping the 12-beat pattern together in unison. After eight measures, one performer transforms the pattern by shifting it forward by one beat, and they clap the new pattern for eight measures. This process is continued until the two patterns align again. The piece was inspired by the clapping patterns in traditional flamenco music of the Roma people in Andalusia, Spain.

We use drum tab to visualize "Clapping Music". Player A claps the same rhythm over and over until the piece ends.

```
Player A:     x x x . x x . x . x x .
```

This pattern can also be written as a set[b] of beat classes: {0, 1, 2, 4, 5, 7, 9, 10}. Player B progresses through a number of patterns, playing each one eight times. Here are the first four, written in drum tab and as sets of beat classes.

1.	x x x . x x . x . x x .	{0, 1, 2, 4, 5, 7, 9, 10}
2.	x x . x x . x . x x . x	{0, 1, 3, 4, 6, 8, 9, 11}
3.	x . x x . x . x x . x x	{0, 2, 3, 5, 7, 8, 10, 11}
4.	. x x . x . x x . x x x	{1, 2, 4, 6, 7, 9, 10, 11}

Each drum tab pattern is formed by shifting the previous one forward and moving the first hit or rest to the end. This shift is called *cyclic permutation* by mathematicians. It will take 12 changes of pattern for the second player to sync up with the first player again in *unison*, meaning that they play the same pattern at the same time.

As sets of beat classes, the patterns are related by subtraction modulo 12 on the beat class circle (note that $(0-1) \equiv 11 \pmod{12}$). The subtraction is more obvious when you write the members of the sets in a different order (remember that order doesn't matter in a set).

$$\begin{array}{llllllll}
\{0, & 1, & 2, & 4, & 5, & 7, & 9, & 10\} \\
\{11, & 0, & 1, & 3, & 4, & 6, & 8, & 9\} \\
\{10, & 11, & 0, & 2, & 3, & 5, & 7, & 8\} \\
\{9, & 10, & 11, & 1, & 2, & 4, & 6, & 7\}
\end{array}$$

Figure 1.8 shows the first four patterns clapped by player B in circular notation. The progression from one pattern to the next corresponds to a 30 degree rotation of the pattern counterclockwise.

[b]A *set* is defined to be a non-repeating collection of objects, called *members*. Curly brackets "{" and "}" enclose a list to indicate that it is a set.

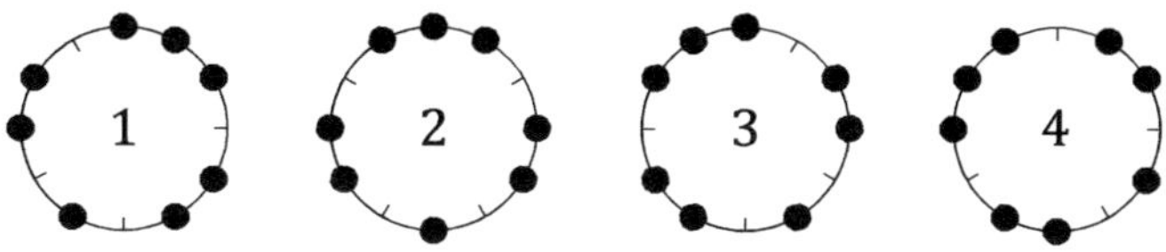

Fig. 1.8. The second player's first four patterns in "Clapping Music".

Analysis of "Clapping Music". As we have seen, the variation in sound follows from the second player repeatedly shifting their rhythm, while the first player repeats the same pattern. The tension created by the musicians clapping different patterns is resolved when the second player's rhythm completes a full cycle, bringing the two players back into unison and giving closure to the piece. However, the fact that the piece ends exactly as it began suggests that "Clapping Music" might continue indefinitely, following the same pattern as before.

Though I don't know "why" Reich chose this particular rhythm pattern and not another, there are a few features that give extra interest to the music. Trying the same process with a different rhythm can also give us insight into why this pattern works so well. Here are a few observations I have:

(1) The fact that the rhythm has no adjacent rests means that in the penultimate pattern (the one before the final unison), the resulting rhythm is equal to the set of all 12 beat classes in the measure. This gives the maximum feeling of tension before the end.
(2) The resultant rhythm is usually not equal to the set of 12 beat classes, but something more interesting. In fact, the situation in which all beat classes are heard only happens three times.
(3) The "Clapping Music" rhythm cannot be divided into smaller repeating patterns of, say, six beats. If it could, the players would come into unison after only six different patterns.

Exercise 15. Write all shifts of the rhythm `xx.x.` in drum tab, as sets of beat classes, and in circular notation.

Exercise 16. Working with a partner, follow the same basic structure as "Clapping Music" but use the rhythm **xx..** or one of your own choosing. How many different resultant rhythms are there? List them.

Exercise 17. How many times do you have to shift **....xx** to make **..xx..**? Write these rhythms as sets of beat classes. What is the mathematical relationship between these sets?

1.9. Introduction to Rhythm Class: Classroom Activity

This is a set of creative exercises inspired by "Clapping Music" and the mathematical concept of symmetry. I begin by creating groups of approximately four students.

(1) Introduce yourselves and decide on a group name.
(2) Make up a 6-beat rhythm pattern. Write it in all three notations we learned: as a set of beat classes, using drum tab, and on a circle. Send a delegate from your group to write the pattern on the board in circular notation, labeled with your group's name.
(3) Practice your pattern as a group and get ready to perform it for the class.
(4) The shift of a pattern is the rhythm that results by moving the first hit or rest to the end of the pattern and shifting all the other hits or rests forward by one place, as in "Clapping Music". Using drum tab, write all the shifts of your rhythm.
(5) The *retrograde* of a pattern is the rhythm that results when playing that pattern backwards. Find the retrograde of your pattern.
(6) Using drum tab, write all the shifts of the retrograde.
(7) Count the number of different shifts of your pattern and the number of different shifts of its retrograde.
(8) Two sets are equal if they contain exactly the same elements. Is the set of shifts of the original pattern equal to the set of shifts

of its retrograde, or not? If not, do they have any elements in common?

(9) The complement of a rhythm pattern A is the rhythm pattern B that has rests wherever A has hits and hits wherever A has rests. In other words, exchange the hits and rests to find the complement. A and B are called *complementary rhythms.* Find the complement of your rhythm using drum tab.

Discussion. The students created the rhythm patterns shown in Fig. 1.9. Here are some of the class responses and some observations I have about the exercise.

- The number of different shifts of a pattern is always equal to the number of shifts of its retrograde. Although most groups had six shifts and six shifts of the retrograde, a few groups had fewer: some had three and others had two. It is also possible to have one if your rhythm was either no drum hits (......) or all hits (**xxxxxx**). Since we didn't have John Cage in the class, no one tried this (except me!).

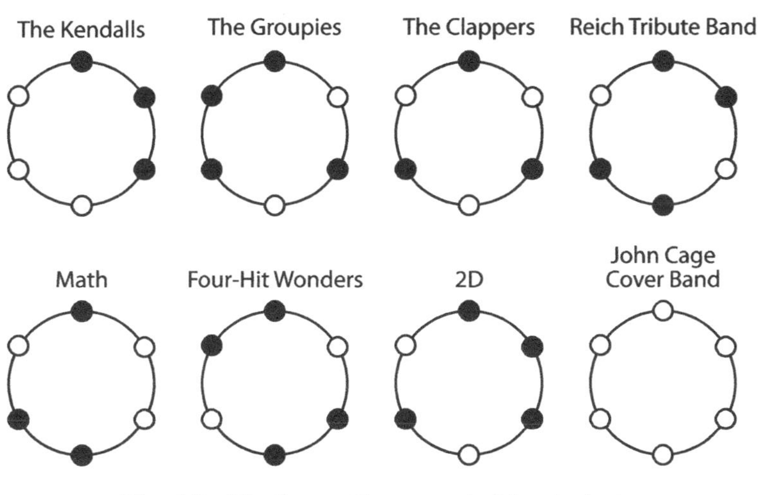

Fig. 1.9. Rhythm patterns created by students.

- There are only two possibilities for Question 8: either the two sets are equal or they do not contain any of the same elements. (Equivalently, if a pattern in one set is the same as a pattern in the other set, the two sets must be equal because they are made up of shifts of the same pattern.) For the majority of groups, the sets were equal. The exception was the group "Math" in 1.9, top. What is special about their pattern?
- As the class discussed each group's answers, looked at the circular representation of their pattern, and heard the rhythm they chose, we saw that some rhythms had special properties that determined the answers to Questions 7 and 8. In particular, we noticed that some patterns could be "flipped" over an axis to produce the same pattern, while others could be rotated by some fraction of the circle to produce the same pattern. These properties are called symmetries.
- One question that puzzled us was "aren't the shifts of a rhythm really the same rhythm?" Does repeating `xxx.xx` over and over sound the same as repeating `xxxxx.` over and over? The answer depends on the musical context: if we have a strong sense of where the downbeat is, the two patterns are completely different. In the absence of a sense of downbeat, however, they sound the same. This is the second of many examples of musical objects that are considered the same in one context and different in another. The first example we studied was the idea of beat class, which is connected to modular congruence in math. As it turns out, mathematicians are also very interested in the idea of "equivalence" and have studied it extensively.
- Can a rhythm pattern ever be the same as its complement? Can a rhythm pattern be a rotation of its complement? Is that true of any of the patterns you chose? Is there an answer that no one chose? (The answer to the first question is "No" and the other three questions are "Yes": The Kendalls pattern, or any rotation of it, is a rotation of its complement. The other pattern that's a rotation of its complement is `x.x.x.` or some rotation of that.)

1.10. Classifying Rhythm Patterns

Some patterns created by the students in the previous exercise are the same forwards or backwards; these are called *non-retrogradable.* Rhythms that are not the same as their retrograde are called *retrogradable.* For example, the rhythm `x.x.` is retrogradable, while the rhythm `x..x` is non-retrogradable.

Other patterns had fewer different shifts than the students expected. A rhythm pattern with n beats is called *reducible* if you can shift it less than n times (but at least once) to produce the same rhythm. Reducible rhythms in an n beat measure repeat more often than once a measure. The rhythm `x..x..` is reducible because shifting it three times produces the original rhythm. The rhythm `x.x...` is irreducible because it has six different shifts.

Exercise 18. Which of the students' rhythm patterns in Fig. 1.9 are retrogradable? Which are not? Which of the students' rhythm patterns are irreducible? Which are reducible?

1.11. Rhythm Class

We saw earlier that beats that occupy the same position in a measure belong to the same beat class. The notion of two rhythms being similar if one is a shift of the other gives us a concept of similarity for rhythms.

Definition 1.5 (Rhythm class). Suppose there are n beats per measure. The *rhythm class* of a given rhythm pattern is the set of all the shifts of that pattern. Equivalently, two n-beat rhythms belong to the same rhythm class if and only if one can be repeatedly shifted to align with the other. A rhythm class has at most n elements.

Example. The rhythm class of the 5-beat pattern `x..x.` is a set of five rhythms. I've written them without the normal commas between members, because commas are easy to confuse with periods in drum tab. Try clapping each pattern eight times. Do they sound similar? Identical?

$$\{\texttt{x..x.} \quad \texttt{..x.x} \quad \texttt{.x.x.} \quad \texttt{x.x..} \quad \texttt{.x..x}\}$$

Example. There are eight 3-beat rhythms:

$$\{\texttt{xxx} \quad \texttt{xx.} \quad \texttt{x.x} \quad \texttt{x..} \quad \texttt{.xx} \quad \texttt{.x.} \quad \texttt{..x} \quad \texttt{...}\}$$

These patterns may be grouped into four rhythm classes:

$$\{\texttt{xxx}\}, \quad \{\texttt{xx.} \quad \texttt{x.x} \quad \texttt{.xx}\}, \quad \{\texttt{x..} \quad \texttt{..x} \quad \texttt{.x.}\}, \text{ and } \{\texttt{...}\}$$

Example. In "Clapping Music", the second player claps all 12 members of the rhythm class of the basic pattern.

Example. *Flamenco* is a music and dance form from Andalusia, Spain that is associated with the Roma peoples. Within the genre of flamenco, there are a number of styles having 12 beats per measure but different characteristic accent patterns. For example, the guajira pattern is `x..x..x.x.x.` while the seguiriya pattern is `x.x.x..x..x.` [6, p. 267]. Shifting the guajira eight times produces the seguiriya. Therefore, the two patterns belong to the same rhythm class. The relationship is easy to recognize using circular notation, as in Fig. 1.10.

Exercise 19. What are the patterns in the rhythm class of `xxx.x..`? Do the patterns `xxx.x..` and `..x.xxx` belong to the same rhythm class?

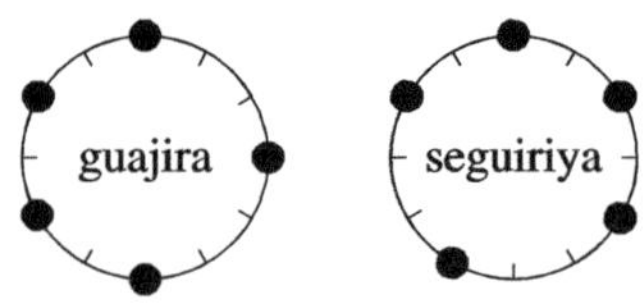

Fig. 1.10. Flamenco rhythms in circular notation.

Exercise 20. What are the patterns in the rhythm class of `x..x..`? Under what circumstances will a rhythm class of 6-beat rhythms have fewer than six members?

1.12. The Mathematics of Transformations

We have learned three transformations of rhythms: shift (S), retrograde (R), and complement (C). Let's represent these mathematically. We'll be using function notation, so that $C(\texttt{x...}) = \texttt{.xxx}$ means "the complement of the pattern `x...` is the pattern `.xxx`" and $R(p)$ means "the retrograde of pattern p".

We can abstract away from referring to patterns and just study the mathematics of transformations. For shifts, we'll use an exponent to indicate the number of shifts. So S^1 means shift by one place, moving the contents of the first beat to the end and moving all the other symbols to the left by one place, S^2 means repeat S^1 twice, etc. Also, S^0 means shift by 0 places — in other words, do nothing — and S^{-1} means shift in the opposite direction by one place.

Shifts can be combined with each other. For example, shifting by three places followed by shifting by four places results in shifting by seven places. We write $S^4S^3 = S^{4+3} = S^7$. In general,

$$S^aS^b = S^{a+b}.$$

Moreover, notice that if there are n beats per measure, the result of shifting n times is the same as doing nothing. We write $S^n = S^0$. In addition, $S^0 = S^n = S^{2n}$ etc. and $S^0 = S^{-n} = S^{-2n}$ etc. In fact, if there are n beats per measure, $S^a = S^b$ if and only if $a \equiv b \pmod{n}$.

We can make some mathematical generalizations about how transformations combine with each other. For example, the complement of the retrograde of any pattern is the same as the retrograde of that pattern. Note that $C(R(\texttt{x...})) = R(C(\texttt{x...}))$, and, in fact, $CR(p) = RC(p)$ for any pattern p — that is, the order of retrograde and complement doesn't matter. It's also true that the order of shifts and complement doesn't matter. That is, $CR = RC$ and $S^aC = S^aC$.

Notice also that a retrograde followed by a retrograde, or a complement followed by a complement, return the original pattern, so that $RR = R^2 = S^0$ and $CC = C^2 = S^0$.

Combining shifts and retrograde is more complicated. We showed in class that $RS = S^{-1}R$, and therefore, in general, $RS^a = S^{-a}R$.

The SRC Formulas. The relationships between S, R, and C are given by the following formulas:

(1) $S^aS^b = S^{a+b}$;
(2) $S^a = S^b$ if and only if $a \equiv b \pmod{n}$ where n is the number of beats in a measure;
(3) $RR = R^2 = S^0$;
(4) $CC = C^2 = S^0$;
(5) $RC = CR$;
(6) $S^aC = CS^a$;
(7) $RS^a = S^{-a}R$.

1.13. Application of Rhythm Transformation: Canons

The most familiar type of canon is a *round*, such as "Row, Row, Row Your Boat" or "Frere Jacques". In this case, the first person starts the melody, then the second person sings the same melody after a delay of several measures. The transformation used in this example is a shift — the second group's melody is a delay of the original melody.

Two-part rhythmic canons. A *two-part canon* occurs when one player plays a melody or pattern and the other player plays a transformation of that melody or pattern. This transformation is typically a shift. Occasionally it can be a different transformation, such as retrograde, inversion, or some combination of shift, retrograde, and inversion. A *rhythmic canon* is a canon on the rhythmic level, though not necessarily a canon of melodies, as in Schumann's "Kind im Einschlummern".

The rhythms are

```
Voice 1:      x.xxxx..x.xxxx..
Voice 2: x.xxxx..x.xxxx..
```

Rhythmic tiling canons. A *rhythmic tiling canon* occurs when there are two or more players and exactly one player plays on every beat. If there are two players, this means that the rhythms they play are complements of each other. Unless specified otherwise, rhythmic tiling canons are assumed to be rounds, where the second player plays a shift of the original pattern.

Suppose you choose the first six beats of a 12-beat canon. When will you get a tiling canon? The only way you can fill in the next six beats to make the canon tile is to use the complement of the pattern you chose for the first six beats. Therefore, a rhythm forms a tiling canon precisely when its first half is the complement of its second half. As a consequence, a tiling canon for two people must have an even number of beats. With 12 beats, the first half is beats 1 through 6, and the second half is beats 7 through 12.

An example of a rhythmic tiling canon starting with the pattern $p =$ `xx.x` is:

```
Drum A:  x x . x . . x . x x . x . . x .        etc.
Drum B:              x x . x . . x . x x . x . . x .   etc.
```

If p is any pattern, a two-part tiling canon may be formed by following pattern p by its complement (that is, the pattern "$p\,C(p)$"). The second player starts when the first player plays the complement, like this:

Drum A: $p\,C(p)\quad p\quad C(p)\quad p\quad C(p)\quad p$ etc.
Drum B: $\quad p\quad C(p)\quad p\quad C(p)\quad p\quad C(p)$ etc.

Crab canons. A *crab canon* occurs when a melody or rhythm is played simultaneously with its retrograde. A tiling crab canon must be formed from a rhythm that is the complement of its own retrograde. An example starting with the pattern $p =$ `x x . x` is

```
Drum A:   x x . x . x . .
Drum B:   . . x . x . x x
```

If p is any pattern, then the pattern p followed by the complement of its retrograde forms a tiling crab canon:

$$\begin{array}{ll} \text{Drum A:} & p \quad CR(p) \\ \text{Drum B:} & C(p) \quad R(p) \end{array}$$

This formula works because retrograde and complement may be done in any order: $RCR = RRC = C$, so that

$$R(\text{Drum A}) = (R(p, CR(p))) = (RCR(p), R(p)) = (C(p), R(p)) = \text{Drum B.}$$

See [3] for examples of rhythmic tiling canons with more than two voices and more complex structure.

Exercise 21. Choose a 6-beat theme and use it to create a rhythmic tiling canon and a rhythmic crab canon. Do you think you made a good choices?

1.14. Solutions to Selected Exercises

2. (a) `x...` (b) `.x.x`

3. If each symbol in the drum tab counts as one beat, the drum pattern repeats every measure (16 beats) and the guitar pattern repeats every six beats. The entire pattern repeats after $\text{lcm}(16, 6) = 48$ beats, which equal three measures.

5. (a) `x...` (b) `.x.x` (c) `...x` (d) `x.x.`

6. Merengue: `xxx.xxx.xxx.x.x.`; cumbia: `xx.xx.x.xx.x.x.x`; mambo: `x.x.xxxx.xxxx.xx`; bintin: `x.x.xx.x.x.x`; lesnoto: `x..x.x.`; bomba: `x..x..x.`; guajira: `x..x..x.x.x.` (this is the rhythm of "America" in West Side Story); clave: `x.x..x.x.x..`

7. (a) 144 mod 13 = 1 because $144 \div 13 = 11\,r.1$ and (b) 169 mod 13 = 0 because $169 \div 13 = 13$ (remainder is 0). Determine whether the statements are correct:

(a) $25 \equiv 61 \pmod 6$ because $(25 - 61)/6 = 6$, which is an integer.
(b) $-4 \not\equiv 4 \pmod 3$ because $(-4 - 4)/3 = -8/3$ is not an integer.

8. The downbeats start on beats 0, 6, 12, 18, etc. (It is equally correct to say that the first, seventh, thirteenth, etc. beats are downbeats.) Beat 50's beat class is 2 because $50 \div 6 = 8\,r.2$. Beat 90's beat class is 0 because $90 \div 6 = 15\,r.0$.

9. You clap on beat classes
$0 \bmod 4 = 0$;
$3 \bmod 4 = 3$;
$(3 + 3) \bmod 4 = 2$;
$(3 + 3 + 3) \bmod 4 = 1$;
$(3 + 3 + 3 + 3) \bmod 4 = 0$, etc.
So you clap on bc 0, 3, 2, 1, 0, 3, 2, 1, ... — that is, on the first, fourth, third, second, first, fourth, etc. beats of the measure.

10. Since $np \bmod n$ is the remainder when np is divided by n, and p is an integer, $np \bmod n = 0$. Musically, any pattern that is repeated n times, where n is the length of a measure, results in a duration equal to a whole number of measures.

11. If $p = n - 1$, then $p \bmod n = n - 1$ and so $p \equiv -1 \pmod n$. The sequence of beat classes on which you clap is $0, n - 1, n - 2, \ldots, 1, 0$, etc. In a 4-count measure, that is `1 . . 4| . . 3.|. 2 . .|1`

12. The repeating pattern `xxxxxx.` has seven beats, while the measure has eight beats. A 7-against-8 polyrhythm repeats after $\text{lcm}(7, 8) = 56$ beats, which equals seven measures.

13. In this case,

$$(3p + 2g) \bmod n = (3 \cdot 3 + 2 \cdot 5) \bmod 6 = 19 \bmod 6 = 1$$

The possible patterns are `x.x.....x.x.....x.x` and `xxx.....xxx.....xxx`. Since $(3 \cdot 4 + 2g) \bmod 6 = (12 + 2g) \bmod 6 = 2g \bmod 6$ is even, it cannot equal 1. Since $(3p + 2 \cdot 3) \bmod 6 = 3p \bmod 6$, which equals either 0 or 3, a 3-beat gap is not possible.

14. First note that if p is even, then $3p + 2g$ is even and therefore $(3p+2g) \bmod 8 \neq 1$. For each odd value of p there are two values of g. The (p, g) pairs are $(1, 3)$, $(1, 7)$, $(3, 0)$, $(3, 4)$, $(5, 1)$, $(5, 5)$, $(7, 2)$, and $(7, 6)$.

15. Shifts: `xx.x.` `x.x.x` `.x.xx` `x.xx.` `.xx.x`
Sets of beat classes: {0, 1, 3}; {4, 0, 2}; {3, 4, 1}; {2, 3, 0}; {1, 2, 4}. I solved this problem by subtracting 1 each time. Note that sets may be written in any order. For example, {4, 0, 2} = {0, 2, 4}.

16. The resultant rhythms are, in order, `xx..`, `xx.x`, `xxxx`, `xxx.`, `xx..`. There are four different ones, since the first and last are the same.

17. You must shift 2 times. The sets are {4, 5} and {2, 3}. Mathematically, you subtract 2 from the first set to get the second.

19. The rhythm class of `xxx.x..` is

{`xxx.x..` `xx.x..x` `x.x..xx` `.x..xxx` `x..xxx.` `..xxx.x` `.xxx.x.`}

The pattern `..x.xxx` does not belong to this class.

20. The rhythm class is {`x..x..` `.x..x.` `..x..x`}. If a rhythm contains repeats, its rhythm class will have fewer than 6 members. Therefore, it is possible for a rhythm class in a 6-beat measure to have 1, 2, 3, or 6 members. In general, if n is the number of beats in a measure, then the sizes of rhythm classes are divisors of n, and every divisor of n is represented.

Bibliography

[1] M. Clayton, *Time in Indian Music: Rhythm, Metre, and Form in North Indian Rag Performance* (Oxford University Press, Oxford, 2008).

[2] T. Gross, James Brown: Feeling good, Radio interview, Fresh Air on WHYY, Philadelphia (2005).

[3] R. W. Hall and P. Klingsberg, Asymmetric rhythms and tiling canons, *Amer. Math. Monthly* **113**(10), (2006) 887–896.

[4] J. London, *Hearing in Time: Psychological Aspects of Musical Meter* (Oxford University Press, Oxford, 2004).

[5] T. Murthy, 16 beat tala — Indian rhythms, (2009), https://www.youtube.com/watch?v=BCkxRxdcwX0. Retrieved on January 21, 2018. Excerpt uploaded by user I Am Alfredo entitled "Tala: Raja Vidhyadharam" from "108 Talas, Mohara & Korvai", DVD by Dr. T. K. Murthy.

[6] G. T. Toussaint, *The Geometry of Musical Rhythm: What Makes a "Good" Rhythm Good?* (CRC Press, Boca Raton, FL, 2013).

Chapter 2

Creating a Level Playing Field for Non-music Majors

Timothy A. Johnson

Ithaca College, Ithaca, NY, USA
tjohnson@ithaca.edu

2.1. Introduction

Although mathematical music theory provides a rich environment for interdisciplinary courses for non-music majors, discrepancies between the inevitably and widely varied musical backgrounds and experiences of students can be a difficult problem to overcome. Some students attracted to such a course may have strong musical backgrounds developed through instrumental or vocal lessons, traditional ensemble experiences, participation in popular music groups of diverse styles and shapes, and even formal instruction in music theory. Other students, on the other hand, may have little to no prior musical experience on which to draw, yet become attracted to a course of this kind because of their mathematical interests or backgrounds, or due to their love of music. The result is a diverse collection of students, some of whom already know intervals, scales, and chords, and others of whom cannot name a note. Some students can relate course activities to their experiences on an instrument, while others are not personally familiar with any instrument. Although non-music major courses in mathematical music theory also contain students with a wide range of experiences in *mathematics*, this diversity in mathematical backgrounds seems easier to overcome than the musical disparity because the range of differences is less acute and often can be overcome relatively easily as the course progresses due to the nature of the mathematical material or the pacing of the introduction of new concepts.

2.1.1. *Teaching fundamentals of music theory*

The solution seems simple enough: Teach music fundamentals. It is a solution that I have employed multiple times with non-music major courses in mathematical music theory; however, each time I am left not fully satisfied with the progress of the class. The students with weak or no musical backgrounds complain about the steep learning curve in music fundamentals, while the more musically experienced students are bored beyond consolation. This approach is flawed. Fundamentals of music theory is a course that many music majors need to take due to poor or non-existent musical experience with music theory in high school. These music majors can draw on their experiences playing musical instruments or singing, and even some of them struggle. To expect non-music majors with little to no prior musical experience to learn this separate subject, while at the same time encountering principles of mathematical music theory, is not realistic in a single course. Although it is possible, in some sense, to cultivate basic music theory survival skills in students with little to no musical experience, their understanding of music theory typically will remain deficient, and they will lag significantly behind their more musically experienced classmates, creating a sense of privilege that they cannot overcome in attempting to succeed at a high level in a mathematical music theory course.

Although this unfair situation is not their fault, the less musically experienced students may find it difficult or impossible to overcome their lack of a musical background every time they encounter music-theory based contexts associated with the course. Teaching these students to use the piano keyboard to help them navigate intervals and scales, for example, remains an abstract construction for most of them. They can point to notes on a drawing of a keyboard and calculate whole and half steps, but they have little understanding of notes beyond their alphabetical A–G classification, with sharp and flat modifiers only complicating the matter, not to mention the complications of enharmonic equivalence. Meanwhile their more musically experienced classmates are using the pianos in the practice rooms, enthusiastically exploring the mathematical concepts encountered in actual musical contexts, and enriching their experience in a desirable and beneficial way. These students, and often only these students, obtain a truly interdisciplinary experience with music and mathematics when a course requires even a basic understanding of concepts from music theory, unless all students already possess that understanding or are otherwise equipped to study it simultaneously due to their other previous experiences in music.

2.1.2. *A textbook example*

This problem is easily encountered. My textbook, *Foundations of Diatonic Theory: A Mathematically Based Approach*, is intended for both music majors and non-music majors, and it faces this issue with the latter population [1]. Aspects of basic music theory appear throughout the book, making it necessary to introduce fundamentals of music theory in courses for non-music majors either before they work through the textbook or simultaneously with it. This approach creates the uneven playing field described above between students with varied musical backgrounds. Although this problem remains unaddressed, at least one reviewer strongly disagreed with the idea that the book poses this problem for non-music major students. This reviewer acknowledged the lack of instruction in music fundamentals in the textbook but did not criticize the textbook for this omission, and even praised the textbook's potential for this audience [2]. Nevertheless, adopting several modifications to the diagrams and musical notation in this textbook allows it to be used in a much more ecumenical way with non-music major populations. In this chapter I provide pathways to a more effective use of this material in mathematical music theory courses for non-music majors, which also are applicable to other pedagogical approaches that combine music fundamentals with mathematical principles. At the same time some of these approaches provide a platform for a richer mathematical exploration of concepts from diatonic theory. Although most of these alterations are very simple fixes on the surface level, they can prevent access if left unaddressed. Because this altered approach to the diagrams and musical notation moves students further from the musical side of the materials, it is imperative that instructors supply the musical contexts and content that become displaced. Nevertheless, in so doing courses can be enlivened musically by bringing more musical activities and musical examples into the classroom and by ensuring that all students, not just those with strong musical backgrounds, fully engage with the material in an musical way. Moreover, this approach mitigates the potential for students to work around or gloss over the musical content due to their lack of prior experience.

2.2. Musical Structures from Geometric Figures

The first problem encountered in this textbook, labeling notes on circle diagrams in Exercise 1.4 in the textbook, is easily remedied. Instead of labeling circles with note names, the process used throughout the textbook, circles may be labeled with integers in mod 12, in the usual manner of a clockface (with 0 replacing 12), as shown in Illustration 2.1. (This chapter uses illustration, rather than figure, to avoid confusion with references to the figures in the textbook

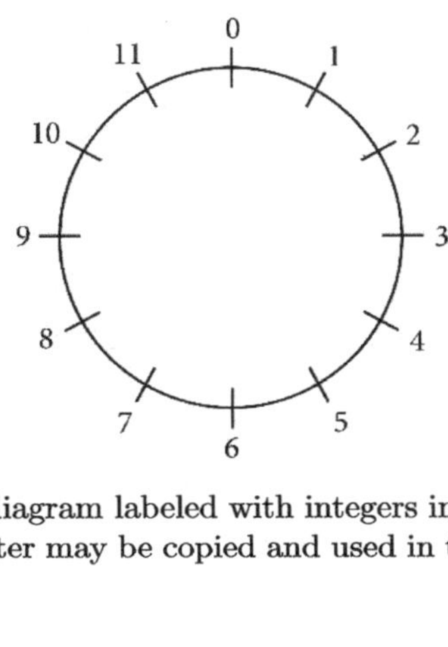

Illustration 2.1. Circle diagram labeled with integers instead of note names. (All illustrations in this chapter may be copied and used in teaching contexts without seeking permission.)

discussed here.) Musical names associated with dot patterns on the clockface would need to be developed in class, but more even success for students is possible with classroom attention on this issue than having students work out the note names for themselves using a piano in conjunction with the textbook alone. I have had decidedly mixed results with non-major populations working these musical patterns out on the keyboard for themselves. Working through the problem in class provides an opportunity for everyone to be involved as each musical structure is introduced, rather than only a few students racing ahead with their prior knowledge of musical structures, such as diminished seventh chords, pentatonic and whole tone scales, and the like, due to their extensive prior musical experiences. As students work through the remainder of the textbook, they may relabel all the circles employed using numbers outside of the circles (with the letter names still shown inside the circles) and only gradually begin to associate numbers with notes.

For figures and exercises involving staff notation in the first chapter of the textbook, substituting circle diagrams obtains equivalent results, and no musical notation must be employed. In some cases, such as Fig. 1.5 (p. 20), the textbook includes both circle and staff notation and can be adapted quickly and easily. However, in other cases, such as Exercise 1.5 (p. 22) and similar exercises, circle diagrams, labeled with integers as described above, can be substituted for the staff notation used in the textbook without diminishing the impact of the experience. Specifically, the diagrams that students developed earlier to form maximally even structures can be used directly to solve the problems in Exercise 1.5, instead of using the musical notation, simply by rotating the circle diagrams instead of transposing musical structures on the staff. Class time must be spent to associate the circle diagram work with the musical sounds, but the intricacies of staff notation can be postponed, or even avoided completely, without hindering the progress of all members of the class, irrespective of prior background with musical notation.

Similar adaptations may be used throughout the remainder of the first chapter in order to facilitate the completion of the exercises. For Exercise 1.6 (pp. 31–32), the instructor simply can provide the

Table 2.1. Exercise 1.6 (pp. 31–32) in *Foundations of Diatonic Theory* adapted from note names to integers.

Exercise	Numerical equivalents for notes
1.6a	4, 10
1.6b	2, 6, 10
1.6c	1, 3, 7, 9, 11
1.6d	0, 2, 4, 5, 7, 9, 11
1.6e	0, 2, 3, 5, 6, 8, 9, 11

Table 2.2. Exercise 1.7 (pp. 35–36) in *Foundations of Diatonic Theory* adapted from whole and half steps in scales to numerically based interval patterns.

Scale	Interval pattern
Major	2-2-1-2-2-2-1
Natural minor	2-1-2-2-1-2-2
Harmonic minor	2-1-2-2-1-3-1
Melodic minor	2-1-2-2-2-2-1

numerical equivalents for the notes on the staff, as shown in Table 2.1. For later examples, such as Exercise 1.7 (pp. 35–36), on the other hand, in order to increase the self-reliance of students, scales may be introduced using numerically based interval patterns. For example, the major scale and the three forms of the minor scale may be defined by the interval patterns without reference to staff notation with no loss of content, as shown in Table 2.2. With these patterns and the introduction of integer equivalences (C $= 0$, C-sharp and D-flat $= 1$, D $= 2$, etc.) indicating the starting notes of the scales, students with or without musical backgrounds may proceed through the reminder of the first chapter on the same level, with no real advantage to either group.

At the same time the mathematical context of these exercises may be enriched by using this numerically based approach in place of note names. All calculations of c distances may be made using mod 12 math, instead of counting. This shift in approach becomes even more important in the ensuing chapters of the textbook, where the intervallic distances become larger.

2.3. Exploring Diatonic Patterns Graphically

The main ideas explored in the second chapter of *Foundations of Diatonic Theory* concern how diatonic patterns change or retain their shapes as they are transposed through the diatonic collection. Staff notation forms the basis of these explorations in the first half of the chapter, and also the identification of intervals uses terms from music theory (such as major third and perfect fifth) combined with numbers of half steps. For non-music major classes with students from varying backgrounds, these musically-oriented approaches create a wide discrepancy in the fluidity of completing the assignments and the amount of time necessary to devote to each exercise. The exercises are far easier to complete for students comfortable with the staff and intervals than for students who are just learning these concepts and approaches for the first time. Students with backgrounds in staff notation even are able to use their understanding of intervals to avoid counting the actual half steps, a time-intensive and rather unrewarding process. The *musical* concepts can be grasped by both groups in classroom demonstrations focusing on the sounds of the patterns, but the staff-based apparatus, both for naming notes and for identifying intervals, remains a significant barrier for many students.

Again, one way to circumvent gaps between students with different backgrounds is to use a graphically-based approach to these exercises, rather than a staff-based approach. Twelve-line circle diagrams can show the underlying *scalar* patterns by using solid lines for the notes in the scale and dashed lines for the non-scalar notes. This approach is one way to present the information necessary for students to complete the exercises in a manner that promotes understanding of the concepts without reliance on musical staves. Illustration 2.2 shows a circle diagram for the C major scale that can be used for any of the exercises corresponding to this scale (Exercises

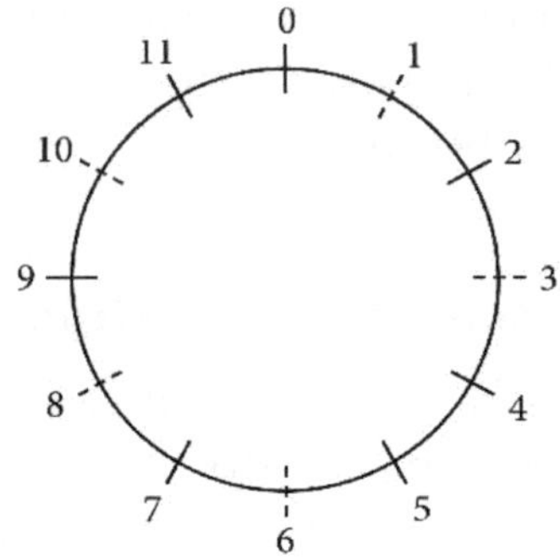

Illustration 2.2. A circle diagram corresponding to the C major scale in a chromatic context that may be used to substitute for staff-based notation without loss of content.

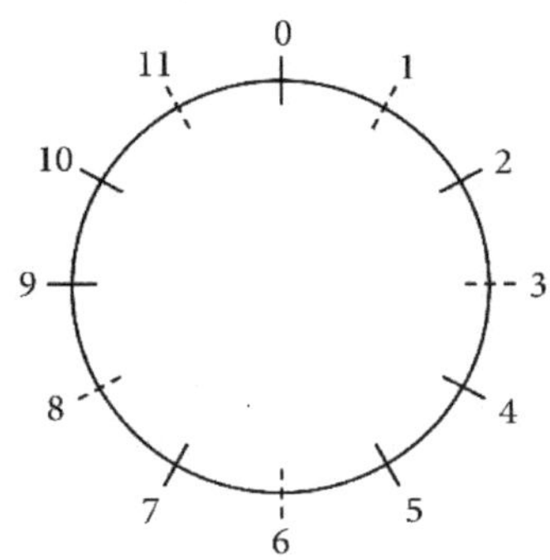

Illustration 2.3. A circle diagram corresponding to the F major scale, a rotation of the C major scale illustration.

2.1a, 2.1b, 2.2a, 2.4a, 2.4c, and 2.5a–f). As students transpose groups of notes diatonically on the circle diagrams, they must preserve the shape of the patterns while placing dots only on the solid lines. However, when they count intervals, they count both dashed and solid lines (for example to identify the distance of 1 between E and F and the distance of 2 between G and A).

Similar diagrams can be used for the other scales in the chapter, simply rotating the pattern of solid and dashed lines to correspond to the other keys, where C = 0, as shown in Illustration 2.3 for F major (Exercises 2.1c and 2.2c) as a model. The diagram corresponding to each major scale may be formed by rotating the C major diagram seven places (a perfect fifth) clockwise for each sharp added to the key signature or seven places counterclockwise for each flat added.

Altered diagrams also are necessary for the various forms of the minor scale and for the other scales explored in the chapter. Illustration 2.4 shows the diagram for the D harmonic minor scale (Exercise 2.6a), and Illustration 2.5 shows the E ascending melodic minor scale (Exercise 2.6b).

Using diagrams rather than staff-based notation for the other scales explored allows students to perform the rotations of the series of notes independently, rather than using the completed series on the

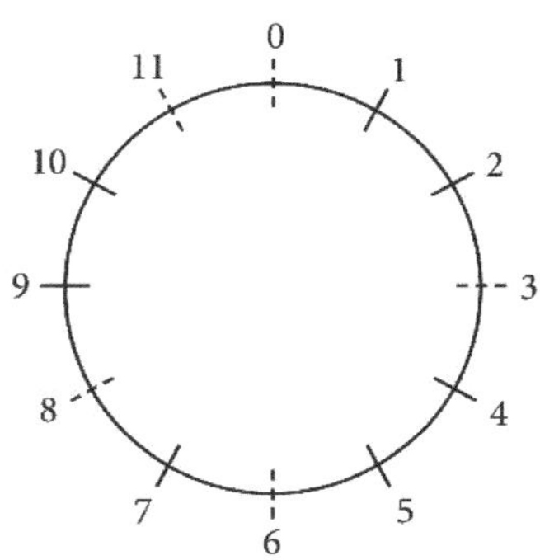

Illustration 2.4. A circle diagram corresponding to the D harmonic minor scale.

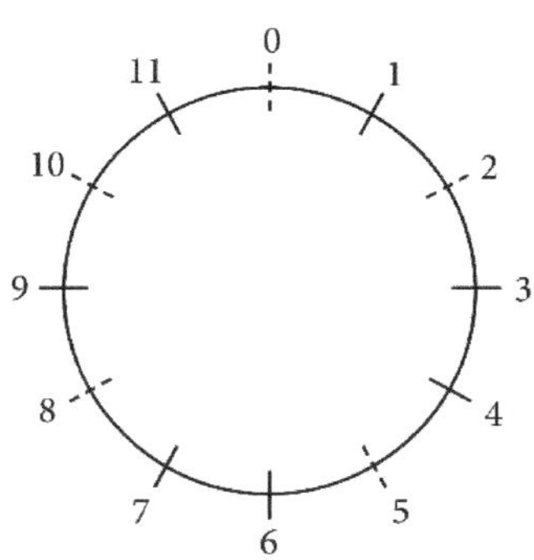

Illustration 2.5. A circle diagram corresponding to the E ascending melodic minor scale.

staves in the textbook, which were provided to facilitate transposition of series within these non-diatonic (and therefore not staff-based) scales. Without the staff these rotations are not cumbersome for the student, and students will have no trouble working out these exercises on their own, simply rotating the series using the solid lines. Since an important part of the approach in the textbook is developing student independence, this modification enhances the experience, provided that the instructor maintains focus on the musical aspects of the exercises during class time. The diagram for Illustration 2.6 shows the pentatonic scale (Exercise 2.7a), again with solid lines indicating the scale. Illustration 2.7 shows the whole tone scale

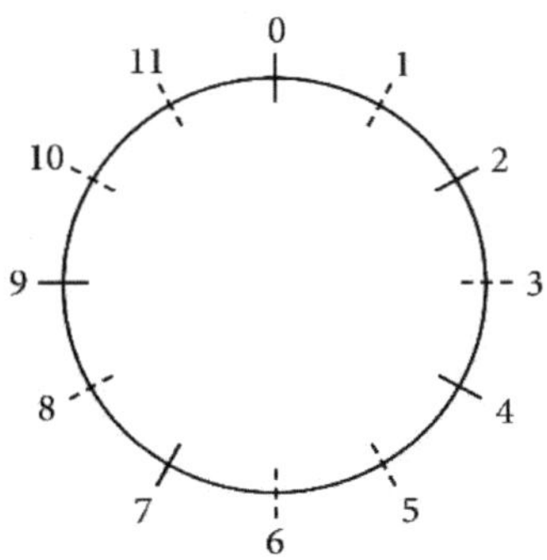

Illustration 2.6. A circle diagram corresponding to (C major) pentatonic scale.

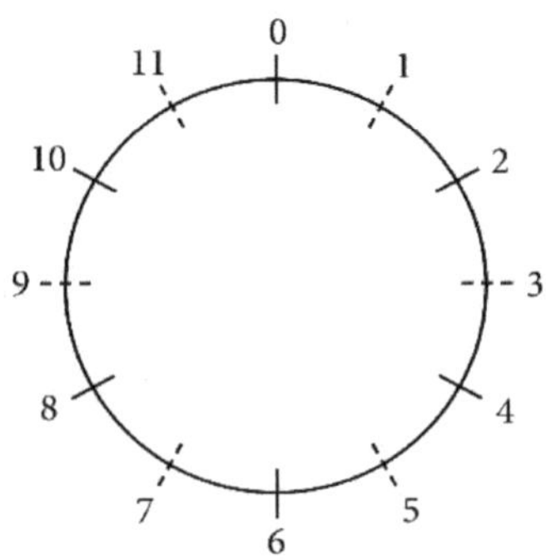

Illustration 2.7. A circle diagram corresponding to the (even) whole tone scale.

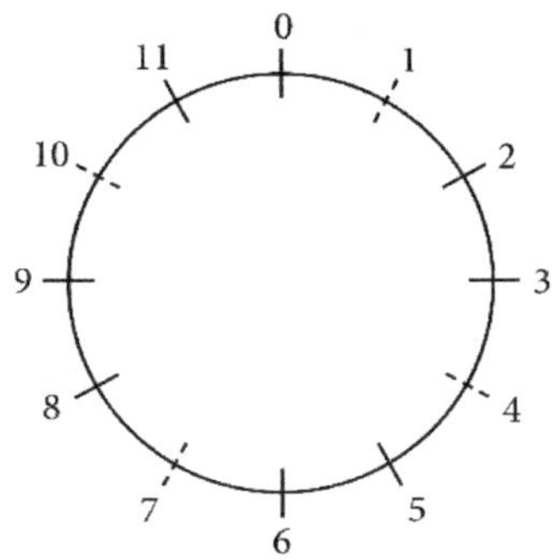

Illustration 2.8. A circle diagram corresponding to the (2, 3) octatonic scale.

(Exercise 2.7b), with its even pattern of alternating solid and dashed lines around the circle. And Illustration 2.8 shows the octatonic scale (Exercise 2.7c).

The remainder of the chapter already employs circle diagrams and may be completed by students both with and without backgrounds in music theory without modification. However, these circle diagrams model the circle of fifths, rather than the scales depicted by the circle diagrams presented above, and care must be taken to avoid confusion. Students will refer to their scale-based circle diagrams in order to create diagrams based on the circle of fifths, and they will compare results using the two types of diagrams to observe occurrences of interval patterns as depicted by both types of diagrams. In so doing they will be able to discover the properties introduced in the chapter independently by their manipulation of note series and their observations of interval patterns. In this way they have an opportunity to explore cardinality equals variety and structure implies multiplicity in detail. Again the musical sounds associated with these diagrams must be brought out in class by the instructor in order to provide direct musical contexts for these mathematically oriented concepts and to mitigate for the more abstract approach presented by circle diagram substitutions for musical staves — though musical staves represent a musical abstraction too, just one that musicians, perhaps, take for granted.

2.4. Graphing Triads and Seventh Chords

The third and final chapter of *Foundations of Diatonic Theory* primarily works with circle diagrams developed earlier in the textbook. Students plot triads and seventh chords on these diagrams, and these new musical structures must be introduced in order for students to complete the exercises. In this case a discrepancy between the backgrounds of students with and without prior musical experience is most likely to be pronounced. Students with musical backgrounds in non-music major courses often have developed an understanding of chords through experience with popular music and the chords that form an integral part of much of this music. Nevertheless, once students understand that triads and seventh chords are formed by skipping diatonic steps to create the structures (in thirds, to use musical nomenclature), students usually are able to proceed with the graphically based exercises without difficulty.

For the final exercise of the chapter, however, staff-based notation returns. Exercise 3.6 provides opportunities to write triads and seventh chords on each note of four major scales. With the same modification described previously, these exercises may be completed both by students with musical backgrounds and students without musical backgrounds. Again the use of circle diagrams with solid and dashed lines, based on the underlying major scale allows students with a wide range of prior musical experiences to complete the exercises and understand the concepts of how cardinality and structure relate to these essential musical formations.

Making this modification, and the modifications developed throughout this chapter, levels the playing field for self-directed, independently experienced explorations with these exercises. Taking a similar approach to other pedagogical material that relies on note names, staves, intervals, and other concepts from the fundamentals of music theory enhances the experience for all students. Keeping a focus on the varying backgrounds of students in mathematical music theory courses that are designed for non-music majors, and making alterations in the presentation and development of materials, can provide richer interdisciplinary experiences for all students.

Bibliography

[1] T. A. Johnson, *Foundations of Diatonic Theory: A Mathematically Based Approach to Music Fundamentals* (Scarecrow Press, Lanham, MD, 2008).
[2] M. Santa, Review of foundations of diatonic theory, by Timothy A. Johnson, *Gamut* **4**(1) (2011) Article 12, http://trace.tennessee.edu/gamut/vol4/iss1/12.

Chapter 3

Mathematics in Music: An Undergraduate Course

James R. Hughes

Mathematical Sciences Department, Elizabethtown College,
Elizabethtown, PA 17022, USA
hughesjr@etown.edu

3.1. The Reasoning Behind the Course

Every two years since 2009, I have offered an undergraduate course entitled "Mathematics in Music". The main impetus for the course was a desire to introduce students to some of the principal ways mathematics is currently being used in the creation and study of music. In designing the course, I placed a high priority on interdisciplinary authenticity, focusing on clear and effective application of mathematical approaches and tools to problems of mainstream interest to music practitioners. I also sought to present the course at a level midway between the popular level (which assumes no prerequisite knowledge of either discipline) and the research level (which assumes graduate-level familiarity with both disciplines). A constant guiding principle of approach was the facilitation of connections between students' actual experience of music with mainstream use of mathematics in musical research. My own review of contemporary scholarly literature on connections between mathematics and music eventually led me to design the course around six main units: Fundamentals, Acoustics, Tuning, Theory and Analysis, Composition, and Education.

I have previously discussed my course in a paper published in the *Journal of Mathematics and Music* [3]. In that paper, I focus primarily on the culminating activities for the six main course units. This chapter is more of a general overview.

My course is offered to undergraduates of all years and majors at my home institution of Elizabethtown College (Pennsylvania). To help ensure an audience for the course, I designed it to be part of the College's Core (a.k.a. general education) curriculum, in the area of Creative Expression. (In [3], I go into more detail about how requirements of the Core curriculum helped drive some course design decisions.) The course is also designated as part of the College-wide Honors program, which helps justify somewhat higher-than-usual expectations for prerequisite knowledge and academic maturity. Finally, the course is deemed to have sufficient mathematical content to count as an elective in the Mathematics major. Thus, for a Mathematics major in the College-wide Honors program, the course can potentially fulfill three different requirements, in the Core, Honors, and major programs.

Although I do a small amount of lecturing from time to time, the overall style of the course is that of a seminar, emphasizing discussion, interaction, and collaborative work among students. There is no required text for the course; rather, I make available to the students some writings of my own (which I may assemble into a text in the future), and items by other authors via the reserve desk at the College library. The course description, as it appears in the syllabus, is as follows:

This is an interdisciplinary, Honors, Creative Expression Core course. Participants will deepen and enrich their creative experience of music by learning about the principal ways that mathematical ideas are applied to the creation of music, and by incorporating these ideas into their own creative repertoires. Of particular interest will be notation, acoustics, tuning systems, theory and analysis, composition, and education.

The course has no formal college-level prerequisites, but the following list of informal prior expectations is given in the syllabus:

- Basic music-reading ability, including rhythmic notation and pitch notation in both treble and bass clef.
- Basic keyboard familiarity (i.e., ability to find a given note on a standard piano keyboard).
- Rudimentary performance capability on at least one instrument (including voice).
- Familiarity with terminology and notation of basic mathematical set theory (unions, intersections, etc.).
- Familiarity with basic mathematical terminology and notation for functions (f(x), domain, range, etc.).
- Facility with high school algebra.
- Familiarity with elementary functions, including exponentials, logarithms, and trigonometric functions.
- Familiarity with the Cartesian coordinate plane, and the graphs of functions listed above.

In an effort to reconcile my own ideas for the course with the College's requirements for a Creative Expression Core course, I articulate two main goals in the syllabus:

(1) Deepen and enrich the creative experience of music by developing mathematical ways of understanding, analyzing, and synthesizing elements of music (including, but not limited to, acoustics, tuning, theory, composition, and performance) on various levels.
(2) Instill appreciation for the idea that the emotive and intellectual aspects of creative expression are intertwined parts of a related whole.

I also list in the syllabus learning outcomes specific to the Creative Expression area of the Core curriculum:

(1) Examine concepts employed in the creation and analysis of like artworks.
(2) Develop and articulate informed aesthetic judgments.

(3) Create or perform artistic work representative of the discipline.
(4) Express the intrinsic value of an artistic medium.
(5) Define the ways in which creative art forms show and affirm human feelings, desires, experiences, and/or values.

Finally, I list learning outcomes for each of the main units, and for the term project for the course.

(1) Identify mathematical aspects of basic notational and analytical issues in music.
(2) Apply mathematical of models of sound to the creation of music.
(3) Utilize the mathematics behind scale construction to make aesthetically significant distinctions between tuning systems used in music.
(4) Apply the mathematical concepts of pitch-class sets and transformational theory to simple analysis of written musical passages.
(5) Utilize mathematical ideas and techniques in the creation of a short musical composition.
(6) Discuss intelligently how connections between mathematics and music can be incorporated into primary and/or secondary school curricula, and the value of doing so.
(7) Be able to research, write, and speak about a particular aspect of mathematics in music, making appropriate and effective use of the resources, concepts, language, and symbols of both disciplines.

By design, there is a learning progression built into each unit, manifested by recurring sequences of different types of assignments: readings, collaborative worksheets, quizzes, and creative experiences. There is also a Term Project that students develop in stages during the semester, and present to their classmates at the end of the term. In keeping with the seminar style of the course, there are no exams.

In the sections that follow, for each main unit of the course I briefly summarize the content, and give examples of questions that appear on worksheets and quizzes. I also describe the culminating creative experience for each unit, and mention some pitfalls I have experienced. I then give a brief description of the research project.

3.2. Fundamentals

3.2.1. *Content summary*

We first review the basic elements of musical notation, and connect them with formal mathematical notions of order and distance. We learn (or review) that ordinal (scale) numbers (third, fourth, etc.) and counting semitones give two ways of measuring musical distance. We observe that the musical staff can be considered a version of the Cartesian plane, and suggest that other musical situations can be modeled by mathematical spaces. We review rhythmic notation and terminology, again invoking relevant mathematical ideas.

We then review intervals, together with the musical notions of transposition and inversion, and take the opportunity to introduce the mathematical formalism of transformations and equivalence relations. We deepen our study of rhythm, and mathematical aspects thereof, by introducing ties and tuplets. Next we do a quick study of chords (triads and seventh chords), scales and modes. Finally, we go through a brief introduction to rhythm from the point of view of timelines, pulse number and onset number, reading excerpts from a recent book by Toussaint [8].

3.2.2. *Examples of worksheet and quiz questions*

In designing worksheet and quiz questions, I strive to keep in mind the guiding principle of connecting any mathematical model we study to students' actual experience of music. In some cases this results in questions that ask students to come up with their own examples, as in the worksheet question below:

Give another musical example (other than pitch or time) of an ordered set. That is, give an example of an ordered set that occurs in music, by describing precisely the elements of the set, and the order relation that holds among them.

The next sample worksheet question also asks students to generate their own examples, in this case of intervals occurring in actual music. The table referenced by the question has a column listing intervals from a minor second through an octave, a column for listing a song in which the interval occurs, and a column for specifying the precise location when the interval occurs. Although it may seem like a pedestrian exercise, it serves the very important purpose of demonstrating to students that intervals are not merely a remote mathematical abstraction, but rather a ubiquitous musical phenomenon, the precise awareness of which can enhance one's creative experience of music.

Create your own table of aural interval recognition examples that differ from the ones given in the reading and are verifiable (via score or recording) if necessary.

The following quiz question is meant to illustrate to students that even (or especially) in the midst of creativity, one may encounter mathematical problems to solve:

In the musical Carousel, the character of Mr. Snow encounters his betrothed, Carrie, in a seemingly compromising situation, and, in a comically overbearing and straight-laced manner, proceeds to declare that they cannot possibly continue with their marriage plans. The libretto calls for Carrie to "whimper" at this point, whereupon Mr. Snow sings a song, "Geraniums in the Winder", lamenting what might have been. The composer, Richard Rodgers, sought to have the introduction to the song mimic Carrie's plaintive cries. He accomplished this by writing a tuplet consisting of a descending 5-note fragment of an A major scale that has the collective duration of an eighth note. What symbol (quarter note, eighth note, etc.) should be used for the individual notes of the tuplet in this case? To help you out, here is the relevant passage from the reading: In general, a tuplet of n notes that ordinarily would each have duration d consists of n notes of equal duration that together comprise a duration of $2^k d$, where k is the largest positive integer such that 2^k is less than n. Here, you are being asked to find d; in your answer, identify n and k in order to help explain how you find d.

3.2.3. *Culminating creative experience*

At the end of this unit, I ask the students to transcribe a roughly 30-second passage of a musical work of their own choosing. The assignment is very definitely transcription and not dictation; students are permitted unlimited hearings of the passage, and encouraged to draw the passage from their own listening repertoires (as long as they have not previously seen written music for the passage). The intent of the assignment is for students to apply the mathematical aspects of symbolic music representation they have learned to a task that is intricate enough to facilitate deeper appreciation of a previously familiar work. In one recent case, this intent was borne out with unusual intensity and clarity. A student chose to transcribe a passage from the song "Do You Wanna Build a Snowman" from the soundtrack of the movie *Frozen*. In order for the passage to have the required length, the student extended the transcription to a background part, played by a flute, at the end of the passage. When the transcription was complete, we realized with astonishment that the flute part is actually a fragment of the tune for the famous anthem "Let It Go" that occurs later in the movie — a subtle musical foreshadowing that is not at all obvious to a casual listener.

3.2.4. *Pitfalls*

In an early incarnation of the course, I expected too much of the students — who are not usually music majors — in the way of ear training and sight singing. As helpful as it would be for students to have a thorough grounding in these skills, there is not nearly enough time in my course to develop such grounding from scratch. In more recent versions of the course, I have been much more modest in my ear training expectations, and do not require sight singing at all.

An unfortunate early experience with the transcription assignment taught me that a transcription passage with too much *rubato* can be impossible to grade or critique rhythmically. As a result, I now formally screen for and disallow such passages.

Another potential pitfall that has not actually occurred would be that a student is interested in transcribing a passage from the rap genre, which does not use traditional pitch structures. Were that to occur, I would have the student use alternative transcription tools as presented in a recent article by Nathaniel Condit-Schultz [1].

Students' prior experience and skills in both music and mathematics can vary considerably, raising the possibility of intimidation (on the part of those who perceive their prior skills are lacking) or boredom (on the part of those whose prior skills are strong). To help mitigate these negative effects, I have the students work collaboratively on the worksheets, and change the size and composition of the working groups frequently, to facilitate student-to-student transfer of skills. On the transcription assignment, I encourage students to work to their level, and (perhaps due to a sense of buy-in or ownership of the task) they usually do. One student with a limited background proposed transcribing the melody line of "Love Me Tender" performed by Elvis Presley. It seemed like an overly simple passage, but once I began working with the student, it became clear that the level of challenge was appropriate. At the other extreme, a music major with a great deal of prior experience ended up producing a full score to lengthy instrumental section of the soundtrack of a recent movie (*Dr. Strange*).

3.3. Acoustics

3.3.1. *Content summary*

Of course, the study of music from the point of view of acoustics, and its related mathematics, is an enormous area of inquiry. With the limited time in my course, we focus on establishing some basic ideas, and the mathematical and computational tools used to model them. Specifically, we review periodic functions and frequency, and learn about formulas relating frequency to pitch (as a signed number of semitones from a fixed pitch, such as A4). We then learn about (harmonic) overtones. After some reading in Roederer's book [7] about the physiology of the ear and sound perception, we conduct some in-class experiments on pitch perception, Just Noticeable Difference, and acoustical beats. Finally, we learn a little bit about Fourier transforms, and use a computer application (Sonic Visualizer) to study the spectra of various musical sounds.

3.3.2. *Examples of worksheet and quiz questions*

One of the first exercises is to construct a table of (approximate) frequencies corresponding to specific standard pitches (i.e., those found on a piano keyboard).

Later, after the Roederer reading, students are encouraged to think critically about the particulars of chord construction:

Go to chordfind.com and click on chord info for a G major (guitar) chord. Find the frequencies of all the notes for the suggested fingering. Then comment critically on the suggested fingering, in light of Roederer Section 2.4 Figure 2.13.

The students construct a table of frequencies of (harmonic) overtones of middle C, then proceed to the following exercise:

Using the Sonic Visualiser program open the file Middle C piano.wav. Hit the Play button to hear the sound and see its graph simultaneously. Pull down the menu under Pane, and select Add Peak Frequency Spectrogram. You should see a dark window with some faint, colored, thin, horizontal bands, corresponding to frequencies the software is detecting in the sound via discrete Fourier analysis. By hovering the cursor over these bands and looking at the little windows that pop up, you should be able to find the "peak frequency for each band. List the peak frequencies (actually narrow ranges) for the first 8 bands (counting from the lowest one). Do they correspond (approximately) to the frequencies listed in the table above?

Other exercises follow, exploring the spectra produced by various instruments.

3.3.3. *Culminating creative experience*

For the culminating creative experience in this unit, students are encouraged to apply the mathematical and computational tools we have studied to the critical analysis of sounds produced by a musical instrument, preferably one on which they have performance experience. Again, the emphasis is on students connecting their own musical experiences directly to the mathematical approaches introduced in the unit. Specifically, students are asked to prepare and give a 10 to 15 minute demonstration of an acoustical phenomenon utilized in music, including

(1) a brief description of the phenomenon and how it is modeled mathematically,
(2) manifestation of the phenomenon on an instrument or electronic device,
(3) at least one example of the phenomenon being used in actual musical practice, and
(4) discussion of how knowledge of the mathematical model enhances creativity.

Memorable examples of student work on this creative experience include a study of how positioning of the hand in the bell of a French horn affects the pitch produced, modeling and demonstrating the use of pinch harmonics on an electric guitar, "wolf tones" on the cello, and the use of beats in tuning.

3.3.4. *Pitfalls*

The main pitfall in this unit is the wide variability in students' mathematical backgrounds. Those who have taken (and done well in) multiple Calculus courses take in stride the technical aspects of Fourier analysis, while those with no background in Calculus have more difficulty with it. In recent years, I have varied the level of presentation according to the students' backgrounds (in one offering, all had had Calculus; in the next offering, a majority had not). I have also used the expedient of assigning students to collaborative groups in such a way that each group has at least one student with a sufficient Calculus background.

3.4. Tuning

3.4.1. *Content summary*

In a natural segue from the study of harmonic intervals from an acoustical point of view, we introduce scales constructed using whole-number frequency ratios, focusing mainly on the just major scale and the Pythagorean major scale. We compute frequencies and frequency ratios for these scales, and compare differences between them, and also differences between each of them and equal temperament (ET), to Just Noticeable Differences (JNDs) studied in the preceding unit. We also explore asymmetries in these scales.

We read an article by Neuwirth [5] and learn about the syntonic and Pythagorean commas. We do some associated computations, and compare the commas with the JND in various registers. We also learn about meantone tuning. Finally, utilizing some Mathematica code provided by Neuwirth, we listen to the various scales and associated intervals, and drill each other on being able to distinguish them by listening.

3.4.2. *Examples of worksheet and quiz questions*

The following is one of my favorite exercises for students. Juxtaposing their eventual finding that the trumpet interval as played is closest to an equal tempered major third, with the natural (presumably harmonic) acoustics of the instrument — a difference that is subtle but audible — drives home the point that equal temperament is learned (albeit unconsciously). Few, if any, teachers of brass instruments point out (or are even aware) that learning to play "in tune" involves overriding some of the natural tendencies of the instrument.

In the class directory, in your instructors folder under Worksheet materials, find sound files for a trumpet playing C (concert Bb) and E (concert D). Using Sonic Visualiser or other software, find the (fundamental) frequencies for the notes (as played) as accurately as possible, and then compute their ratio. Is the interval between the notes as played closer to a just, Pythagorean, or equal tempered major third? Comment on what you observe. Why is it interesting to ask this question?

The question below helps me gauge students' level of engagement with the Neuwirth reading in general, and the syntonic comma in particular.

Explain carefully, in your own words and in complete sentences, precisely how the ratio of 81/80 measures the degree of incompatibility between the pure third and the pure fifth.

3.4.3. *Culminating creative experience*

In the creative experience for this unit, students have the opportunity to apply the mathematics of tuning and scale construction to the critical analysis of the sound combinations made by musical instruments (including voices). Specifically, students prepare a short report (in both written and oral form) on a few particular intonation distinctions one can make between tuning systems using actual instruments or recordings of musical sound. Again the connection with actual music in their listening experience is paramount. Some recent examples include studies of actual intervals (particularly thirds) sung by *a capella* vocal ensembles, guitar tuning using harmonics, gamelan tuning, and modeling and demonstrating how an ocarina produces different pitches. In the latter, the student reported on mistakes in a model for ocarina sound production the student had found in a website online. Despite a considerable background in differential equations, the student found it difficult to formulate a correct model, but the close critical analysis of a proposed model made the report more than sufficiently interesting and worthwhile.

3.4.4. *Pitfalls*

Some of the distinctions between intervals in scales are admittedly subtle and hard to hear. In the creative experience, it is quite possible that an expected deviation from equal temperament is not borne out by observation, either because of limitations of perception, or the limitations of the sound analysis software used. For some students, the difficulty is compounded by lack of a clear understanding of what they are supposed to be observing or computing.

3.5. Theory and Analysis

3.5.1. *Content summary*

My course is a work in progress; each time the course is offered I make modifications to the content of every unit, refining the presentation, examples and exercises. But the unit on Theory and Analysis has undergone more substantial changes than the other units, due to the burgeoning variety of fruitful avenues of exploration, and the need to make hard choices due to time limitations. The topics I list here represent those aspects of mathematical music theory covered in the most recent incarnation of the course, but past versions of this unit have differed, and it is likely future versions will differ even more.

We first read excerpts from Forte's classic text [4] and learn about pitch class sets, normal order and prime forms. We revisit transposition and inversion in the context of Forte's writing. We then learn about other musically important properties of pitch class sets that have been studied in recent years, such as maximal evenness and the deep set property, in the context of familiar scales, and some unfamiliar ones (e.g., octatonic). In a bit of a stretch for undergraduate students (albeit honors students) we read the paper "A Transformational Space for Elliott Carter's Recent Complement-Union Music" by John Roeder [6], which provides a nice pivot from combinatorial analysis of pitch class sets to transformational theory. Finally, we learn some of the basic elements of neo-Riemannian transformational theory (e.g., the R, P, and L transformations, and Tonnetz representations), and related mathematical group theory (including group actions).

3.5.2. *Examples of worksheet and quiz questions*

In case it is not already sufficiently obvious, the sample worksheet exercise below helps illustrate that analysis of atonal music as practiced by Forte and others differs from traditional analysis of tonal music.

Represent a major triad by a prime form. Apply the inversion mapping I to the prime form, and interpret the result as a tonal chord. Keeping in mind that Forte would consider the new chord to be equivalent to the major triad, are you outraged or intrigued? Explain.

The next sample worksheet exercise follows a table of some familiar (and unfamiliar) scales and chords. It helps set up the next exercise, in which students check each scale or chord for maximal evenness.

Represent each of the collections listed above by a diagram formed by placing hash lines at the hour locations around a circle (to correspond with the twelve pitch classes), and then placing dots at the locations corresponding to pitch classes in the collection. Then, for each collection, determine how many distinct transpositions it has. (Hint: on the circle, a transposition is just a rotation.) Can you draw any conclusions about how 12, the cardinality d of each collection, and the number of transpositions it has are related?

The following worksheet exercise, concerning the Roeder paper and the All-Trichord Hexachord (ATH), involves a fair amount of combinatorial work, but the students (working in groups of three) dove into it.

Roeder makes the following observation about the ATH: Not only does it have the complement-union property (CUP), but it actually exhibits the property in two different ways! Not only could X be 0167 and Y be 04, but we also could take X as 048 and Y as 016. Verify this by pairing each member of the set class 048 with each (disjoint) member of the set class 016, and checking that the result really does belong to the ATH set class.

This last sample worksheet exercise illustrates how mathematics can inform questions of interest to music theorists, and also what I mean by "interdisciplinary authenticity". It requires introducing the notion of "voice leading distance" to students, but is well worth the extra effort.

The minimal number of L, R, and P operations needed to get from one triad to another can be taken as a metric on the set of all major and minor triads. (a) In this metric, how far is an F major triad from a C major triad? (b) How far is an F minor triad from a C major triad? (c) What is the largest distance possible in this metric? (d) Music theorist Dmitri Tymoczko uses the results of (a) and (b) above to argue that this LPR (or Tonnetz) metric is inferior to one based on voice leading distance. Explain his point of view by finding efficient voice leadings from F to C and from Fm to C.

3.5.3. *Culminating creative experience*

In the creative experience for this unit, students have the opportunity to apply what they have learned about musical sets and transformations (and the mathematics thereof) to the critical analysis of music they hear (and possibly perform). They find their own examples of a musical passages that can be studied utilizing some (not necessarily all) of the analytical tools we have seen (e.g., pitch-class sets or chords, properties of pitch-class sets, transformations between sets or chords), and prepare written analyses of these passages using those tools. Once again, the *in vivo* aspect of the assignment is crucial: students are not applying the analytical tools to unfamiliar, contrived examples, but to music they know and care about. Since the unit is introductory, the expected analysis is not particularly deep: in most cases, it just involves enumeration of the pitch class sets present, and the basic combinatorial or transformational relationships between them. Some memorable examples of student work on this assignment include a transformational analysis of a traditional Israeli folk song, "Darkeinu" (the particular arrangement used involved a key change that made the analysis more interesting), a study of the use of dissonance in a "neo-impressionist" choral work by Eric Whitacre, and a Tonnetz-based analysis of "When the Sun Goes Down" by the Arctic Monkeys.

3.5.4. *Pitfalls*

One obvious pitfall is the considerable mathematical and musical demands this unit puts on students. For the unit in its most recent incarnation, various combinatorial and algebraic tools needed to be developed in a relatively short time. I have had to give up on covering some recent, very promising trends in mathematical music theory due to the involvement of mathematical tools (e.g., category theory) that are inaccessible even to most undergraduate math majors. Likewise, some of the motivating musical examples come from the early twentieth century atonal repertoire, which is completely unfamiliar to most students. Since the progression from learning the requisite mathematical and music-theoretical background to the culminating creative experience is so rapid, it is unrealistic to expect analysis that resembles current research. Hence, even with the *in vivo aspect* mentioned above, there is some risk that lack of realism will get in the way of interdisciplinary authenticity. In short, students may not see the point of what they are doing. In this unit especially, I am still working on finding an undergraduate-appropriate balance between accessibility and authenticity.

3.6. Composition

3.6.1. *Content summary*

The reading for this section is less extensive than that of previous units. We learn about incorporating the transformational tools studied in the preceding unit into the process of tonal music composition. We then read a brief introduction to formal 12-tone composition, and then an excerpt from Leon Harkleroad's book [2] on probabilistic composition. I also do a brief presentation on David Cope's work with automated composition.

3.6.2. *Examples of worksheet and quiz questions*

Since, by this point in the semester, students are working more intensively on their research projects, there are no worksheets or quizzes in this unit or the next.

3.6.3. *Culminating creative experience*

In this creative experience, students have the opportunity to apply what they have learned about tonal musical transformations, probabilistic music, or 12-tone music (and the mathematics thereof) to the composition of a short passage of music. Specifically, students compose a short (16–32 measures) passage of music that incorporates the use of one of the following:

(1) Tonal transformations, such as transposition (chromatic or diatonic), inversion (chromatic or diatonic), or harmonic moves to relative or parallel minor/major and leading tone exchange.
(2) Probability, such as eighteenth-century dice music, or twentieth-century schemes for randomization of individual notes, as described in the Harkleroad reading.
(3) A 12-tone row and its variations as enumerated in a row box, as described in the reading.

Students are also asked to document their efforts by writing out a short paragraph in which they indicate which of the three options above they chose, and which transformations or schemes they utilized to develop the composition.

We take a class meeting to perform the compositions, either on a traditional instrument, or via a computer playback feature.

3.6.4. *Pitfalls*

Other than making sure the *pro forma* elements specified above are present, there are not a lot of criteria on which to base grades for the student compositions. Perhaps because of my background as a mathematician, I am uncomfortable making grading distinctions based on aesthetic matters, even though I personally may prefer one piece over another. If time would allow for longer pieces involving more development, then this difficulty might be mitigated.

In earlier incarnations of the course, there were some compatibility problems with computer playback software. More recently, though, such problems have largely disappeared.

3.7. Education

3.7.1. *Content summary*

In this unit, students "close the loop" and take on the roles of educators, considering the implications of what they have learned about mathematics in music for the way each discipline is taught to middle school level children. As a point of departure for discussion, they read the current Pennsylvania educational standards for music and for mathematics at or around the 7th grade level. They then engage in discussion regarding the case for interdisciplinary learning. Discussion moves from general considerations to the specifics of designing classroom activities that introduce middle school students to the use of mathematics in the study or creation of music, which is the culminating creative experience for the unit. At this point in the semester, the students are accustomed to working with one another, so it is both feasible and effective to limit my own participation in discussions as much as possible, letting the discussion be mostly student-driven. As in the previous unit, there are no worksheets or quizzes.

3.7.2. *Culminating creative experience*

In the creative experience for this unit, students have the opportunity to apply what they have learned about mathematics in music to education, by designing and implementing one or more engaging classroom activities for middle school students. This Creative Experience is a group project on which we all will work together. Of necessity, I take care of some logistical details (i.e., arrangements with the middle school, classroom, and teacher with whom we will work) months in advance. I also provide the following task sequencing guidelines:

(1) Choose one or two general topic area(s). Your instructor will have some suggestions, based on past experience, but you need not feel constrained by these.
(2) Identify Pennsylvania Department of Education Standards for Mathematics and Music that might be addressed by an activity in your general topic area(s).
(3) List possible activities in your general topic area (brainstorming).
(4) Decide, as a group, on one to three specific activities to develop and deliver.
(5) Make detailed list of tasks that need to be done in order to prepare the activity (writing up learning outcomes, creating materials, finding resources, writing up plans, etc.), and delegate responsibilities for these tasks.
(6) Produce materials needed for the activity (displayed items, manipulatives, software, recordings, detailed plan for the activity, documentation, etc.).
(7) Test run of activities and last minute adjustments.
(8) On-site delivery.
(9) De-briefing, reflective questionnaire (individual) and submission of report (group).

Beyond providing these rough guidelines, I let the students organize themselves, make decisions, and create the activities. Ironically, taking the "hands off" approach is unfamiliar (and therefore difficult) for me, but it is worth it to watch the students take ownership of the task.

In recent incarnations of the course, the students have designed classroom activities involving rhythms as timelines (with a pulse number and onset number), and composition of a simple 12-tone row. The latter was particularly interesting because it was obviously the first exposure to atonal music for most of the schoolchildren.

3.7.3. *Pitfalls*

If the class is large (e.g., 12 or more), discussion involving everyone is difficult to maintain. Under such circumstances it is advantageous to break up into smaller groups. Likewise, it may make more sense to design several different activities, with (smaller) working groups assigned to each.

The school students' level of preparation is difficult to obtain in advance. E-mail exchanges with the middle school teacher have helped to some degree, but in some cases (e.g., some of the rhythm activities), the activity was pitched a little low (although the school students were polite about it).

3.8. Research Project

3.8.1. *Description*

There are two options for the research project in this course. The traditional option is an expository paper of roughly 2500 words, on a topic that is related in an essential way to the use or occurrence of mathematical ideas in music. The other option is to create an item, such as a computer program, musical composition, or musical instrument, incorporating the application of mathematics to music in some essential way. The second option will still involve some writing, in the form of documentation, performance notes, or similar explanatory text. The task of creating the paper or item is divided into stages, so that we can focus carefully on the processes of research and writing. The stages are Research Proposal, Bibliography, Outline, First Draft, and Final Draft. For non-traditional projects, students substitute Progress Reports for the Outline and First Draft. Students also prepare and deliver an oral presentation of their projects.

3.8.2. *Examples*

The most memorable project for me was a non-traditional one, a computer program that would automatically produce variations on an input MIDI file. Anecdotal details on that project are given in [3]. Almost as memorable was another non-traditional project, in which a student built a simple distortion pedal for an electric guitar. A memorable traditional project was a survey of automated transcription methods that went into considerable depth with respect to mathematical and computational tools used.

3.9. Conclusion

I still do not consider my course a finished product, but like to think I come reasonably close to achieving my goal of mathematical approaches to the study of music in a way that is true to both disciplines. In any case, it has been an interesting and worthwhile endeavor.

Bibliography

[1] N. Condit-Schultz, MCFlow: A digital corpus of rap transcriptions, *Empir. Musicol. Rev.* **11** (2016) 124–147.

[2] L. Harkleroad, *The Math Behind the Music* (Cambridge University Press, New York, 2006).

[3] J. Hughes, Creative experiences in an interdisciplinary honors course on mathematics in music, *J. Math. Music* **8** (2014) 131–143.

[4] A. Forte, *The Structure of Atonal Music* (Yale University Press, New Haven, 1977).

[5] E. Neuwirth, The mathematics of tuning musical instruments: A simple toolkit for experiments, in *Mathematics and Music: A Diderot Mathematical Forum*, eds. G. Assayag and H. Feichtinger (Springer, Berlin, 2002).

[6] J. Roeder, A transformational space for Elliott Carters recent complement-union music, in *Mathematics and Computation in Music*, eds. T. Klouche and T. Noll (Springer, New York, 2009).

[7] J. Roederer, *The Physics and Psychophysics of Music: An Introduction*, 4th edn. (Springer, New York, 2008).
[8] G. Toussaint, *The Geometry of Musical Rhythm: What Makes a "Good" Rhythm Good?* (CRC Press, Boca Raton, 2013).

Chapter 4

Phenomenally Loud: Music, Mathematics, and the Diversity of Musical Experience

Jon Kochavi

Swarthmore College, Swarthmore, PA, USA
jkochav1@swarthmore.edu

4.1. Introduction

Music is experiential. This statement hardly seems debatable, at least not when considered from the usual perspective. Standard musical actors — performers, audience members, composers — may have differing relationships or reactions to a musical event, but each gauges his or her understanding of music based on an interpretation of the sounds produced or implied. The music theorist, at least the effective one, engages directly with perceptual experience when analyzing a piece. Even "soundless" music — whether in the mind's imagination when "reading" a score or in the vibrational sensations produced in the alertly responsive deaf musician — creates an experiential event.

And yet, in the typical music theory classroom, there is often tension between the subject matter and the experience of music. This is not particularly surprising in a discipline that, while grounded in an art form inextricably linked to human perception, was so deeply shaped by its emergence from the Enlightenment ideals that placed a premium on objective truth. To provide just one extended quote to illustrate this epistemology, the following is taken from Diderot's "Encyclopédie" entry from his influential eighteenth-century compilation:

> One must therefore make the most serious attempt to explain the reasons that lie at the roots of things, when these exist. One must assign causes when they are known, indicate effects when these are certain, resolve difficulties by the direct applications of fundamental principles, demonstrate truths, expose errors, skillfully discredit prejudices, teach men to doubt and to wait, dissipate ignorance and put a just value on the different kinds of human knowledge, distinguish the true from the false, the true from the probable, the probable from the miraculous and the incredible, the common event from the extraordinary, the certain fact from the doubtful one, and the latter from those that are absurd and contrary to the laws of nature, understand the general course of natural events and take each thing only for what it is, and — consequently — inspire in men a taste for science, an abhorrence of lies, a hatred of vice and a love of virtue....
>
> A thing that I consider intolerable is that one should lean on some ancient writer's authority in questions that require the use of reason.... In scientific writings, it is the logical connections of ideas or of phenomena that directs our progress step by step as we advance....
>
> The world has long awaited a reasoning age, an age when the rules would be sought no longer in the classical authors but in nature, when men would come to sense the false and the true that are mingled in so many of the arbitrary philosophies of art, whatever field one works in.
>
> Diderot [2, pp. 294, 298]

The reaction against reliance on intellectual scaffolding handed down from previous generations is stark here, with its vigorous argument for replacing this mode of "arbitrary philosophy" with an appeal to natural law and scientific inquiry.

Richard Parncutt discusses the pitfalls emerging from this approach when it was applied to music, most notably by Rameau. The problem arose from the reductionism necessitated by this epistemological vantage point at a time when availability of the tools for application of this methodology to music was limited:

> The trouble with Rameau's approach seems to be that the *corps sonore* [the resonating body producing various overtones] is an objective, *physical* entity, but the musical harmony which it is supposed to explain is a subjective, psychological *experience*.... Rameau was working long before the major developments in psychoacoustics of pitch perception..., and so was in no position to realize the implications of a perceptual approach to the relationship between harmony and the *corps sonore*.
>
> Parncutt [8, pp. 16–17]

The tension, then, between the *objective* — with its claims of universality — and the *subjective* — as expressed through phenomenological experience — is a constant undercurrent in the music theory classroom. In cases when there is a more flexible syllabus, this background disquiet can be confronted directly, opening up the possibility of interdisciplinary discussion that organically ranges into the fields of philosophy, neuroscience, psychology, and disability studies among others. At first blush, a course on music and mathematics may not seem to be the most natural place to explore these issues. However, I have found that by situating such a course at the boundaries of both fields, rather than at the center of one with the "aid" of the other, pedagogical space is expanded, allowing for the possibility of considerations that fall well beyond the typical scope of either.

4.2. Mathematics and Music: Humanities in the Era of STEM

In the Mathematics and Music course that I teach at Swarthmore College, the focus is on the intersection of the two disciplines as examples of lines of intellectual inquiry, modes of understanding and organizing the world, and foundational approaches to conceptualizing and contextualizing thought and knowledge. In short, the course is designed as an introduction to studies in the liberal arts tradition using music and mathematics as a rich playing field for relatively straightforward questions prompting discussions, if not always answers, that are anything but. The population of students in the course generally falls into two (not necessarily discrete) categories: (1) music students who are interested in finding out more about the connections between mathematics and the art form they practice, and (2) math and science students who are interested in applying their knowledge to a field that they are connected to informally (though often passionately). In previous work characterizing the course philosophy [4], I focused on the role of boundary transgression between the theoretical (*musica*) and the practical (*cantor*) in the course, and how this can help open the door to introducing important advances and trends in the field of music theory at an early point of study. This goal benefits everyone involved, but can be especially useful to the first category of student, giving them a taste for the variety and manner of theoretic investigation that lies ahead for them if they choose to continue their academic music studies.[a]

In recent years, especially since the economic downturn in 2008, there has been a trend in higher education towards increased enrollments in STEM disciplines as major fields of study. This development is in evidence even at colleges with strong liberal arts traditions, like Swarthmore College.[b] Perhaps as a consequence of this, I have noted an uptick in the overall enrollment numbers and interest in the Mathematics and Music course, with an increasing proportion of these students coming from the STEM disciplines, the second category above. Applications of tools and methods of scientific

[a]This was the motivation beyond the radically revised undergraduate theory curriculum proposed by Richard Cohn in his Plenary Session address at the meeting for the Society for Music Theory in 1997 [1].

[b]The housing bubble burst took place in late 2006, with the banking collapse beginning in September 2008. Seniors and juniors at this time were most likely locked in to the majors they had chosen, but the effect could be detected in choices made by younger and incoming students. In graduating class of 2009 at Swarthmore, 30% of students had majored (or, in the case of double majors, had at least one major) in the Natural Science division and 30% majored (or had at least one major) in the Humanities division. By 2014, these numbers were 39% and 20%, respectively.

investigation — both theoretical and experimental — provide a level of comfort and security to many of the students involved in the course who come from majors in the natural sciences and engineering. However, one of the objectives of the course, with respect to this segment of the student population, is an active engagement in discourse characteristic of the humanities. This is particularly important because a number of these students are using the course, which is housed in the Department of Music and Dance and consequently in the Humanities Division, to fulfill a divisional distribution requirement. The pedagogy aspires to lead students through investigative terrain that feels comfortable and familiar, but then locates that journey in an epistemology representing a marked contrast to what the students might be used to from their STEM courses.

A topic that I have found to be particularly useful in this regard is the study of acoustics. The irony of using acoustics as means for a progressive introduction to the methodologies of humanities in a twenty-first century math and music course should not be lost here. Some decades back, if a course on mathematics and music were to be offered, acoustics would likely be the primary (if not the only) area of concentration. These early courses resembled courses on applications of physics, rather than music courses or even interdisciplinary liberal arts courses. This said, I have always included a unit involving acoustics in my course, if only to represent the broad reach the study of music has across the curriculum, not to mention to provide the foundation for the deep historical roots common to the two fields of study.

4.3. Measuring Loudness

The specific aspect of acoustics that my course focuses on is, by design, one that seems on the surface to be the simplest: loudness. All students have an intuitive understanding of the concept, and most will have some cursory experience with the idea of measuring loudness on a decibel (dB) scale. But even limiting the investigation of loudness to purely physical phenomena, the topic is deceptively

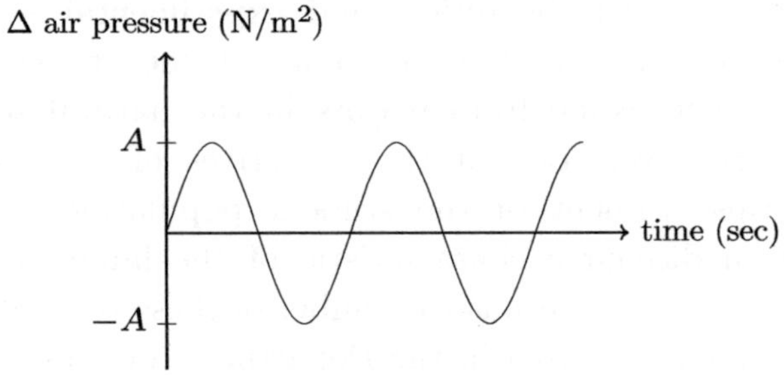

Fig. 4.1. Function $f(t) = A\ \sin(t)$ representing the idealized sound wave as the air pressure differential at a fixed point over a span of time.

complex. We can begin by modeling the physics of sound with an idealized sine wave representing sound pressure (air pressure deviation from the baseline reading at equilibrium in N/m^2) at a given point in space over a time interval (shown in Fig. 4.1). In a discussion of the aspects of this pure tone model which affect volume, important distinctions need to be make between the *instantaneous sound pressure* (the deviation from equilibrium at a given snapshot in time), the *peak sound pressure* (the amplitude **A** on the graph), and the *effective sound pressure.*

In an introductory acoustics course, the effective sound pressure would simply be defined with an equation and folded in to the overall discussion. In the context of this course, the path towards conceptualizing this value is more germane. We can understand effective sound pressure to be an adjustment to the basic sound pressure information gleaned from the sound wave itself, an adjustment that brings the measurement in line (or more closely aligned) with our perception of relative volume of sound. Intuitive discussions of altered sound waves graphs lead the class to two quick conclusions:

(a) the peak amplitude does not precisely correspond to loudness (comparing two graphs with identical amplitudes and periods, but varying overall particle displacement); and
(b) the amount of air displaced does not precisely correspond to loudness (comparing two graphs with identical particle displacement and periods, but varying amplitudes).

In fact, even a correlation between these properties and loudness is in question (at least in the general case).

To provide context, at this point in the class, it is necessary to dive into some physics. The concepts of energy and energy over time (or power) are natural acoustic explanations upon which to ground our understanding of human perceptions of loudness. It is not difficult to show that energy is directly proportional to velocity squared, where the velocity in this case is the particle velocity. Delving briefly into the concept of acoustic impedance, we can motivate the fact that particle velocity and sound pressure themselves are linearly related, justifying the fact that sound intensity (the measure of sound energy per second, per unit area) is proportional to the square of sound pressure. Finally, if we really want to understand the overall energy contained in a sound wave, from these basic facts it is clear that we will need to look not at the "peak" sound pressure or at the total (or even average) air displacement. Instead, we will need to consider the average sound pressure squared (over time), or the root mean squared value of the sound pressure, in order to compare sound intensities produced by varying sound waves.

With a grasp of the basic physics of sound, we can start to correlate this understanding with our sensation of loudness. Converting very small amounts of energy carried by a sound wave into the sensation of sound is a particularly impressive human (and animal) activity. The threshold of hearing typical in young humans corresponds to an air pressure change of $0.00002\,\mathrm{N/m^2}$, in the context of the standard sea-level air pressure of $101{,}325\,\mathrm{N/m^2}$. Translating this value into sound intensity, the energy threshold is tiny: $10^{-12}\,\mathrm{W/m^2}$. Rather than dealing with such small numbers in order to discuss loudness, we can convert sound intensity to sound intensity level, measures in decibels (dB), designating 0 dB to be the level corresponding to $10^{-12}\,\mathrm{W/m^2}$.

While this step is logical, convenient, and utterly unproblematic for a classroom of students who have been exposed to the concept of decibels all of their lives, it is also a step that needs to be carefully examined. Up to this point, the discussion of sound has been grounded in the physics of waves, work, energy, and related equations. Here, we are making a decision based on a human understanding of the aural sensations produced by the physics. The demarcation of 0 dB is one that presupposes a common ("normal") human experience, a collective agreement that sound intensity level represents a sensory breaking point, a norm by which each person can be measured: if one can hear a sound at −5 dB, their hearing is "exceptional" if one cannot hear a sound at 5 dB, their hearing is "deficient".[c]

But the decibel level interpretation goes beyond this assumption, of course. As a logarithmic scale, a 10 dB increase corresponds to a 10-fold increase in sound intensity. The reason for this adjustment to the more standard linear scale is again perceptual, at least in general terms. While human perception of loudness does not correspond to the logarithmic scale suggested by dBs, the range of human hearing necessitates a compression of the scale in order to meaningfully represent the human auditory experience in the world's sonic landscape. This concept is quite confusing, as we need to match the acoustic (sound intensity) and the representational (decibels) with the psychoacoustic (loudness). At middle range volumes and middle range frequencies, a 10 dB increase will correspond to an approximately 2-fold increase in the perceived loudness of a sound for the typical listener.[d] Conversion of decibel measurements to **sones** creates a measurement that lines up with typical human perception of loudness, but in order for this measurement to be meaningful, one must first take human auditory processing of frequency into account.

In 1933, Fletcher and Munson first defined and determined equal-loudness curves, which essentially correct sound intensity level for the differing psychoacoustical perception of loudness level depending on the frequency of the underlying tone [3]. This loudness level

[c]Straus [12] would call these two types of hearings "prodigious" and "disablist", which he contrasts with "normal" (see below).

[d]This baseline was established by Stevens [11] and remains the International Organization for Standardization (ISO) standard today, though competing research exists.

measurement, calibrated to decibels at the 1000 Hz frequency, came to be known as **phons**. The phon curves represent the experience of "otologically normal persons in the age range from 18 years to 25 years", as stated by the International Organization for Standardization (ISO). The Fletcher–Munson curves have been updated and are frequently subject to refinement, but their original formulation has been relatively stable, despite the fact that it was based on a study involving just 11 subjects. The current ISO 226 standard, as derived and discussed by Suzuki and Takeshima [13], is given in Fig. 4.2. The take-away from this for students in my introductory course is clear: the mediation of the human ear, with its widely divergent pitch frequency sensitivities, creates a disconnect between the popularly conflated concepts of "loudness" and "decibels".

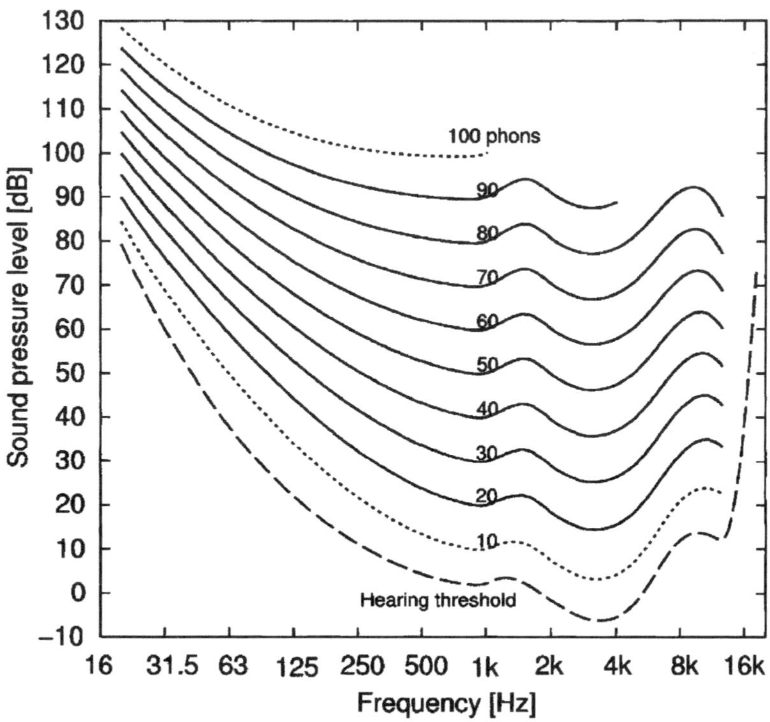

Fig. 4.2. Equal loudness level contours (phons) as proposed by Yôiti Suzuki and Hisashi Takeshima. Reprinted with kind permission from [13, Fig. 11]. Copyright 2004, Acoustical Society of America.

4.4. The Phenomenological Perspective

And so what had begun as an objective study of acoustic power gradually transforms into a discussion of psychoacoustics, the filtering of scientific relations and properties through human perceptual interpretation. But we can push further in this direction, as we begin to skirt with rather vivid demonstrations of phenomenological inquiry, broadening the disciplinary palette of the course.

Husserl's framing of the natural attitude as distinct from experiential interpretation is starkly on display, and not easily ignored, as we consider the concept of loudness. When we operate our audio playback devices, we click a button or turn a knob to make our music "louder" or "softer". When a teenager is blasting her dance jam, the parent asks her to make it "quieter", which she responds to (hopefully) by reducing the sound intensity level. If she did so just as the pitch frequency changed from low- to mid-range, the music could actually become louder, prompting the parent to anger at her disobedience, which would quickly be responded to with vehement denial. By being unaware of the physical act of "turning down" the device's volume, the parent has effectively bracketed her natural attitude which posits a direct correlation between the act of turning a volume knob and the perception of loudness.

From a more abstract vantage point, the conceptualization of loudness in terms of phons and sones, with their baselines determined by empirical perceptual data, is a notable example of phenomenological reduction. Our human experience of sound is primary in the determination of these loudness relationships, regardless of the physical reality of the sound waves, the volume of displaced air particles, the power that the waves generate, or even their effect on the hair cells on the basilar membrane. We are bumping up against a problem described in Thomas Nagel's foundational 1974 article "What Is It Like To Be a Bat": there are limits to investigating perceptual phenomena through reducing them to their materialist, objectively observed core. Conveniently for us, Nagel's discussion of consciousness and its role in the mind-body problem uses the bat's interpretation of sound waves as its central thought experiment. Both bats and humans perceive sounds, but the two species use sounds in radically different ways to interpret the world around them. For Nagel, this essential difference is a defining feature of the experience for each of the two species. To reduce the experiences to the physics underlying both actually puts further distance between the investigation and the "real nature" of the conscious interpretation of that physical input:

> In discovering sound to be, in reality, a wave phenomenon in air or other media, we leave behind one viewpoint to take up another, and the auditory, human or animal viewpoint that we leave behind remains unreduced. Members of radically different species may both understand the same physical events in objective terms, and this does not require that they understand the phenomenal forms in which those events appear to the senses of members of the other species. Thus it is a condition of their referring to a common reality that their more particular viewpoints are not part of the common reality that they both apprehend. The reduction can succeed only if the species-specific viewpoint is omitted from what is to be reduced.
>
> Nagel [7, p. 445]

In other words, trying to understand the bat's sonic experience by finding the common acoustic features it has with the human processing of sound simply trades one line of questioning for another, less interesting one.[e]

Luckily for us, in our class, we are focusing almost exclusively on human perception of sound, so we can assume that there is a more common basis for understanding and interpreting sound, generally. In fact, this is the premise of phon and sones: the Fletcher–Munson equal-loudness curves are products of phenomenological intersubjectivity, an agreed upon summary of a typical human interpretation of the soundscape. That these curves are situated and described with elements of acoustics and mathematics is simply a communicative convenience, in this view. But if the relationship

[e]It should be noted that human echolocation, especially among the blind population, has been extensively documented and studied over the past 25 years, suggesting that avenues for phenomenological connections between the species may be more prevalent than they initially appear.

between hearing and acoustics is this indirect for young, "otologically normal persons", what can we take away from the experiences of listeners who fall outside of this category (the vast majority of the population)?[f]

4.5. Normal and Disablist Hearing

The question that we must confront in the classroom here is a fundamental one. Where do we place the non-normative experience of loudness in the spectrum of our understanding of the concept? The bias is to exclude the experience of these listeners in our theorizing, a tendency that has deep roots in the field and in our culture.[g] From a societal view, these listeners are disabled in some way, unable to directly access the experience of the "otologically normal".

Tichkosky and Michalko [15] discuss the intricacies of viewing disability from a phenomenological frame. Trying to frame disability in a Husserlian intersubjective lifeworld necessitates interpreting the experience as both inside and outside of the experience of that "taken-for-granted" space:

> This taken-for-granted life-world and the natural attitude that represents, for us, the genesis of disability frameworks. It is within and from this conception of human life that disability experience... springs and frames disability as a meaning-full phenomenon. Disability is a frame that can, upon analysis, teach us much about the life-world that generates it. But herein lies an irony — disability is framed as a phenomenon located and locatable

[f] According to recent data, only about 9% of the U.S. population is between the ages of 19 and 25, and only a subset of these would be considered "otologically normal". See [14]. The next section of the paper is primarily concerned with non-normative hearers who may or may not fall outside the age ranges represented to establish the ISO standards.

[g] Straus [12, pp. 152–157] discusses this disciplinary assumption within the field of music cognition, which "creates and depends upon normal listeners hearing normally" [12, p. 153]. From the perspective of experimental psychology, normal hearing is limited to the experience of "cognitively and physically normal American college students with modest musical training and ability..., [presenting] at best a partial and exclusive picture of human music cognition" [12, p. 156].

> only outside of the taken-for-granted life-world as well as outside the natural attitude.... Disability can, and often does, disrupt the taken-for-granted character of the world and our life in it.
>
> Tichkosky and Michalko [15, p. 132]

It is this paradox that leads to societal treatment of disability as a problem in need of a solution, an experience that lies outside the good, the natural, and the reasonable. The frame of disability, phenomenologically, forces even those with disabilities into the subjective perspective that they are experiencing the world not just through their disability, but an understanding that their disability is a problem for them and for others, as "a threat to the unquestioned versions of normalcy".

In the context of the interpretation of the concept of loudness, this phenomenal marginalization of those with non-normative hearing demands from them the goal of overcoming their "problem" by understanding the concept in the natural attitude, and by implication, understanding that their processing of the input is "flawed", a distorted perception of the real. The acknowledgement here is that there is a "correct" and "incorrect" perception of the sound input. The disabled listener experience is "incorrect", and she must understand this. The non-normative hearing student's own sensory experience is irrelevant to the learning going on in the classroom—they have a hearing problem that must be solved, and that solution involves intellectually framing themselves in the normative hearing realm. As Tichkosky and Michalko note, "Framed as people *with* a disability, individuals become those who do not live *through* their bodies, minds, senses, or emotions, but *with* them..." [15, p. 140, italics added].[h]

[h]Martiny [5] makes a similar observation from the clinical vantage point. He distinguishes between living **through** a disabled body and living **with** that body. The first is subjective, involving experiencing the world through the body you are in. The second is objective, treating the body as the object as observation, turning your attention to it, or experiencing the world while consciously mitigating the effects of your body on your interpretation. The shift in phenomenological frame is similar to the one that Tichkosky and Michalko argue is demanded by the normatively oriented society.

It is helpful to unpack the notion of "normal" hearing in the context of the music theory classroom. In his writings on music and disability, Joseph Straus [12] identifies three types of hearing: prodigious, normal, and disablist. Each of these has become associated with different aspects of the landscape of music theory. Prodigious hearing is demanded by many of the fully explicated theories developed within the discipline over the past 100 years, including analyses based on atonal pc sets and long-range harmonic processing common to Schenker's approach to tonal music. Normal hearing is assumed as the foundational core of the music theory curriculum at the undergraduate level: in order to succeed in such courses, the student must either learn to hear "normally" or at least be able to demonstrate the knowledge of what a "normal" listener hears. Disablist hearing includes modes of listening that are generally excluded from traditional music theory pedagogy, and even more explicitly excluded from most studies in the field of music cognition. Straus breaks disablist hearing into four separate types — autistic hearing, deaf hearing, blind hearing, and mobility difference hearing — with no claim that these are the only types possible [12, p. 160].

Opening up the possibility of alternate "hearings" contextualizes the acoustics and psychoacoustics of loudness in meaningful ways. The foregrounding of normal hearing is baked in to all aspects of the scientific characterization of loudness, most bluntly in the ISO standards themselves. Awareness of this foundational assumption can reveal truths that lie below a surface that is crowded seemingly unquestionable mathematical equations and graphs. Altering the phenomenological frame allows one to place alternate modes of hearing (whether prodigious or disablist) on equal planes to the normal, revealing unexpected varieties in the ways that humans process and understand sound input. Rather than fitting their own hearing experiences into the normative models, the students can compare their sonic experiences to multiple possibilities, and even to one another's understanding of loudness.

One tangible way to accomplish this in the context of the loudness unit in my class is to spend some time talking about the history and evolution of the Fletcher–Munson curves, or more generally and accurately, the equal-loudness curves, found in Fig. 4.2. In 1956, Robinson and Dadson published a study proposing fundamental changes to Fletcher and Munson's original study [10]. These were subsequently adopted by the ISO as the standard. Later studies, however, called the results into question, leading to another change in the standard in 2003, which remains in force today. Figure 4.3, taken from Suzuki and Takeshima's study that led to the new standards, shows the discrepancies among 11 empirical experiments determining the 40 phon equal-loudness curve, including the 1956 standard. The deviations arise from multiple causes, but one can quickly glean from the comparisons that precise determinations of phon curves are tremendously sensitive to experimental design and procedure. Most of the post-1980 studies represented here use fewer than 30 subjects to determine the contour data points, and these subjects are all between the ages of 18 and 30.

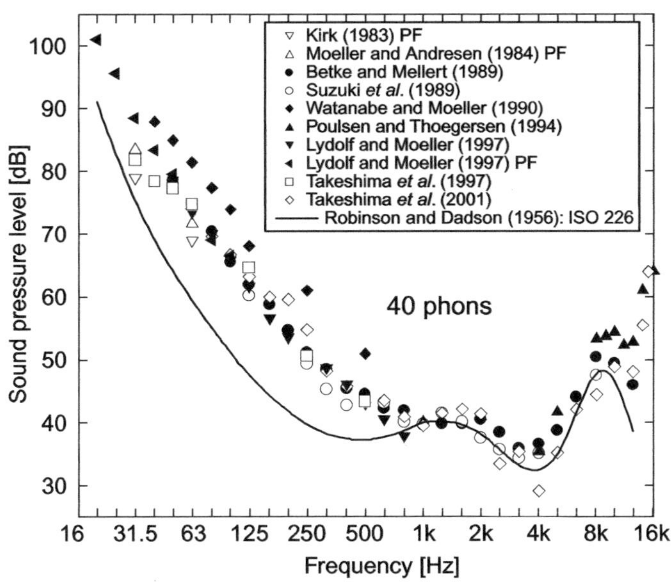

Fig. 4.3. A reproduction of Fig. 1 from [13] showing equal-loudness curves at 40 phons as determined by empirical data from various studies from 1983 forward, compared to the Robinson and Dadson standard from 1956. Reprinted with kind permission from [13, Fig. 1]. Copyright 2004, Acoustical Society of America.

As perceptual curves representing the mean perceptual loudness judgments of the narrowly defined normal listener, we can reasonably question the universal application of these curves in modeling human experience of loudness sensation. As an exercise, I have the student in the course model their own personal equal-loudness curves, easily completed via rudimentary experiments that can be done online.[i] The results are often surprising. In truth, the college classroom setting is one of the closest matches to the expected experimental study population (young people whose hearing is likely to closely match the societal norm). And yet, there are always a handful of participants (including their older instructor) whose results differ quite markedly from the expected contour configuration. Such differences lead to important class questions involving the purpose of standard equal-loudness curves, the nature of hearing, and the phenomenological differences that the varying individual curves might imply. How close do our loudness curve contours need to be in order to claim that we share the same phenomenological frame? The differences, if suitably significant, imply experiential interpretations that extend far beyond mere measures of loudness. As argued by Merleau-Ponty, "the blind man's world differs from the normal person's not only through the quantity of material at his disposal, but also through the *structure* of the whole" [6, p. 261].

4.6. Conclusion

In a recent study on the interplay of the humanities and the sciences in modeling tonal understanding, Parncutt critiques the de-emphasis of perception in traditional music theory circles. In this discussion, he explores the nature of the musical interval, or even more fundamentally, the musical pitch. Arguing from a stance of mind-body dualism (one that he further characterizes as "ecologically informed [and] minimal"), Parncutt concludes that "perceived pitches . . . are like any other phenomenal experiences: they can depend on both

[i] As of 2018, acoustician Joe Wolfe at the University of New South Wales maintains a fantastic website enabling such informal experimentation. Available at: http://newt.phys.unsw.edu.au/jw/hearing.html.

auditory/neural physiology *and* the affordances of relevant sound sources. To equate musical pitch with frequency, periodicity or any other physical measure in the air or brain is to jump to conclusions about the nature of consciousness" [9].

The temptation to fall into this reductionist mode of thought is arguably even greater in a course that purports to specifically address the interconnectedness between the fields of mathematics and music. However, by treating the topics in the course with care, circling back to questions of perception and the phenomenal experience, we can both enrich and problematize the objective lines of inquiry simultaneously.

Acknowledgments

The author would like to thank Carr Everbach for helpful and illuminating conversations about acoustics which have informed both this paper and pedagogical aspects of the course discussed here. Also, thanks to Cheryl Grood for lending her mathematical expertise.

Bibliography

[1] R. Cohn, Music theory's new pedagogability, *Music Theory Online* **4**(2) (1998).

[2] D. Diderot, Encyclopédie, in *Encyclopédie, ou Dictionnaire raisonné des sciences, des arts, et des métier*, eds. D. Diderot and J.-B. le Rond d'Alembert, (1751–1772). Translation in *Diderot, Rameau's Nephew and Other Works*, by J. Barzun and R. H. Bowen, Doubleday (1956).

[3] H. Fletcher and W. A. Munson, Loudness, its definition, measurement and calculation, *J. Acoust. Soc. Am.* **5** (1933) 82–108.

[4] J. Kochavi, *Musica speculativa* for the twenty-first century: Integrating mathematics and music in the liberal arts classroom, *J. Math. Music* **8**(2) (2014) 117–123.

[5] K. M. Martiny, How to develop a phenomenological model of disability, *Medical Health Care Philos.* **18** (2015) 553–565.

[6] M. Merleau-Ponty, *Phenomenology of Perception* (Routledge and Kegan Paul, London, 1962). Transaction by Colin Smith.

[7] T. Nagel, What is it like to be a bat? *Philos. Rev.* **83**(4) (1974) 435–450.

[8] R. Parncutt, *Harmony: A Psychoacoustical Approach* (Springer, New York, 1989).

[9] R. Parncutt, Understanding major-minor tonality: Humanities meet Sciences, *Proc. Ninth Triennial Conf. European Society for the Cognitive*

Sciences of Music, eds. J. Ginsborg, A. Lamont, M. Phillips and S. Bramley (2015).

[10] D. W. Robinson and R. S. Dadson, A re-determination of the equal-loudness relations for pure tones, *British J. Appl. Phys.* **7**(5) (1956) 166–181.

[11] S. S. Stevens, A scale for the measurement of the psychological magnitude: loudness, *Psychol. Rev.* **43**(5) (1936) 405–416.

[12] J. N. Straus, *Extraordinary Measures: Disability in Music* (Oxford University Press, New York, 2011).

[13] Y. Suzuki and H. Takeshima, Equal-loudness-level contours for pure tones, *J. Acoust. Soc. Amer.* **116**(2) (2004) 918–933.

[14] The Kaiser Family Foundation's State Health Facts, Population distribution by age; timeframe 2016, Data Source: Census Bureau's March Current Population Survey, CPS: Annual Social and Economic Supplements (2017), available at: https://www.kff.org/other/state-indicator/distribution-by-age.

[15] T. Titchkosky and R. Michalko, The body as the problem of individuality: A phenomenological disability studies approach, in *Disability and Social Theory: New Developments and Directions*, eds. D. Goodley, B. Hughes and L. Davis, (Palgrave Macmillan, New York, 2012), pp. 127–142.

Section II

Chapter 5

Mathematical Music Theory: Integrated Course Pairing with Mathematics and Music Students from the USA and China*

Mariana Montiel

Department of Mathematics and Statistics, Georgia State University, Atlanta, GA 30303, USA
mmontiel@gsu.edu

5.1. Genesis

In this section we will explain the genesis of two integrated courses in which the topics of mathematics and music are intertwined, and whose objective is to strengthen mathematical knowledge at varying levels. One of these courses took place at the East Chinese University of Science and Technology (ECUST) in Shanghai. In the context of a study abroad program with participation from the Mathematics and Statistics Department and the School of Music at Georgia State University (GSU) in Atlanta, this course was planned as an interdisciplinary and cultural experience. The GSU students took the course together with a group of ECUST mathematics students.

---

*I would like to recognize, in many of the exercises and examples, the work of students. In particular I want to thank Robin Baidya and his Shanghai group for some of the symmetry examples in Section 5.3.1, and Robin Baidya in Section 5.3.4.1 and Emiliano Nieto-Montiel in Section 5.3.4.2 for their course-pairing projects.

The population was not homogeneous in terms of their major subject areas, as they were from both mathematics and music, nor were they identical with respect to their levels of sophistication, as there were undergraduate and graduate students from each discipline. For this reason, the course and the form of delivery were designed taking into account this particular circumstance. There was emphasis on group work in which the members were selected so as to have an equal distribution of disciplines and levels; additionally, the student evaluations were individualized according to the discipline and stage of studies in their respective areas. The subjects will be described, as well as examples of the materials and assignments that were carried out, in Section 5.3. There is a public YouTube video, titled *Mathematical Music Theory in Shanghai,* in which the participants in the study abroad program present their experience and some of the subjects that were covered [14].

The second course arose as a response to a solicitation published by the College of Arts and Sciences of GSU in which it was announced that students would be able to obtain six credit hours during the amount of classroom time that is usually employed for three credit hours. This would be done through a new pilot program called *Integrative Course Pairing* in which each course would be programmed once a week in the classroom with the respective professor. To complement the needs and requisites of hours for both courses, video lectures would be programmed, as well as assigned readings and online interactive tasks for each course.

To justify the pairing of the two courses, *Mathematical Music Theory* listed in the Mathematics and Statistics Department's catalogue, and *Analysis Postonal*, a standard course at the School of Music, two fundamental arguments were given:

(1) As the titles of the course indicate, one is theoretical and one is analytical.
(2) The analysis of postonal music includes different styles, many of which have been approached mathematically. Thus, it was suggested that each style could combine the analytical techniques with the underlying mathematics.

It was explained that, in particular, the established postonal analysis course focuses upon music written since 1880. Modern music embraces a variety of styles and the majority have been rigorously analyzed the context of the boom of mathematical music theory during the last few decades. The basis of the course pairing, it was argued, would be the study of each one of the styles and the mathematics used in their analysis, such as: musical set theory which includes mathematical structures such as groups; neo-Riemannian theory and toroidal models that also employ group theory as well as other constructions from modern algebra; non-Euclidean geometries; serial theory and combinatorics mod 12.

On the other hand, the mathematical music theory course offered by the Department of Mathematics and Statistics studies the mathematics that underlie the structures and patterns that result from the organization of musical material. For example, even a musical note as a basic unit consists of parameters such as pitch, duration, onset, volume, timbre, etc. and a complete piece is formed by notes, rests, and other elements that appear in the score. For this reason music offers a rich and varied subject for the study and advance of certain mathematical areas that do not always form part of the general study plan. Postonal music has always been a fertile source for composition and analysis that feed upon these mathematical subjects.

In the proposal for the pilot course in course pairing it was necessary to explain the reasons why the integration of the two selected courses would enhance student commitment to the material. One aspect of the argument in favor of this pairing is that the possibility of studying postonal analysis from multiple complementary angles leads, in a natural way, to a deeper comprehension of the topic. It was also emphasized that music students would not only learn the classical analytic techniques, but would also be able to comprehend the mathematics on which they are based. This is especially important, it was contended, when a beginner in this kind of analysis is not sure which technique to use. On the other hand, for the mathematics students, the common abstract presentation of specific subjects in their study plan actually comes to life in the context of music theory. Indeed, in the context of mathematical music theory, some of the mathematical operations and transformations studied can be *heard* by means of aural examples.

It was also argued that another advantage of taking the mathematical music theory course for mathematics students is the study of certain mathematical tools, techniques and theories that are not always covered in the traditional program for the major. For example, in a first modern algebra course where the emphasis is on the study of groups, it is not always possible to cover notions such as the semidirect product or the wreath product, which are included in a unit of the mathematical music theory course. Additionally, the program includes some of the basic constructions of category and topos theory, such as limits and colimits, in the context of applications to music analysis and to the use and understanding of the software Rubato Composer®, developed by Guerino Mazzola [10], Gerard Milmeister [13], and others [11]. In the same way, music students have the opportunity of learning several formal aspects that underlie postonal theory or to carry out rhythmic analysis, an aspect that is usually delegated in traditional music theory courses, whether tonal or postonal.

5.2. Logistics

In the context of these courses the most evident challenge is how to achieve that both mathematics and music students, whose levels of sophistication vary, acquire the knowledge that is expected of them according to their disciplines and stage of advance in their area. This is not a trivial achievement, given that there is no time to fill "gaps" before the course and that much of the materials used for study, such as texts and articles, take for granted certain previous knowledge. On the other hand, those that are versed in the basic antecedents of both disciplines should not have to be held back.

In the general lectures the goal was to standardize the language with which the students would be confronted in the written materials and in the interdisciplinary communication. This process includes the representation of musical notes as numbers, the concept of the octave and the chromatic scale modulo 12 (or the diatonic scale modulo 7) and the formalization of musical operations as functions, among other subjects. In terms of language, this last item implies the notions behind the equivalences between geometric translation and musical transposition, geometric horizontal reflection and musical inversion, horizontal translation and musical repetition, and so on.

The course held in China consisted of 3 credit hours and the contact time was distributed among lectures and group work. The groups were formed in such a way that there could be an even distribution of students of both disciplines and of different level of advance in their majors. It should be mentioned that some of the mathematics students also had at least a basic level (some had more) of musical knowledge, due to their having studied a musical instrument or participated in bands or orchestras at the secondary level. On the other hand, the music students had taken, at the most, a calculus course; however, some had taken the postonal analysis course in which the use and application of discrete mathematics and group theory concepts is implicit. In this chapter the content studied by the different groups will be described, and the subjects covered and the materials that were developed for each one of them will be presented.

The course pairing was also formed by students of both disciplines. The levels were either advanced undergraduate or graduate students and the two courses together (6 credits) had the amount of contact hours of one 3-credit course, as was explained above. In this chapter the postonal analysis course as such will not be included in the analysis, as it is a standard course in music schools and the content is found in innumerable texts. However the content will be referred to, as the mathematical music theory course was synchronized with the aspects of postonal analysis that lend themselves to further mathematical study. In particular, it will be seen later in this chapter that the final projects reflect techniques learned in postonal analysis together with the mathematical explanation.

It should be mentioned that the prerequisite of the four tonal music theory courses for music students was waived for the mathematics students. However, for readers that are familiar with the content of postonal analysis it should be clear that the classical Roman numeral background is not required so as to be able to employ the techniques of musical set theory. In a certain sense, the mathematics students had a small advantage over the music students, especially taking into account that none of them were totally exempt of some music background (for that reason their interest in participating in the course pairing pilot).

The delivery format of the course in the hour and a half of weekly contact was the usual lecture. All classes were video-recorded and online activities in which group work was fomented were assigned weekly. The majority of the materials were similar in content to the course at ECUST in Shanghai. What distinguished this course was the final project which will be included in this chapter as part of the materials that can be used for future interdisciplinary endeavors of this nature. This assignment consisted of composing a postonal piece in one of the styles studied in the postonal analysis course, together with the inclusion of structures explicitly subject to mathematical analysis. This project was used to detect elements of the collaboration that contributed to the enhancement of the teaching and learning process in both disciplines. The project had two major components:

(1) Each student had to select one or more notions from the mathematical areas employed in the mathematical music theory course and related them to a concrete postonal composer and piece.
(2) Each student had to compose a piece and, at the same time, analyze it based on the relevant mathematics in terms of style or combination of styles chosen. It was allowed and encouraged to employ the style of the composer chosen in 1.

5.3. Content

In this section, we describe the different subjects covered in both mathematical music theory classes (delivered at ECUST and at GSU) with the intention of orienting the reader in relation to the reach of the material.

The organization is according to topic and, after a brief explanation of each subject, the materials used to communicate the concepts and to facilitate mastery by the students are presented. Some of the materials presented arose from the assigned exercises and projects of the students themselves and, this way, can be seen as results of the interdisciplinary experience as well as part of a collection that is constantly being created as these courses are implemented.

It should be emphasized that the order in which the topics are presented is not the sequence in which they appeared in the courses. To begin with, there were certain subjects that were seen at the initial stage of the course with the objective of creating a common language and achieving homogeneity with respect to certain concepts, especially those that permit a smooth transition between mathematics and music.

For example, it is mandatory to know that in mathematical music theory often the 12 notes of the chromatic scale are conceptualized as the elements of a group isomorphic to $\mathbb{Z}_{12}$. Of course, the concepts of isomorphism and group, as will be explained later, are treated with more or less formality according to the students' characteristics. However, at the end, all university students have taken a course in which the notion of bijective functions is taught (a very intuitive notion, needless to say). In Fig. 5.1 it is shown how the transition from the group $\mathbb{Z}_{12}$ to the group of 12 notes, with the operation of "summing intervals" is achieved. Beginning with C, numbers from 0 to 11 are assigned to each note. As an example, if we take the note D, represented by the number 2, it is conceived as a static element of the group. On the other hand, D can be conceived as the result of the intervallic operation that consists of summing 2 semitones to the

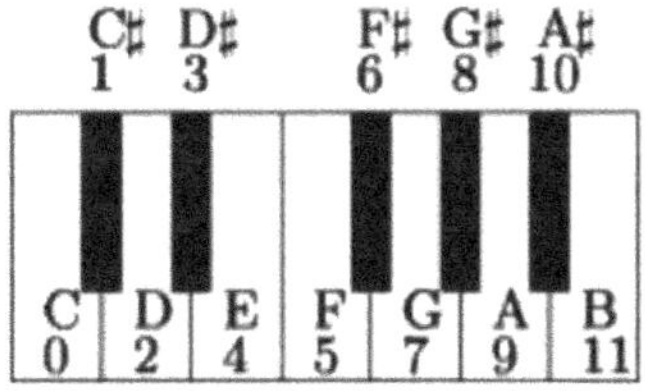

Fig. 5.1. Isomorphism between $\mathbb{Z}_{12}$ and the chromatic scale.

origin $C = 0$. Abstraction is made of the frequencies and reference is made to the *class of* C or *the class of* D, etc. What is more, if only the white notes are taken into account the result is the diatonic scale of 7 notes (if we begin with C we obtain the usual major scale), isomorphic to $\mathbb{Z}_7$.

Many of these aspects, which are essential for homogenizing language and concepts of the material covered in the present chapter, are explained in more detail in this volume in Chapters 2 (Johnson), 6 (Cohn), 11 (Mannone), 1 (Hall), 3 (Hughes), and 4 (Kochavi).

5.3.1. *Symmetries and transformations*

The presentation in this section is based on [1, 7].

Three common operations in music composition are denoted as follows:

(1) **Inversion**, I_s, with respect to the fixed pitch s;
(2) **Retrograde**, R;
(3) **Retrograde inversion**, RI_s.

Let us define an n-motive as a sequence $\{x_i\}_{i=1,\ldots,n}$ with $x_i \epsilon \mathbb{Z}_{12}$. We denote $T(n)$ as the set of all n-motives (a set of sets). Then the operations can be formalized as follows:

(i) $I_s : T(n) \to T(n), \quad \{x_i\}_{i=1,\ldots,n} \to \{y_i = 2s - x_i\}_{i=1,\ldots,n};$
(ii) $R : T(n) \to T(n), \quad \{x_i\}_{i=1,\ldots,n} \to \{y_i = x_{n-i+1}\}_{i=1,\ldots,n};$
(iii) $RI_s : T(n) \to T(n), \quad \{x_i\}_{i=1,\ldots,n} \to \{y_i = 2s - x_{n-i+1}\}_{i=1,\ldots,n}.$

A geometric representation of these transformations is found in Fig. 5.2.

For example, we can take the 5-note motive:

$$\{x_1 = A = 9, \quad x_2 = G = 7, \quad x_3 = F = 5, \quad x_4 = E = 4,$$
$$x_5 = G = 7\},$$

which appears in the 29th bar of Figure 6 in D minor from the first book of "Das Wohltemperierte Klavier" by J. S. Bach. If we invert

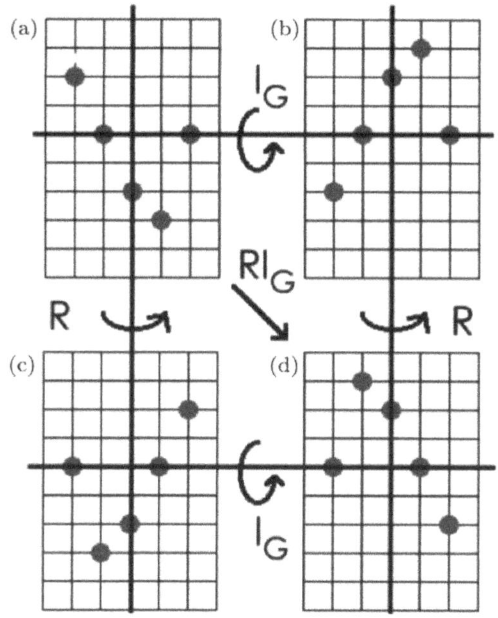

Fig. 5.2. Geometric representations of the three symmetries.

it with respect to the pitch $G = 7$ (recalling that $2 \cdot 7 = 14 = 2$), we obtain:

$$\{y_1 = 2 - x_1 = -7 = 5, \quad y_2 = 2 - x_2 = -5 = 7, \quad y_3 = 2 - x_3 = 9,$$
$$y_4 = 2 - x_4 = 10, \quad y_4 = 2 - x_5 = 7\},$$

that is:

$$\{y_1 = F, y_2 = G, y_3 = A, y_4 = B\flat, y_5 = G\},$$

and is found in bar 33. See Fig. 5.3.

Now, armed with the definitions and images and, of course, with the adequate explanations, there are many types of exercises that can be generated. In the case of the courses at hand, it was necessary to focus the assignments for mathematics and music students in a more personal manner and, especially in the case of the mathematics students, the level of sophistication must be taken into account. The

Fig. 5.3. Motive with symmetries.

majority of the exercises were designed to be carried out in mixed groups of mathematics and music students with a leader.

Exercise 1. Invent a musical motif (a pattern of 5 notes in the pentagram) and apply the operations I_s, R, IR_s. Make a geometric diagram of your motif as in Fig. 5.2.

Exercise 2. (the musicians and those that read music are responsible for the identification of the motif). Identify a motif in a Bach fugue and find where at least one of the three operations is applied.

The concept of symmetry, present in both mathematics and music, can be studied via the *musical plane*, defined in the following manner. The *musical plane* refers to any subset of $\mathbb{R}^2$ that possesses musical significance in a given context.

For example, we can define a unit of time, say a quarter note, on the $x-$axis and the semitone interval, seen as a unit, on the *y-axis*. This way we define our musical plane as a grid that, mathematically, is the Cartesian product of the integers $\mathbb{Z}^2$, as can be seen in Fig. 5.4.

We can also define a *rotation* as a function $R : \mathbb{R}^2 \rightarrow \mathbb{R}^2$ such that $R(x, y) = (x \cos\theta - y \sin\theta, x \sin\theta + y \cos\theta)$. In particular, when $\theta = 180°$ the musical term is retrograde inversion.

Additionally, we define *vertical and horizontal reflections* as well as the mathematical *translation* and show their musical meaning (see Figs. 5.5 and 5.6).

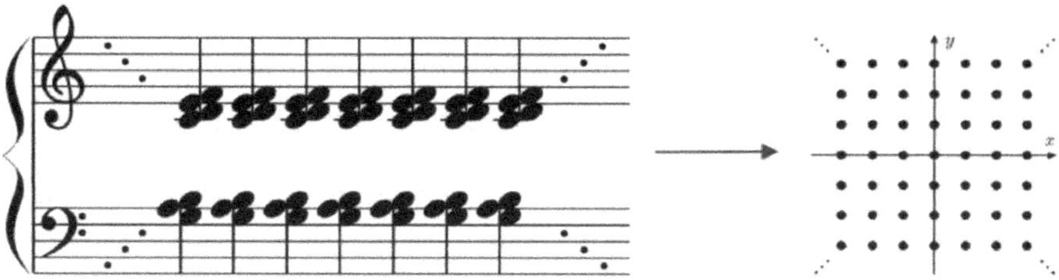

Fig. 5.4. The musical plane.

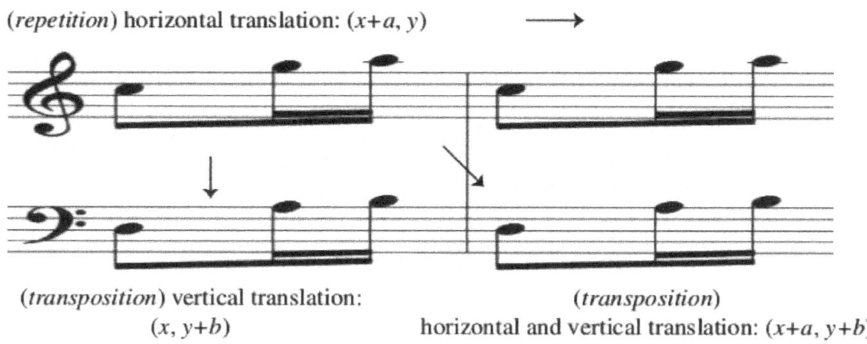

Fig. 5.5. Musical representation of geometric operations.

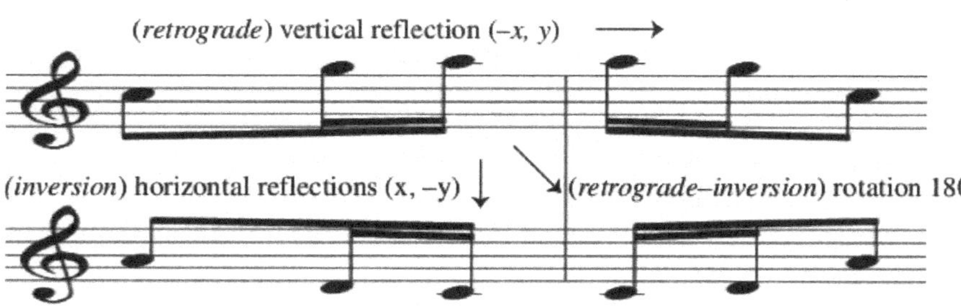

Fig. 5.6. Musical representation of geometric operations (the vertical reflection — inversion — is about the third horizontal line of the pentagram).

$V : \mathbb{R}^2 \to \mathbb{R}^2$ such that $V(x, y) = (-x, y)$;
$H : \mathbb{R}^2 \to \mathbb{R}^2$ such that $H(x, y) = (x, -y)$;
$T : \mathbb{R}^2 \to \mathbb{R}^2$ such that $T(x, y) = (x + a, y + b), a, b \in \mathbb{R}$.

Figures 5.5–5.8 illustrate these transformations musically and geometrically. The musical term is found in italics in the parenthesis.

Fig. 5.7. The frieze group of translation (or musical repetitions), $\langle T \rangle \approx \mathbb{Z}$.

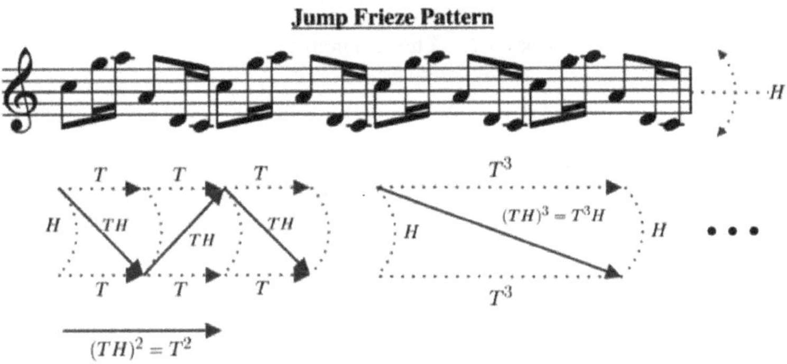

Fig. 5.8. The frieze group of translations and horizontal symmetry, isomorphic to the integers $\mathbb{Z}$ and generated by $\langle TH \rangle$.

The vertical reflection, V, is the same operation as the inversion I_s studied above.

Exercise 3. Create combinations ("compositions" — in mathematical terms!) of the different operations, both geometrically and musically.

Exercise 4. (for mathematics students, in particular those who know the definition of an isometry). Show that, in the musical plane, any isometry is a composition of a translation T, a vertical reflection V, and a horizontal reflection H.

Some other symmetry-based constructions, studied in both courses, are the frieze groups. Of course, those without mathematical sophistication were only responsible for identifying the patterns and explaining them in terms of the operations mentioned above; the formal aspect of symmetry groups was not mandatory for them, although some expressed an interest in the formal mathematics.

In the simplest terms, as a pattern, a frieze is a covering of a strip with infinite horizontal repetition and finite width, obtained by the application of plane movements of a particular figure or cluster of figures. Friezes can be constructed by the combinations of translations, reflections, rotations, and glide reflections (a composition of a translation followed by a reflection about a horizontal line).

A more formal definition presents frieze groups as two-dimensional *line groups*, having repetition in only one direction. The symmetry groups are formed by the operations, which comply with the group axioms, given that these operations are closed under composition, the identity transformation always exists and is unique, and they are invertible and associative. Seven different subgroups (groups in themselves) of friezes have been classified by convention:

(1) the frieze group of translations;
(2) the frieze group of translations and horizontal symmetry;
(3) the frieze group of translations and vertical symmetry;
(4) the frieze group of translations and glide reflections;
(5) the frieze group of translations and 180° rotations;
(6) the frieze group of translations, 180° rotations, and horizontal symmetry;
(7) the frieze group of translations, vertical symmetry and glide reflections.

Of course, at the end, if we take into account the identity transformations, there are really only four different classes, but the convention is to classify the seven listed above.

Once again the geometrical and musical representations were contrasted. The group exercises, especially the ones carried out in China, will serve as an example of the reach of this subject in the pedagogic context of interdisciplinary mathematics and music courses.

For example, the translation frieze pattern (Fig. 5.7) is generated by only one design and is isomorphic to the integers. The concept of isomorphism as a one-to-one and surjective group homomorphism is known by students with mathematical sophistication but, at the same time, is subject to a more general and intuitive explanation, given that functions are studied at the secondary school level. Additionally, the intuitive concept of group arises continuously in the course, as will be seen when the other units are presented. This is not surprising, as groups are implicit in the standard material of postonal analysis music courses as well. In the exercises, as is habitual, the work in mixed teams with different degrees of mathematical and musical sophistication is assumed.

Another concept that was studied was the dihedral group. For those without mathematical sophistication it was sufficient to explain the different isometries of the triangle and square. There are excellent online materials that can help with this task, for example [4]. The mathematics students studied specific materials that relate these isometries to the condition of dihedral groups. Of course, any participant that had taken a first modern algebra course would have already studied the subject of dihedral groups.

Figures 5.7–5.18 are examples of musical frieze patterns. We will give them the names invented by [3] and revisited in [7], because they are suggestive and light-hearted in the pedagogical context.

Exercise 5: Graph at least one frieze pattern and transform your graph into a score.

Next we will present some of the exercises carried out by the transformation and symmetry team in the mathematical music theory course delivered in China. The scores were transformed to sound by music students using the appropriate software, such as Finale®. These examples should serve as models and motivation for future courses.

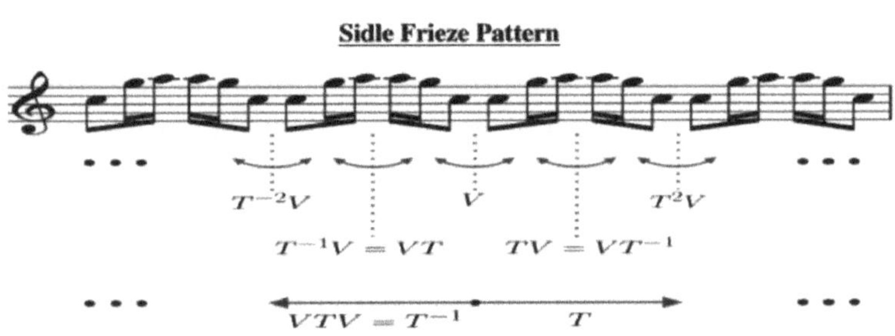

Fig. 5.9. The frieze group of translations and vertical symmetry, isomorphic to the infinite dihedral group D_∞. The hypothetically infinite translations play the role of the rotations in the finite dihedral groups, and the vertical reflection plays the role of the "flips".

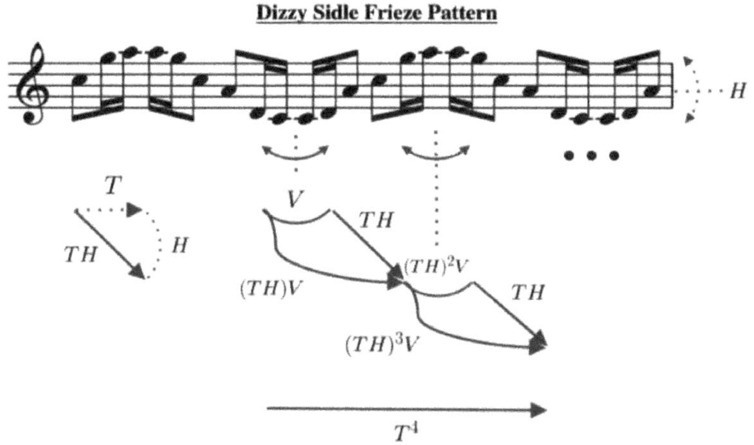

Fig. 5.10. The frieze group of translations and glide reflections isomorphic to the infinite dihedral group D_∞.

Fig. 5.11. The frieze group of translations, horizontal symmetry and vertical symmetry, isomorphic to the direct product $D_\infty \times \mathbb{Z}_2$.

5.3.2. *Groups and transformational theory*

Due to space limitations we will only touch on some of the aspects covered in this unit. There is more material, much of it covered in [1], especially in Chapter 4 where abundant exercises with solutions can be found.

The emphasis in this unit is on *triads*, that is, 3 notes that are played simultaneously. Now, there are $\binom{12}{3}$ or 220 combinations of 3-note sets from the entire 12-note set of the chromatic scale, but

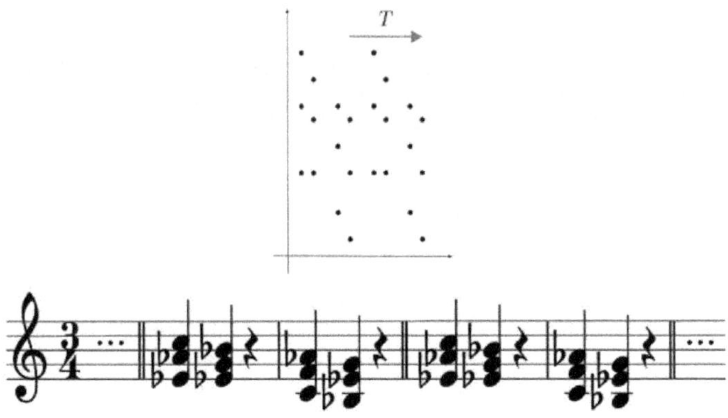

Fig. 5.12. Hop frieze pattern.

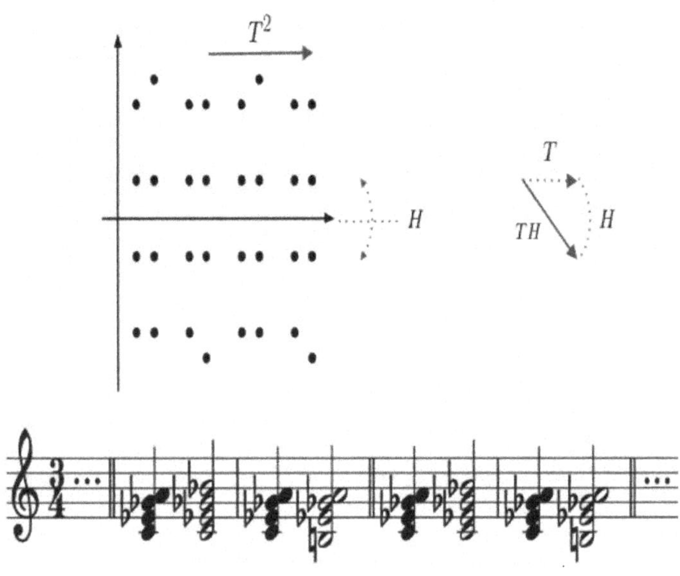

Fig. 5.13. Step frieze pattern.

only *major* and *minor* chords are included in this unit. The three notes in a triad are respectively known as the *root*, the *third* and the *fifth* where each triad is named after its root. We define the major and minor triads mathematically as follows.

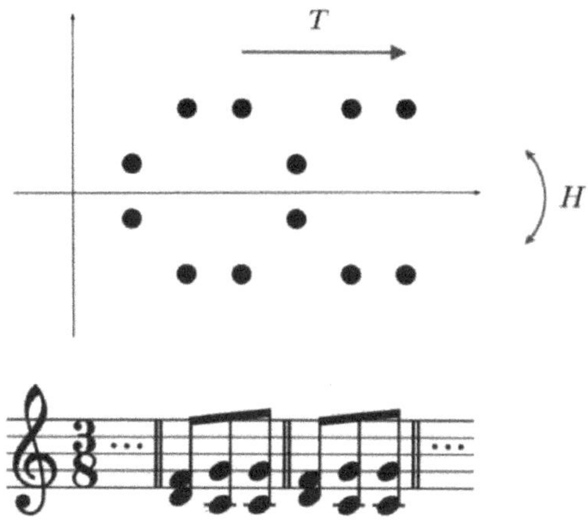

Fig. 5.14. Jump frieze pattern.

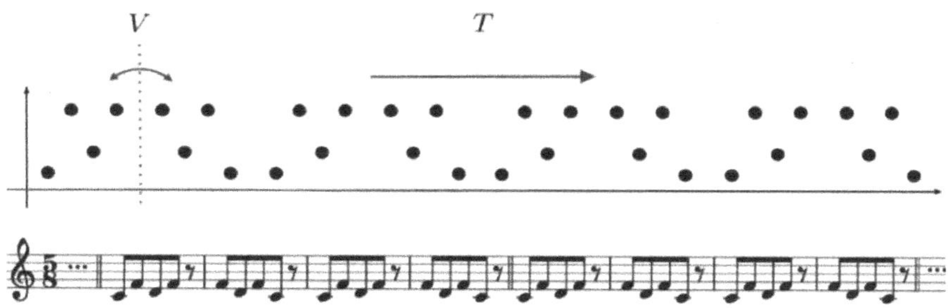

Fig. 5.15. Sidle frieze pattern.

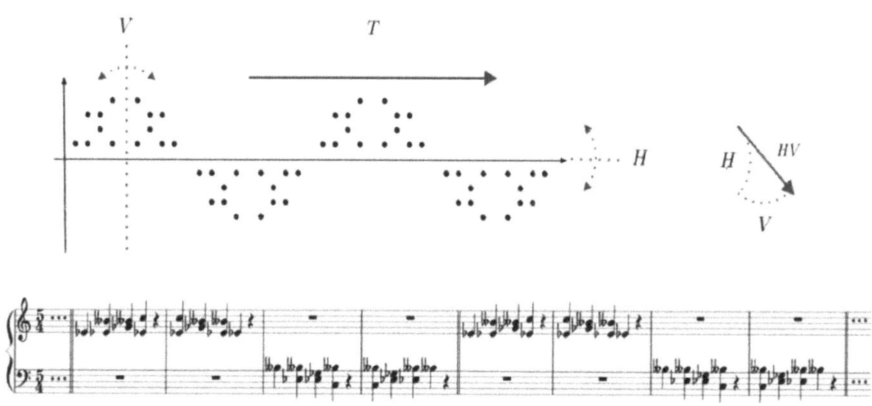

Fig. 5.16. Dizzy hop frieze pattern.

Fig. 5.17. Dizzy sidle frieze pattern.

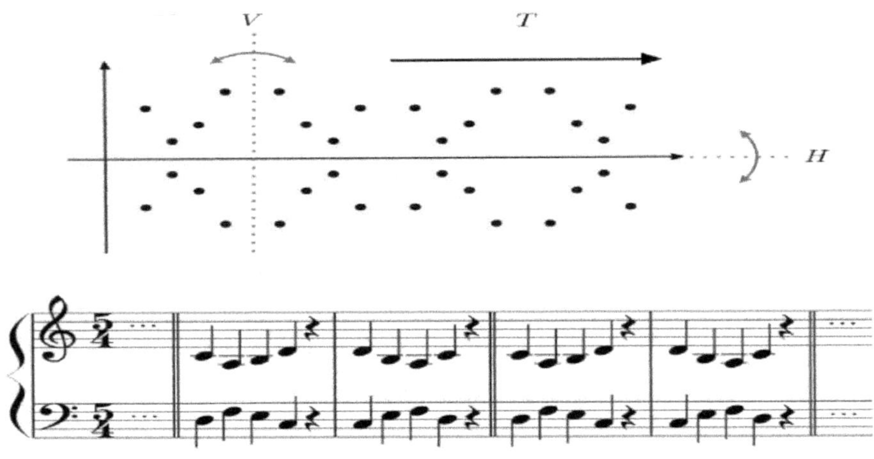

Fig. 5.18. Dizzy jump frieze pattern.

Definition 3.2.1. Let $\langle a, b, c\rangle$ be a **major** chord; then $b = a + 4$, and $c = a + 7$ where $a, b, c \in \mathbb{Z}_{12}$.

Major chords in this form are said to be in *root position* and are generally denoted by upper case letters, such as $G\# = \langle 8, 0, 3\rangle$. In the case of $G\#$, the root is $G\# = 8$, the third is $B\# = 0$, and the fifth is $D\# = 3$.

Definition 3.2.2. Let $\langle a, b, c\rangle$ be a **minor** chord; then $b = a + 3$, and $c = a + 7$ where $a, b, c \in \mathbb{Z}_{12}$.

Table 5.1. Set of all major and minor triads.

Major chords		Minor chords	
C	$\langle 0,4,7\rangle$	C	$\langle 0,3,7\rangle$
$C\sharp/D\flat$	$\langle 1,5,8\rangle$	$c\sharp/d\flat$	$\langle 1,4,8\rangle$
D	$\langle 2,6,9\rangle$	D	$\langle 2,5,9\rangle$
$E\flat/D\sharp$	$\langle 3,7,10\rangle$	$e\flat/d\sharp$	$\langle 3,6,10\rangle$
E	$\langle 4,8,11\rangle$	E	$\langle 4,7,11\rangle$
F	$\langle 5,9,0\rangle$	F	$\langle 5,8,0\rangle$
$F\sharp/G\flat$	$\langle 6,10,1\rangle$	$f\sharp/g\flat$	$\langle 6,9,1\rangle$
G	$\langle 7,11,2\rangle$	G	$\langle 7,10,2\rangle$
$A\flat/G\sharp$	$\langle 8,0,3\rangle$	$a\flat/g\sharp$	$\langle 8,11,3\rangle$
A	$\langle 9,1,4\rangle$	A	$\langle 9,0,4\rangle$
$B\flat/A\sharp$	$\langle 10,2,5\rangle$	$b\flat/a\sharp$	$\langle 10,1,5\rangle$
B	$\langle 11,3,6\rangle$	B	$\langle 11,2,6\rangle$

Minor chords in this form are said to be in *root position* and are generally denoted by lower case letters, such as $f = \langle 5,8,0\rangle$.

The set of these 24 major and minor triads, denoted *pitch class triads*, is referred to as$M$. The entire set is displayed in Table 5.1 and, in set builder notation, is

$$M = \{\langle x, x+3, x+7\rangle \text{ and } \langle X, X+4, X+7\rangle | x, X \in \mathbb{Z}_{12}\}.$$

It is important to note that the 3-element sets are not necessarily ordered. In other words, the f-minor chord $\langle 5,8,0\rangle$ is the same set as $\langle 0,8,5\rangle$. Musically the f-minor chord is formed by playing the notes $F, A\flat$, and C simultaneously. If we take $\langle 0,8,5\rangle$ we are still indicating that the notes $C, A\flat$, and F be played together, which would indicate that we intend to play the $f-$minor chord. So the root position of the chord, as in Definitions 3.2.1 and 3.2.2, shows the spelling of the chord and is more of an algorithm for obtaining the elements of the set of all major and minor triads. The individual notes may be distributed in multiple ways without changing the identity of the chord.

The term *pitch class triad* draws our attention to a subtle yet important distinction that must be made. We must be very clear about what elements we are working with, because up to now we have referred to a pitch class triad simply as a triad. An element x in M is a triad, where $x = \langle a, b, c\rangle$, and where $a, b, c \in \mathbb{Z}_{12}$. This notation, however, is used for convenience and simplicity, but to be more precise we must remember that $\mathbb{Z}_{12}$ is a *set of classes*:

$$\begin{aligned}\mathbb{Z}_{12} &= \{[0], [1], \ldots, [11]\}, \quad \text{where}\\ [\mathbf{0}] &= \{\ldots, -24, -12, 0, 12, 24\},\\ [\mathbf{1}] &= \{\ldots, -23, -11, 1, 13, 25, \ldots\}\ldots\\ [\mathbf{11}] &= \{\ldots, -13, -1, 11, 23, \ldots\}.\end{aligned}$$

Therefore, $a, b, c \in \mathbb{Z}_{12}$ actually represents [a], [b], [c] $\in \mathbb{Z}_{12}$. We call these classes *pitch classes* because every note from a to g represents all the pitches which are a multiple of it — in the same way that each class in $\mathbb{Z}_{12}$ represents all the numbers modulo 12 that are multiples. So, $x = \langle a, b, c\rangle$ is actually $[x] = \langle [a], [b], [c]\rangle$. Therefore this idea of pitch classes is extended to pitch class triads where all the elements in M are also classes. As an example, the C-major chord $x = \langle 0, 4, 7\rangle$. If we look at C-major as a triad class, we should represent it in the following way:

$$\begin{aligned}C = [x] &= \langle [0], [4], [7]\rangle\\ &= \{\ldots, \langle -12, -8, -5\rangle, \langle 0, 4, 7\rangle, \langle 12, 16, 19\rangle, \ldots\}.\end{aligned}$$

Note that we have clarified the distinction between basic elements and classes, for simplicity, we will continue to denote $[x]$ simply as x.

As M is a set, certain functions in the mathematical sense can be applied to M that, at the same time, have musical meaning. In particular we define the *parallel* (P), *leading tone exchange* (L), and *relative functions* (R) [11]. There are musical, group theoretic and geometric descriptions of the P, L, and R functions.

Two triads are said to be *parallel* if they have the same letter name but are of opposite parity (parity meaning major or minor). For instance, the parallel minor of F-major $\langle 5, 9, 0\rangle$ is f-minor $\langle 5, 8, 0\rangle$. Two triads are said to be *relative* if they are of opposite parity, and if the root of the minor triad is three semitones below the root of major triad. To illustrate, we take F-major $\langle 5,9,0\rangle$ and count three semitones below 5, which is 2 and then build a minor chord on 2. This yields the d-minor chord $\langle 2,5,9\rangle$, and d minor is the relative minor of F-major. Lastly, the *leading tone exchange* is derived from the fact that a semitone below any pitch is called the *leading tone* of that pitch. Therefore, the leading tone exchange of any triad is also of opposite parity, and the root of the major triad is replaced with its leading tone. F-major $\langle 5,9,0\rangle$ is used once again to illustrate. The root of F is 5, which is replaced with its leading tone, 4. It suffices for now to say that the only minor chord with the pitches 4, 9, and 0 is the a-minor chord, $\langle 4,0,9\rangle$. Richard Cohn [5] describes it as:

> P (for Parallel) which relates triads that share a common fifth; L (for Leading-tone exchange), which relates triads that share a common minor third; and R (for Relative), which relates triads that share a common major third.

Below are the mathematical definitions of P, L, and R, which are then followed by examples. Recall that the triad ordering in Table 5.1 is recommended.

Definition 3.2.3. Let $x, Y \in M$, where $x = \langle a,b,c\rangle$ a minor triad and $Y = \langle A,B,C\rangle$ a major triad; then

$$\begin{aligned}
\boldsymbol{P(x)} &= P(\langle a,b,c\rangle) = \langle C, B+1, A\rangle;\\
\boldsymbol{P(Y)} &= P(\langle A,B,C\rangle) = \langle c, b-1, a\rangle;\\
\boldsymbol{L(x)} &= L(\langle a,b,c\rangle) = \langle C+1, A, B\rangle;\\
\boldsymbol{L(Y)} &= L(\langle A,B,C\rangle) = \langle a-1, c, b\rangle;\\
\boldsymbol{R(x)} &= R(\langle a,b,c\rangle) = \langle B, A, C-2\rangle;\\
\boldsymbol{R(Y)} &= R(\langle A,B,C\rangle) = \langle b, a, c+2\rangle.
\end{aligned}$$

Notice that each function keeps two notes in common with the original chord, but switches their positions. In addition to this, each function converts the original triad from major to minor or vice versa.

Each function has musical relevance, and these transformations are commonly used during modulation (the change from one key to another). The goal is to make the transition as smooth as possible, so the more notes in common between the connecting triads, the less noticeable the change of course. The following examples provide concrete implementation of the definition:

$$P(c) = P(\langle 7,3,0\rangle) = \langle 0,4,7\rangle = C \quad \text{and}$$
$$P(F) = P(\langle 5,9,0\rangle) = \langle 0,8,5\rangle = f;$$
$$L(e) = L(\langle 11,7,4\rangle) = \langle 0,4,7\rangle = C \quad \text{and}$$
$$L(G) = L(\langle 7,11,2\rangle) = \langle 6,2,11\rangle = b;$$
$$R(b) = R(\langle 6,2,11\rangle) = \langle 2,6,9\rangle = D \quad \text{and}$$
$$R(A) = R(\langle 9,1,4\rangle) = \langle 1,9,6\rangle = f\#.$$

What does the set of P, L, and R functions look like? We will start with the geometric representation of the P, L, and R functions, known as the *Tonnetz.* The word *Tonnetz* is German for "tone network" and was coined by Leonhard Euler [5]. Hugo Riemann explored its capacity to chart harmonic motion or the movement from one pitch or triad to another. For various reasons, the original *Tonnetz* has undergone alterations [5], and we will use the version shown in Fig. 5.19. Note that the vertices are pitch classes and the triangles represent major and minor triads. As mentioned before, the P, L, and R transformations preserve two pitches when applied to any triad. Therefore, the rotation of a triangle about any one of its edges yields another triangle which is equivalent to one of the three triads that P, L, or R would produce. Notice that if we expand the diagram with more vertices, we see that they start repeating vertically and horizontally and in effect, the grid wraps around and therefore lies on a torus.

While we are treating P, L, and R as transformations we will determine what sequence of functions maps each element of M to a distinct image. The *tonnetz* makes this exploration visual and in turn much more effortless than having to calculate a series of transformations by hand. We look at Fig. 5.19 to see that there are multiple ways of tracing any triad to itself; however we are concerned with a path that traverses every element in M. Figure 5.20 displays

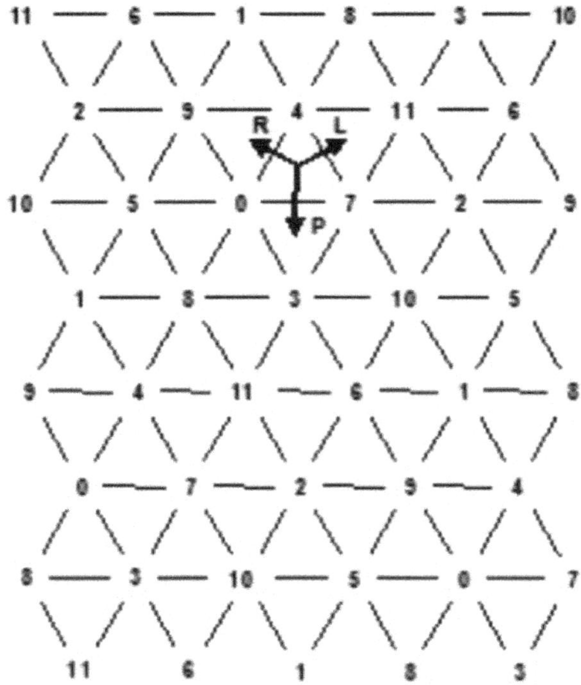

Fig. 5.19. The Oettingen/Riemann *Tonnetz*.

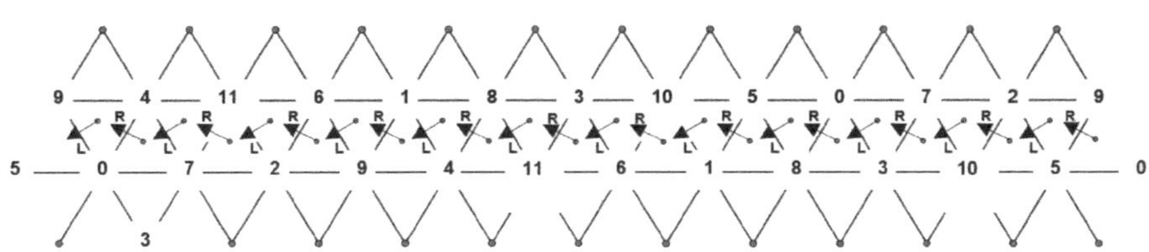

Fig. 5.20. A unique path of functions on the tonnetz.

such a path and we see that a series of R and L functions map the triad $\langle 5, 9, 0 \rangle$ to itself by mapping to every other triad in the process.

We should remember, once again, that the exercises were part of the work in mixed groups of mathematics and music students with varying levels of sophistication in their areas.

Exercise 6. Exhibit a trajectory on the tonnetz, basing yourself on Fig. 5.20, such that a sequence of R and L functions transform the triad $\{7, 11, 2\}$ (G major) into itself after passing through all the other triads of M in the process. Generate the sound.

Exercise 7. Show that the P, R, L operations are well-defined. That is, if $[x]$ is a triad of pitch classes in M, then for every x_1, $x_2 \in M$ we should show:

$$\begin{aligned} P(x_1) = P(x_2), &\quad \text{i.e., } P(\{a_1, b_1, c_1\}) = P(\{a_2, b_2, c_2\}), \\ R(x_1) = R(x_2), &\quad \text{i.e., } R(\{a_1, b_1, c_1\}) = R(\{a_2, b_2, c_2\}), \\ L(x_1) = L(x_2), &\quad \text{i.e., } L(\{a_1, b_1, c_1\}) = L(\{a_2, b_2, c_2\}). \end{aligned}$$

Exercise 8. Prove with details that the P, R, L, operations on M, form a group.

5.3.3. *Signature transformations and spelled heptachords*

5.3.3.1. *Signature transformations*

This section is based on work by Julian Hook in [8, 9].

Signature transformations (Hook [8]) look at changes in tonality in the diatonic context. In an extremely original manner, these transformations provide a tool to analyze the seven diatonic modes that begin on the same tonic. This restriction leads to changes of key signatures, hence the name.

Signature transformations, as functions, act on the set of *fixed diatonic forms* [8, pp. 140–142], which are *equivalence* classes of fragments of diatonic music. If the pitch class content corresponds to the same content (*modulo* 12) we then say they belong to the same equivalence class. That is, if they result in the same diatonic collection, up to enharmonic equivalence, they are considered as part of the same equivalence class.

When a certain number of sharps are appended, the notation s_n, $n \in \mathbb{N}$ is employed for the number n of sharps that are added; in an analogous manner, s_{-n} is used for the number $-n$ of flats that are added. The operation of adding sharps (or subtracting flats)

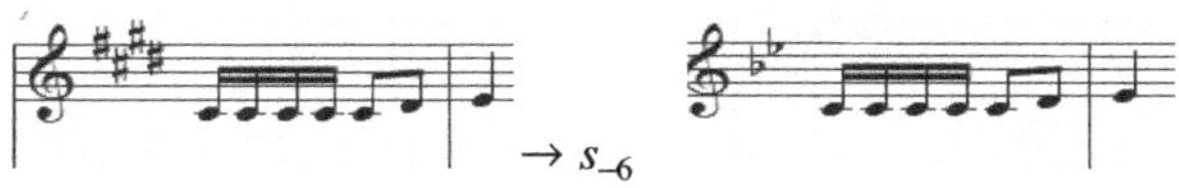

Fig. 5.21. Signature transformations.

is considered "positive", and the operation of subtracting sharps (or adding flats) is seen as "negative". In Fig. 5.21, the key signature of the original fragment loses four sharps by s_{-6}, and then the count becomes negative by appending flats.

Hook's theorem [8, pp. 142–144], on which the following results are based, gives us a theoretical foundation for these novel techniques that analyze changes in music based on the classical diatonic tonality.

The signature transformations form a cyclic group of 84 elements (they pass through the twelve pitches of the chromatic scale and the seven diatonic modes) and are generated by s_1. Of course, it is clear that 84 sharps will not be added to a key signature! Although the signature transformations form a cyclic group, the s_n and s_{-n} can be reached through compositions with T_n (the transposition operator from Section 5.3.1) and t_n (the diatonic transposition operator, which maintains the key signature and does not distinguish chromatic steps, see [8]).

Appending seven sharps to a key signature transposes the diatonic collection by a semitone (for example, from C major to $C^{\#}$ major). Hence, s_7 facts as T_1 and, analogously, s_{-7} operates as T_{11}. It is known that chromatic transposition changes the key signature as well as notes, while the diatonic transposition operator within its diatonic scale without changing the key signature. If t_1 acts on a *diatonic fragment* — or *diatonic form* —, without changing the key signature, we have the same pattern in the pitches but transposed up a scale step. On the other hand, if s_{12} is applied, we also transpose a scale step (see Fig. 5.22 taken from Hook, [8, p. 143], with a diatonic fragment of four notes, where a key signature with six flats arrives to a key signature of twelve sharps by applying s_1 twelve times). Therefore, all transition operators, no matter whether chromatic or diatonic, are equivalent to an s_n for

Fig. 5.22. Transition operators as signature transformations in Hook [8].

some n. As a weak converse, any s_n can be written as a composition of some T_n and t_n because we can arrive to the generator, s_1, by: $t_3T_7 = (t_1)^3(T_1)^7 = (s^3_{12)}(s_7)^7 = s_{36}s_{49} = s_{85} = s_{84}s_1 = s_1$ (with computations *modulo* 84).

Signature transformations explain the transformational aspects of music that shifts its content between different diatonic forms. In other words, the operations always will take place in a diatonic context. This context needs to be identified, which is not the case for other neo-Riemannian-type transformations, say P, L, and R from Section 5.3.2.

Now we present an example of signature transformations using Manuel M. Ponce's Sonata no. 2. The transformations will be traced by a *commutative triangle*, which allows us to see how the composition of the s and t functions is equivalent to a T function. It should be clear that this is a very good way to introduce the language of arrows, so important in modern mathematics, in a relevant and contextualized manner. As will be seen below, the signature transformation perspective can be used to follow certain transpositions in a gestural way [2]. However, this approach uses passages that are not actually found in the piece.

We will use a passage from the first movement of Ponce's sonata no. 2, and analyze the diatonic fragment that corresponds to measures 227 and 228, and to measures 231 and 232. Measures 227 and 228 are in E Aeolian, with one sharp. This can be seen in Fig. 5.23; however, in the original piece the key signature has

Fig. 5.23. Measure 227, 228 and 231, 232 of Ponce's Sonata no. 2.

four sharps. Measures 231 and 232 are in $G^{\#}$ Aeolian, which has five sharps. To transit from E Aeolian to $G^{\#}$ Aeolian four sharps must be appended using s_4 (which takes us to E Lydian); the next step is to transpose diatonically by two tones. As the composition of these functions is commutative, the process could have also been carried out in reverse order (although there are examples in which it is not possible musically to carry out some s_n in particular, due to the diatonic context). Thus, the signature transformation is $t_2s_4 = (t_1)^2s_4 = (s_{12})^2s_4 = s_{28} = s_4t_2$. Of course, we can look at this transformation as simply $T_4 = (T_1)^4 = (s_7)^4 = s_{28}$. The inclusion of E Lydian is gestural, as it does not appear in the piece. However, with respect to the signature transformation perspective, it is implied.

Exercise 9. Create 2 different equivalence classes of diatonic fragments (5 notes) with 2 fragments in each class. Define signature transformations (s_i) between elements in each class.

Table 5.2. Transposition by fifths.

$E_{\flat\flat}$	$B_{\flat\flat}$	$F_{\flat}$	$C_{\flat}$	$G_{\flat}$	$D_{\flat}$	$A_{\flat}$	$E_{\flat}$	$B_{\flat}$	F	C	G
-12	-11	-10	-9	-8	-7	-6	-5	-4	-3	-2	-1
D	A	E	B	$F\sharp$	$C\sharp$	$G\sharp$	$D\sharp$	$A\sharp$	$E\sharp$	$B\sharp$	$F\sharp\sharp$
0	1	2	3	4	5	6	7	8	9	10	11
$C\sharp\sharp$											
12											

Exercise 10. Find in the literature, or create an example, of the s_n, t_n, and T_n transformations and present it as a commutative triangle.

5.3.3.2. *Proper spelled heptachords*

Spelled heptachords are sets of seven pitch classes, with the condition that each class (letter name) is only included one time. Diatonic scales are spelled heptachords. Many "almost diatonic" scales are also spelled heptachords. Proper spelled heptachords are those free of enharmonic doublings or voice crossings.

If τ_k represents transposition by fifths, we obtain Table 5.2.

The symmetry is about D, given its position in the generation by fifths. Through this transposition, the 66τ-classes (fields) of proper spelled heptachords (scales of 7 notes, including the usual diatonic scales) are generated. τ_k is the transposition operator within each one of the classes. In other words, within each class the proper spelled heptachords can be expressed in any of the 12 keys. Each spelled heptachord in the class can be permuted to produce seven modes, see [8, 9]. The diatonic bell [9], available online, is a visual representation of the 66 proper spelled heptachord classes and the "distance" of each class from the usual 7 note diatonic scale forms the bell. The diatonic bell can be accessed at: http://www.cloche-diatonique.ch/world/12-7, and the list of the 66 classes of spelled heptachords is found in [8].

The C# Mixolydian mode appears in measures 89–91 of Ponce's Sonata no. 2 (see Fig. 5.24). Later in the piece, measures 354–356 appear at first to be the ideal candidate for a signature

Fig. 5.24. E Aeolian to G$^\#$ Aeolian, passing through E Lydian.

transformation that would change the mode and maintain the fixed tonic. The apparently logical signature transformation is s_{-1}, because one sharp is eliminated from the passage. Nevertheless, the eliminated sharp is A$^\#$ and, diatonically, it is not possible to go from six to five sharps by removing A$^\#$, as it should be E$^\#$ that would need disappear according to the theory. However, what really happens is that in measures 354–356, with C$^\#$ as tonic, none of the seven diatonic modes appear and what we really can identify is the Hindu scale whose pattern is 2212122 (also known as the Dorian mode of the acoustic scale, or the fifth mode of the melodic minor scale).

Hook's spelled hexachords include non-diatonic collections. We can find, in [8], the classification of a rotation of the scale from measures 354, 355 and 356 under the name of MMIN (for melodic minor).

Exercise 11. Take 2 heptachords from any 2 of the 66 classes listed in the appendix of Hook's article on signature transformations, and apply the transformation τ_3.

Exercise 12. Play with the diatonic bell (not to turn in).

Exercise 13. Create some passages similar to the ones identified in Ponce's Sonata no. 2 in which you change heptachord class and you change, by τ_i, key within the heptachord class. Identify the mode of the heptachord.

5.3.4. *The final projects*

As was mentioned above, a common final project was required in the course pairing for both courses, *Postonal Analysis* from the School of Music and *Mathematical Music Theory* from the Department of Mathematics and Statistics. The guidelines are presented below. First, a synthesized version of the postonal analysis professor's requirements is given, followed the mathematical music theory course specifications, which is the aspect of most interest for this chapter.

Postonal analysis:

For your final composition, you have the choice of writing in three different styles, each associated with analytic techniques we have discussed in class.

Style 1

Please compose a non-functional tonal work of 24 *bars. Make sure that at least* 8 *bars are written in a style devoted to Neo-Riemannian triadic and seventh chord transformations. Your harmonic language of this section will be limited to major and minor triads and dominant and half-diminished seventh chords, for obvious reasons. Please also make sure that another* 8 *bars are written using the scale-based style discussed in class. You can use any of the Gregorian modes or any of the modes of limited transposition in these measures; the harmonic language you employ will be limited only by the scale selected.*

Style 2

Write an atonal work in a free atonal style. Your work must be at least eighteen measures in length and be written either for piano or small instrumental ensemble (three instruments or less, notated on a C score). Please provide a pitch-class set analysis of your work (pitch-class sets circled and labeled according to set type and transposition level throughout the work, as well as a chart showing superset and subset relationships). Finally, your work should be written in the style of the atonal works used as examples in the text; adherence to this style will be rewarded, while deviation from it will be frowned upon.

Style 3

Please compose a serial work of 24 *bars. Make sure that at least* 8 *bars are written in the "Classical" 12-tone style of Schoenberg, Berg and Webern while at least another* 8 *bars are written in one of the post-war serial styles associated with Boulez, Stockhausen, Babbitt, et al.*

Please use a derived row (trichordal or tetrachordal) for your composition and include a matrix along with your finished composition (the prime form of the row should be labeled to show how the derived trichords or tetrachords relate to the opening form of this set in the row). Please also make your row hexachordally combinatorial and be sure that any row form used in the Hauptstimme is always accompanied by a combinatorial row form in the Nebenstimme. Finally, include a 12-tone count of your finished piece, labeling row forms used along with the order numbers next to each note of the row.

Mathematical music theory:

Make use of the following concepts and techniques: PLR transformations; Signature transformations; Heptachord classes; Maximal evenness; Cardinality equals variety; Structure implies multiplicity; Symmetries with frieze patterns; Modulation by symmetries.

You will add another minimum of 14 *measures to your piece. You will use at least two of the techniques. For example, you can create symmetries with frieze patterns and use a maximally even rhythm. Or you can change modes and analyze the change through signature transformations.*

In this case, you will add 14 *measures to the piece, but the techniques may be used throughout the whole piece. For example, if you choose Styles* 2 *or* 3, *you may include, say, the symmetries, or the maximal evenness, or the choice of particular species that correspond to one genre in different places of the piece, you do not need to wait until the last* 14 *measures!*

You will also write, apart from the analysis, "program notes" that explain the mathematics in the music to a general public that is not expert in either mathematics or music (but that does have a good cultural level).

Examples will now be given of two of the actual projects that were carried out, given that from their construction and the details of their creation new materials and accessory exercises can be developed.

5.3.4.1. *Project* 1

To understand the analysis carried out in Figs. 5.25–5.27, it is first necessary to offer some antecedents, definitions, and theory. This will be done as follows.

Literal pitch class sets are subsets of $\mathbb{Z}_{12} = \{0, 1, 2, \ldots, 9, T, E\}$, in other words, elements of the power set of $\mathbb{Z}_{12}$. The elements of a literal pitch class set are often listed in a particular form, called the *normal form* of the set, which can be computed via an algorithm. For example, the normal form of the set $\{0, 6, \mathrm{E}\}$ is [6E0].

The dihedral group D_{24} of order 24 has twelve rotations and twelve reflections. We label the rotations $T_0, \ldots, T_{11}$ and the reflections $T_0I, \ldots, T_{11}I$.

Abstract pitch class sets are the orbits of the power set of $\mathbb{Z}_{12}$ under the action of D_{24} defined by letting

$$T_nX = \{x + n | x \text{ in } X\} \quad \text{and} \quad T_nIX = \{-x + n | x \text{ in } X\}$$

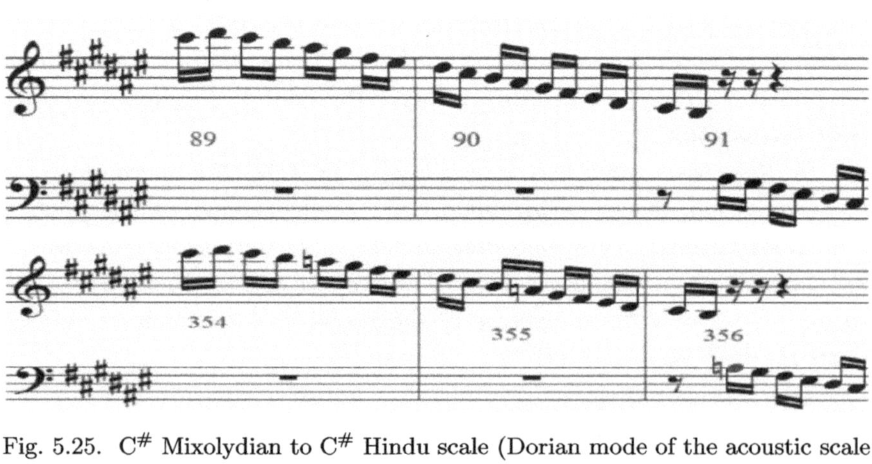

Fig. 5.25. C# Mixolydian to C# Hindu scale (Dorian mode of the acoustic scale or fifth mode of the melodic minor scale). Two different classes of proper spelled heptachords.

Fig. 5.26. Analysis of movement I.

for all X in the power set of $\mathbb{Z}_{12}$ and $n \in \mathbb{Z}_{12}$. An abstract pitch class set is often identified by its representative whose normal form begins with zero, called the *prime form* of the set. For example, the prime form of the orbit of [6E0] is (016).

In the annotation to Figs. 5.25 and 5.26, the literal pitch class sets appear in boxes. Each literal pitch class set X is labeled both by the abstract pitch class set Y to which it belongs and by the elements of D_{24} that take X to the set characterizing the prime form of Y.

For example, the literal set [6E0] is labeled both by the prime form of its abstract set (016) and by the reflection T_0I that takes [6E0] to [016].

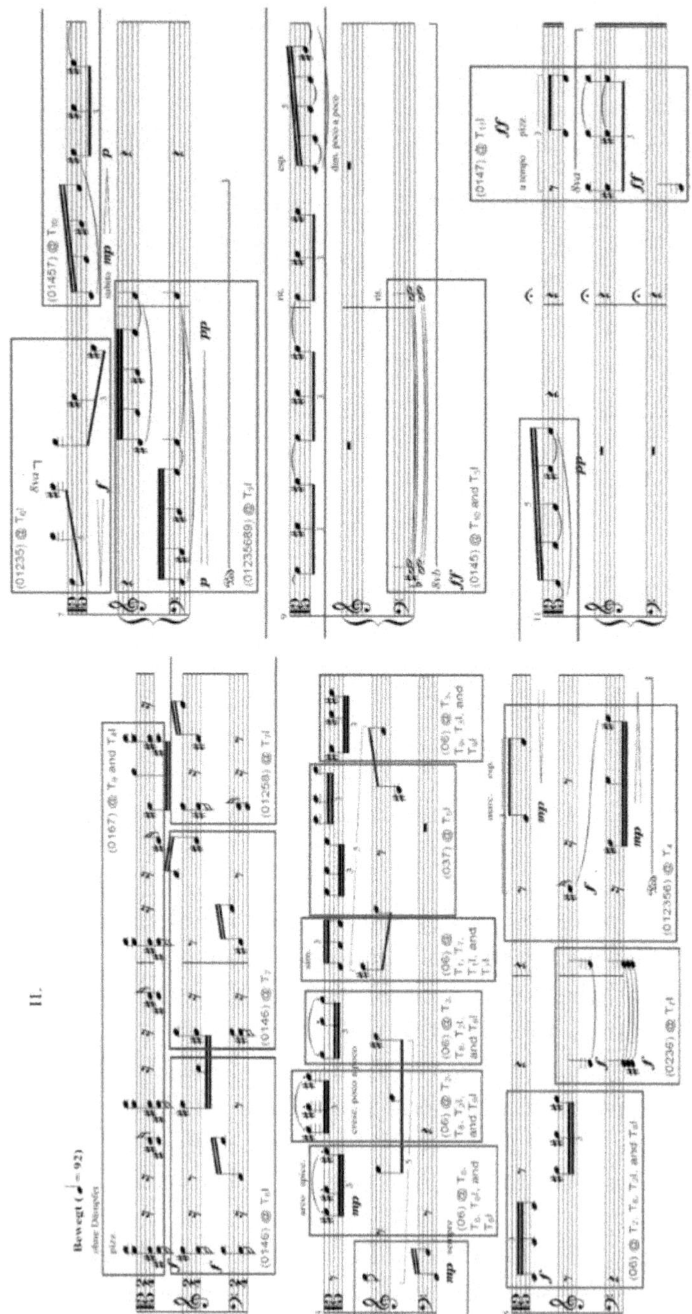

Fig. 5.27. Analysis of movement II.

The pitch classes in movement III are all from a single heptachord: $\{B\#, C\#, D\#, E\#, F\#, G, A\}$. We label these pitch classes with elements of $\mathbb{Z}_7$ as follows: $B\# = 0, C\# = 1, \ldots, A = 6$.

Literal pitch class sets are simply the subsets of $\mathbb{Z}_7 = \{0, 1, 2, \ldots, 6\}$. The elements of a literal pitch class set can be listed in a particular form, called the *normal form* of the set, which can be computed via an algorithm. For example, the normal form of the set $\{1, 5\}$ is [51].

The dihedral group D_{14} of order 14 has seven rotations and seven reflections. We label the rotations $R_0, \ldots, R_6$ and the reflections $R_0S, \ldots, R_6S$.

Abstract pitch class sets are the orbits of the power set of $\mathbb{Z}_7$ under the action of D_{14} defined by letting

$$R_nX = \{x + n | x \text{ in } X\} \quad \text{and} \quad R -_n SX = \{-x + n | x \text{ in } X\}$$

for all n in $\mathbb{Z}_7$ and for all X in the power set of $\mathbb{Z}_7$. An abstract pitch class set can be identified by its representative whose normal form begins with zero, called the *prime form* of the set. For example, the prime form of the orbit of [51] is (03).

In the annotation to Fig. 5.28, literal pitch class sets appear in boxes.

Each literal pitch class set X is labeled both by the abstract pitch class set Y to which it belongs and by the elements of D_{14} that take X to the set characterizing the prime form of Y.

For example, the literal set [51] is labeled both by the prime form of its abstract set (03) and by the rotation R_5 and the reflection R_1S that take [51] to [03].

5.3.4.2. *Project* 2

- Dodecaphonic piece.
- The main row is: $CBDC\#FF\#D\#EG\#GA\#A$.
- Through the use of a matrix we can find from 24 up to 48 variations of the row including its inverse, its retrograde, and inverse–retrograde through all twelve notes from the original row.

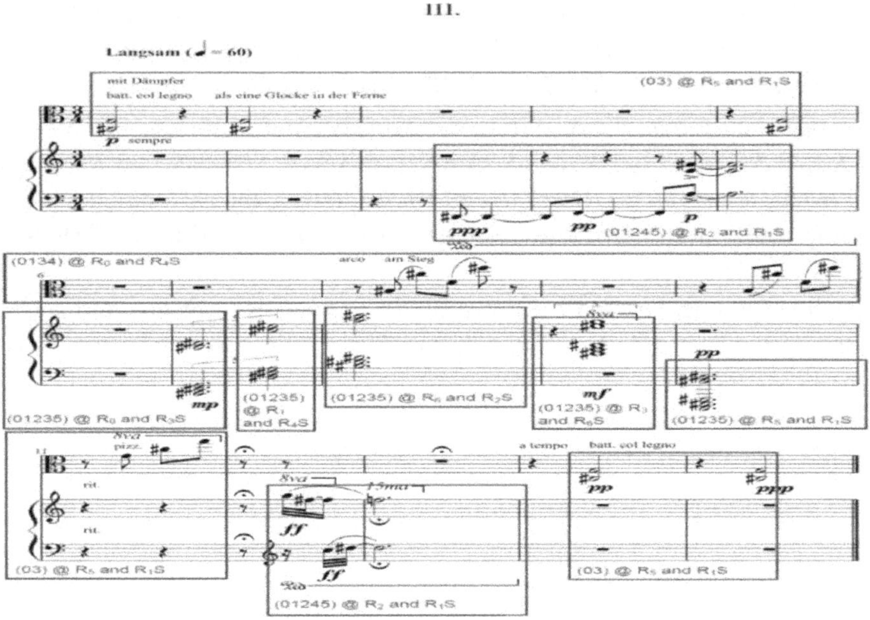

Fig. 5.28. Analysis of movement III.

- The twelve notes of the row are divided into three groups of four notes (tetrachords), with the last two pairs of tetrachords themselves being "derived", which means that they also have retrograde and inverse–retrograde properties.
- For the first 24 measures of the piece, the row is transformed using the aforementioned transformations, as well as classical compositional techniques such as imitation, augmentation and diminution.
- Starting on measure 25, the piece uses a clear mathematical transformation. Using a retrograde inversion, measure 26 on the lower voice in response to measure 25. In mathematical terminology, the musical retrograde inversion is a "rotation". As this rotation occurs in time, the notes do not rotate or reflect around a fixed center or axis. In this case, the result is a reflection of the reflection (Fig. 5.31).

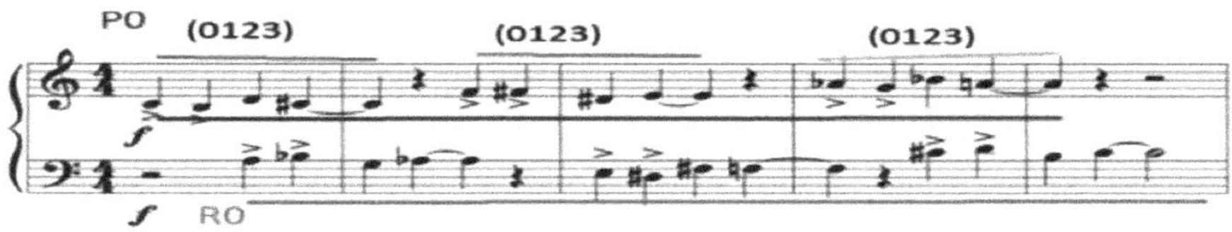

Fig. 5.29. 12-tone row.

	I_0	I_{11}	I_2	I_1	I_5	I_6	I_3	I_4	I_8	I_7	I_{10}	I_9	
P_0	C	B	D	C#	F	F#	D#	E	G#	G	A#	A	R_0
P_1	C#	C	D#	D	F#	G	E	F	A	G#	B	A#	R_1
P_{10}	A#	A	C	B	D#	E	C#	D	F#	F	G#	G	R_{10}
P_{11}	B	A#	C#	C	E	F	D	D#	G	F#	A	G#	R_{11}
P_7	G	F#	A	G#	C	C#	A#	B	D#	D	F	E	R_7
P_6	F#	F	G#	G	B	C	A	A#	D	C#	E	D#	R_6
P_9	A	G#	B	A#	D	D#	C	C#	F	E	G	F#	R_9
P_8	G#	G	A#	A	C#	D	B	C	E	D#	F#	F	R_8
P_4	E	D#	F#	F	A	A#	G	G#	C	B	D	C#	R_4
P_5	F	E	G	F#	A#	B	G#	A	C#	C	D#	D	R_5
P_2	D	C#	E	D#	G	G#	F	F#	A#	A	C	B	R_2
P_3	D#	D	F	E	G#	A	F#	G	B	A#	C#	C	R_3
	RI_0	RI_{11}	RI_2	RI_1	RI_5	RI_6	RI_3	RI_4	RI_8	RI_7	RI_{10}	RI_9	

Fig. 5.30. Tone row matrix.

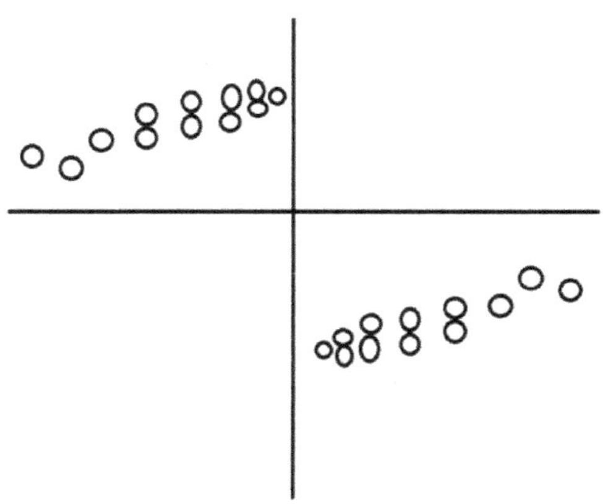

Fig. 5.31. Dizzy hop frieze pattern present in the composition.

Fig. 5.32. Complete score.

5.4. Conclusion

In this chapter we have presented examples of subject areas within mathematics, as well as materials, student work, and ideas for managing interdisciplinary mathematics–music courses in very special contexts. A logical question that arises is, although the results seemed to be very positive and the specific motivations caused engagement of the exceptionally diverse groups of students, how feasible and generalizable is the model that was developed?

It is evident that special conditions are necessary for this concept to be successful; among them, the existence of faculty versed in mathematical music theory. An indiscriminate implementation of this model would lead to caricaturization. However, if there are scholars carrying out research or following the trends in mathematical music theory, a phenomenon that does exist and is growing, the design and implementation of these courses should be encouraged. Additionally, not only the materials that go into the courses, but also the ones that come out of the courses are very important at this stage, where standard texts are still non-existent.

The concept seemed to work very well in the context of cultural exchange. As long as the students possess a certain level of knowledge in at least one of the subject areas the mixed group activities were essential in the learning process. The students showed, through their evaluations (projects, tests, etc.), that they were mastering the objectives of the mathematical and/or musical content, although the objectives were not that same for everyone. To the same extent, as both mathematics and music have a strong symbolic language component, it seems natural to employ these disciplines in study abroad programs.

Bibliography

[1] F. Aceff-Sánchez, O. Agustín-Aquino, E. Lluis-Puebla, M. Montiel and J. du Plessis, *An Introduction to Group Theory: Applications to Mathematical Music Theory* (Bookboon Ventus Publishing, 2012).

[2] Audetat and J. Junod, The diatonic bell, (2006), Retrieved on December 4, 2014, from: http://www.cloche-diatonique.ch/atlas/preview.php?lang=en\&c=12\&d=7.

[3] W. Barker and R. Howe, *Continuous Symmetry* (American Mathematical Society, 2007).

[4] A. Bart and B. Clair, Math and the art of M.C. Escher, (2017), Retrieved from: http://mathstat.slu.edu/escher/index.php/Math_and_the_Art_of_M._C._Escher, Wiki Commons.

[5] R. Cohn, Neo-Riemannian operations, parsimonious trichords, and their "Tonnetz" representations, *J. Music Theory*, **41**(1) (1997) 1–6.

[6] A. S. Crans, T. M. Fiore and R. Satyendra, Musical actions of dihedral groups, (2008), Retrieved on June 1, 2017, from: http://arxiv.org/PS_cache/arxiv/pdf/0711/0711.1873v2.pdf.

[7] V. Hart, Symmetry and transformations in the musical plane, in *Proc. Bridges 2009: Mathematics, Music, Art, Architecture, Culture*, eds. C. Kaplan and R. Sarhangi (Tarquin Publications, 2009), pp. 169–176.

[8] J. Hook, Signature transformations, in *Music Theory and Mathematics: Chords, Collections, and Transformations*, eds. J. Douthett M. Hyde and C. Smith (University of Rochester Press, Rochester, NY, 2008), pp. 137–160.

[9] J. Hook, Spelled heptachords, in *MCM 2011: Mathematics and Computation in Music*, eds. C. Agon, M. Andreatta G. Assayag, E. Amiot, J. Bresson and J. Mandereau (Springer, Heidelberg, 2011), pp. 84–97.

[10] G. Mazzola, *The Topos of Music* (Springer, Berlin, 2003).

[11] G. Mazzola, M. Mannone and Y. Pang Clark, *Cool Math for Hot Music* (Springer, Berlin, 2009).

[12] G. Mazzola and F. Thalmann, Musical composition and gestural diagrams, in *MCM 2011: Mathematics and computation in Music*, eds. C. Agon, M. Andreatta, G. Assayag, E. Amiot, J. Bresson and J. Mandereau (Springer, Heidelberg, 2011), pp. 151–164.

[13] G. Milmeister, *The Rubato Composer Music Software: Component-Based Implementation of a Functorial Concept Architecture* (Springer, Berlin, 2009).

[14] M. Montiel, Mathematical music theory in shanghai, (2016), https://www.youtube.com/watch?v=HiNd3e3UnMc.

Chapter 6

Scaling up to Atonality: The Pedagogy of Small Cyclic Universes*

Richard Cohn

Yale University New Haven, CT, USA
richard.cohn@yale.edu

6.1. The Challenge of Teaching Atonal Theory

The theory of atonality concerns the cyclic universe of 12 elements (C12), interpreted as chromatic pitch classes, focusing on properties of pitch-class sets and relations among them. It is a standard curricular offering at both undergraduate and post-graduate levels in North America and elsewhere, is integrated into at least one comprehensive music-theory textbook [20], and is the sole focus of several dedicated ones [16, 26, 28].

There are several distinct reasons why atonal theory is challenging to teach. The musical repertory is unfamiliar to many students. The degree of abstraction is higher than in elementary theory. The connection from concept to percept is often indirect. Even for students who are interested in atonal repertories, and comfortable with mathematical modes of conception and representation, it takes some time before the techniques of atonal theory help them to achieve satisfying analytic insights. For students who are math-phobic, not drawn to atonal repertories, or lack a high degree of aural

*This chapter revises and expands [12]. I am grateful to the editors of the online journal *MusMat: Brazilian Journal of Music and Mathematics* for permission.

discrimination, the curriculum can be mystifying and alienating, at worst provoking hostility that generalizes to the entire project of thinking conceptually about music.

One part of the challenge can be confronted by broadening the range of repertory. C12 can be interpreted in the rhythmic/metric domain as well as in the chordal/scalar one: not only as a chromatic universe of pitch classes, but also as a 12-beat cycle, which might be realized as a bar of $\frac{12}{8}$, two bars of $\frac{6}{8}$, four bars of $\frac{3}{4}$, a bar of $\frac{4}{4}$ with tripleted subdivisions, and so forth [1]. Musicians become comfortable at any early age with these metric cycles. By the time they have reached intellectual maturity, their deeply embodied knowledge of them is ready for mobilization. Abstract concepts and symbols can be connected immediately to West-African, Latino, global-popular, hip-hop, minimalist, or electronic dance music [2, 23–25]. Application of C12 to these familiar repertories exposes students to central terms and concepts, such as rotational equivalence, invariance, complementation, inclusion, and set classification. Learning C12 in this environment, students acquire abstract knowledge ready for transfer to the isomorphic universe of pitch classes, and to chromatic, atonal and serial repertories. There is a pedagogical advantage in staging the mathematical and musical challenge at different times. And there is a residual benefit: as they travel along the road to atonal theory, students are exposed to a theory of musical meter, which is otherwise neglected in the curriculum [10].

This solution addresses the problems of repertory familiarity and concept-to-percept correspondence, but not the problem of abstraction. C12 is a complex system, with 4096 distinct combinations, including 66 distinct pairs of elements, 220 triplets, and so forth. It is difficult to view such a system holistically, especially if one has not "scaled up" to it through simpler systems. The application of C12 to beat-class cycles suggests a solution. There is only one chromatic universe of pitch classes, but there are many universes of beat classes, some quite small, that are even more familiar than C12. Larger-cardinality universes inherit the simple properties and relations of smaller ones, and add more complex ones. An incremental pedagogical progression from smaller to larger cyclic systems thus has some of the advantages of elementary mathematics curricula that are initially restricted to small numbers, such as a Japanese model for teaching arithmetic to children [14].

Musicians in the west typically learn systems based on 2 and 3 beats, their powers (4, 8, 9), and their composites (6), thus catching every number in the range from 2 to 9, with the exception of 5 and 7. Fortuitously, it is exactly these missing prime cyclic universes that underlie the most familiar pitch-class systems: pentatonic and diatonic scales. Unlike the beat-class and chromatic universes, the elements of these scales are not distributed perfectly evenly. But they are even enough that we can disregard, or "reduce out", distinctions between step-class-equivalent (generic) intervals [3]. Indeed, in the case of the diatonic scale, such reductions are familiar to all music students, who have been taught from an early stage to use evenly distributed small numbers to model unevenly distributed diatonic intervals and scale degrees.

6.2. Objectives and Outline of a Pedagogical Program

I developed this pedagogical program for music majors at Yale, starting in 2009, and it is this form of the program that is described below. In 2014, in conjunction with Andrew Jones, a version was developed for general populations of students in Yale College, seeking to fulfill a quantitative-reasoning requirement. In this form, the material was also taught to general-education students at the University of Sydney. In conjunction with a team of researchers in Australia headed by Andrew Milne (MARCS Institute, University of Western Sydney), I am currently developing a version of this material for school-age populations, using animated-graphic software (see Chapter 9 in this volume).

For music students, the program has the following objectives: (1) to explore rhythm and meter in diverse repertories, otherwise under-served topics in most music-theory curricula; (2) to explore diatonicism from a perspective that complements the standard harmony/part-writing curriculum; (3) to introduce concepts and terms of pitch-class theory, in a simpler and musically more familiar environment (as described in the introductory remarks); (4) to reflect on the special properties of the 5-, 7- and 12-tone universes that are our native scalar habitats; (5) to reflect on the marvelous and often surprising abstract correspondences between pitch and time structure; and (6) to acquire and apply aspects of mathematical set theory, graph theory, combinatoriality, number theory, and modular arithmetic.

The pedagogical program progresses in three stages. In the first stage, which can be worked through in about 30 minutes of class time, power sets of 0, 1, and 2 elements are briefly studied. Basic relations such as null set, universal set, complementation, and cardinality are introduced, as are the basic symbols and conventions of set theory. The second stage studies cyclic universes of 3, 4, and 5 elements, realized respectively as triple and quadruple meter in the rhythmic domain, and pentatonic scales in the pitch domain. Topics that can be introduced at this stage include modular arithmetic, rotational (transpositional) equivalence, classification and labeling procedures, interval class, interval content, set class, and invariance.

The musical applications are not yet surprising. Students are learning a new language to model properties and relations about which they have long cultivated deep intuitions. They may feel skeptical about acquiring a new set of heavy machinery that does not immediately yield new knowledge. I emphasize that it is always good to test-drive a new vehicle on familiar and comfortable ground. Soon enough, they'll see how well it handles the challenging bumps and divots in the terrain just around the bend in the road.

As the size of the cycle increases, intuitions about its structure diminish at roughly the rate that interest in its musical capacities grows. Thus, conceptual and terminological grasp is not overwhelmed at the same moment that students are struggling to gain some intuitive traction on structures that are becoming exponentially more complex. C6 represents a pedagogical watershed: just small enough to be graspable as a *Gestalt*, but large enough to introduce curious features with unexpected musical ramifications. The universes from 6 to 9 all have distinctive features that underlie familiar and compelling musical properties. These universes are large enough that set-class enumeration and classification from scratch becomes a challenge, but small enough that it remains tractable. But enumeration is no longer the central focus at this level. That focus shifts toward the generation of larger sets by recursive stacking of a single interval. Each universe has a unique personality, with special musical ramifications, that results from its number of elements. Generation behaves quite differently according to whether the number of elements is prime (5, 7), a power of a single prime (8, 9), or composed of multiple distinct primes (6, 12).

Three variables, adapted from [5], are used throughout this study:

- **c** counts the number of elements in the cyclic universe, corresponding to the large-case variable in expressions such as "C12".
- **d counts** the cardinality of a pitch-class set. We will label a pairing of c and d values as (c, d). Thus, a major scale in a chromatic universe is classified as (12, 7), and a triad in a diatonic one as (7, 3).
- **g** is a generating interval, and corresponds to one of the $\lfloor c/2 \rfloor$ interval classes within a universe of size c.

An upward progression through the values of c corresponds to a downward progression through the rows of Pascal's triangle, a skewed version of which is Table 6.1. Each entry in the table presents $\binom{c}{d}$, the multiplicity of (c, d). When $d = 0, 1, c-1$, or c, their cardinalities are "exterior", and the structures are of little interest musically or mathematically. Our attention will be focused exclusively on the unshaded cardinalities in the interior of each row, once they begin to appear at (4, 2). The final column of each row indicates the cardinality of the power set, 2^{c}, which sums the entries to its left.

6.2.1. *Non-cyclic universes of* 0–2 *elements*

Since $c = 3$ is the smallest cyclic universe, some instructors may find that this a sensible place to begin. I have nonetheless found it profitable to work quickly through the trivially small, non-cyclic universes first, establishing the most basic definitions (defined terms

Table 6.1. Pascal's triangle, interpreted as number of sets $|d|$ in a $|c|$-universe.

c =	d= 0	1	2	3	4	5	6	7	8	9	10	11	12	2^c =
0	1													1
1	1	1												2
2	1	2	1											4
3	1	3	3	1										8
4	1	4	6	4	1									16
5	1	5	10	10	5	1								32
6	1	6	15	20	15	6	1							64
7	1	7	21	35	35	21	7	1						128
8	1	8	28	56	70	56	28	8	1					256
9	1	9	36	84	126	126	84	36	9	1				512
10	1	10	45	120	210	252	210	120	45	10	1			1024
11	1	11	55	165	330	462	462	330	165	55	11	1		2048
12	1	12	66	220	495	792	924	792	495	220	66	12	1	4096

are here placed in italics). For $c = 0$, there is a single set that is both *null* (ø) and *universal* (U). For $c = 1$, these functions partition into two distinct and *complementary* sets of different *cardinality*. The formal definition of complementation ($B = U \backslash A$ if and only if $A \cup B = U$ and $A \cap B = \emptyset$) gives occasion to introduce fundamentals of mathematical sets, the primary symbolic language to be used throughout this curriculum. The power set of $c = 2$ is completed by augmenting ø and $U = \{A, B\}$ with two singleton sets $\{A\}$ and $\{B\}$, related both by complementation and by *cardinality equivalence*. Introducing this term here provides the simplest possible environment in which to contemplate the distinction between equivalence and equality, and to begin to emphasize that there are many ways to classify a musical object, depending on one's goals.

A rudimentary first application is a two-beat bar, which has 2^2 possibilities: both ($\{A, B\}$), first beat only ($\{A\}$), second beat only ($\{B\}$), neither ($\{\emptyset\}$).

6.2.2. *Cyclic universes of* 3–5 *elements*

With $c = 3$ we arrive at a properly cyclic domain, and the next several universes will gradually introduce the most significant properties, relations, and representational protocols for musically realized cyclic spaces, including modular arithmetic, cyclic graphs, rotational (= transpositional) equivalence, subset/superset (= inclusion), set class, abstract complementation, abstract inclusion, invariance, interval class, interval vector, and interval generation. **c = 3** has eight sets: ø, U, three singletons (3, 1), and their three complements (3, 2). Each increment in the value of c doubles the power set, and the number of distinct combinations will soon require a more systematic labeling protocol. In preparation, *integer labeling* of elements is introduced, from 0 to $c - 1$. Using integers as labels risks confusing the different "registers" in which numbers will be used — for labeling, counting, and measuring — and it is important at this stage to exhort vigilance about these distinctions.

C3 is the appropriate universe in which to introduce *modular arithmetic, cyclic graphs, and transpositional equivalence.* Figure 6.1(a) shows the cyclic graphs for the three sets such that (3, 2), filling circles to indicate the elements in the set. It can be readily seen that the sets are related by rotation. Figure 6.1(b) realizes the same three sets as rhythms in 3/4 meter. A musician

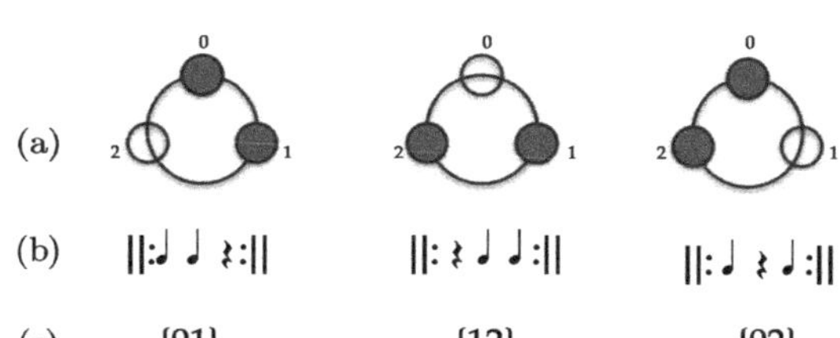

Fig. 6.1. Sets for (3, 2), represented in three different ways: (a) as cyclic graphs; (b) as repeating rhythms; (c) as integers.

can just as easily intuit how rotation is realized in this domain as in the graphic one.

Finally, Fig. 6.1(c) realizes the same three sets using integer notation. Here intuitions are less stable. How can {02}, whose elements seem separated, have the same structure as {01} and {12}, whose elements are obviously adjacent? By comparing these representations with the cyclic graphs and rhythmic sets, students can gain their first foothold on the unfamiliar logic of modular arithmetic, and begin to make sense of such expressions as $1-2=2$. Through comparisons of this sort, students begin to explore the ways that graphic, arithmetic, and musical relations reciprocally model each other, a process whose goal is to allow their pre-loaded intuitions about each of these three domains to inform their understanding of the other two.

As this point ideally marks a juncture between two distinct sessions, I give students detailed class notes and then give them a first problem set, given as "Problem Set 1" at the end of this paper. The focus problem set asks them to scale up to the next level (in this case, C4), generate its power set, classify the contents of that set, and portray them as cyclic graphs. I also prompt them to explore unfamiliar properties of this brave new world, generate new concepts to account for those properties, and explore systems of labeling for those concepts.

C4 has 16 sets, ten of which have exterior cardinalities that advance no new properties. We focus on the $\binom{4}{2} = 6$ sets of intermediate cardinality (4, 2). For the first time, we encounter cardinality-equivalent sets that are not equivalent by rotation (= transposition). These six sets represent two distinct pair-wise distances, or *intervals*, each corresponding to a *transposition class*, or T-class, which can be provisionally labeled as "step" and "leap" (i.e., adjacent and diametric pair). The musical distinction between these two classes is represented by Fig. 6.2, from Mozart, where each measure has four ♪ beats, labeled from 0 to 3. In the first measures, the beats are partitioned into complementary step-related pairs, {12} and {03}. Beginning at bar 5, beats are partitioned into complementary leap-related pairs, {02} and {13}. This simple example illustrates

Fig. 6.2. From Mozart's Variations on "Ah, vous dirai-je, Maman". Measures 1–4 partition C4 as {03} and {12}, representing step class [01]. Measures 5–7 partition C4 as {02} and {13}, representing leap class [02].

how a change of transposition class can model a recognizable change in rhythmic "feel" or *qualia.*

Students are asked to contemplate why the six dyads in C4 contain four steps but only two leaps. An explanation of this curious circumstance introduces the important topic of rotational *invariance.* Musicians easily intuit, from examining Fig. 6.2, that there are more possible step-pairs than leap-pairs, since each leap-pair is indistinguishable from its two-unit rotation (or transposition). The invariance is easy to see in a cyclic graph, but more of a challenge to see when the same sets are represented using modulo-4 integers. It is in mastering challenges of this sort that students who have difficulty adjusting to modular arithmetic gain further traction.

The introduction of T-classes in C4 through the step/leap distinction gives an occasion to confront one of the perpetually confusing aspects of atonal set theory, the distinction between literal sets and abstract set classes. For bookkeeping purposes, Allen Forte [15] assigned each transposition/inversion equivalence class a two-value label whose second value was an arbitrary number. Most atonal pedagogies now prefer to label each set class by algorithmically selecting one of its member sets to serve as its *prime form.* Although this procedure eliminates the arbitrary relation between label and referent, there is still a pedagogical challenge, since the same label evidently refers to objects at two different levels of abstraction. For example, in the pitch-class interpretation of C12, {037} references a specific triad, C minor, whereas [037] references the general transposition class of twelve minor triads that C minor is selected to represent. Unless the distinction between curly and square brackets is emphasized, considerable confusion arises. The step/leap distinction in (4, 2) provides a pretext for introducing the prime-form protocol in an environment that is intuitive and contained: [01] and [02] are introduced as alternate labels for "step" and "leap" classes, respectively.

c = 5 has 32 sets, still small enough to explore and comprehend as a single *Gestalt*. Twenty of these sets are of intermediate cardinality: $\binom{5}{2} = 10$ pairs and their $\binom{5}{3} = 10$ complements. Each cardinality class has two distinct rotation classes: steps [01] and leaps [02] for pairs, and their respective complements, [012] and [013]. The fact that both of these binomial coefficients are multiples of 5 suggests that there are no transpositional invariances, a result of 5's status as a prime number.

I use C5 to introduce two significant concepts that are portable to larger-cardinality universes. The first concept is *total interval content*, a property of each set class that is catalogued by its *interval vector*. Cataloguing the single interval of a two-element set is trivial work, but there is a payoff: cataloguing the three intervals of a (5, 3) set, and comparing that vector to that of its (5, 2) complement brings to light the interval-profile affinities between complement-related sets. This leads to the introduction of a simple form of the complement algorithm, which produces the interval vector of a set from the interval vector of its complement. In addition to the gains realized by introducing complement relations in a universe with a small number of elements, there is also a pedagogical benefit to introducing the complement algorithm in a universe whose cardinality is odd, where the algorithm is not complicated by the invariances of diametric intervals such as the tritone.

Because c is prime, C5 is also a good place to introduce intervallic *generators* (g), marking a shift from a static conception of a cyclic universe to a dynamic one, a space to navigate through time. Each set in $c = 5$ is generable either by step ($g = \pm 1$) or leap ($g = \pm 2$). All of these values of g generate all sets of exterior cardinality. It is the intermediate cardinalities that are distinguishable by their generators: $g = \pm 1$ generates steps of class [01] and their complements of class [012], and $g = \pm 2$ generates leaps [02] and their complements [013].

C5 is musically realized as a pentatonic scale, whose intervals come in two chromatic sizes: "steps" are major seconds and minor thirds, and "leaps" are perfect fourths and a major third. Following John Clough [3], these chromatic distinctions are overlooked, and the pentatonic space is treated as if it were perfectly rather than maximally even. Step-generation involves a sequential pass through the scale, $\langle G, A, B, D, E, G\rangle$; leap-generation involves skipping scalar notes, $\langle E, A, D, G, B, E\rangle$, as in the standard tuning of a guitar's open strings. Dozens of pentatonic pieces that illustrate this universe are found in [13].

6.2.3. *Cyclic universes with* 6–9 *elements*

Half-way to twelve, C6 is the universe in which curious features with unexpected musical ramifications begin to arise. It is also where the size of the power set becomes difficult to control. The intermediate cardinalities consist of 15 pairs (6, 2), 15 pair-complements (6, 4), and 20 triplets (6, 3). None of these numbers are multiples of c, indicating the presence of rotational invariances at each cardinality. Of the 15 pairs, there are three T-invariant diametric leap-sets [03], alongside six step-sets [01] and six skip-sets [02]. Of the 20 triplets, there are two T-invariant skip-generated triplets [024], alongside the six step-generated clusters [012] and twelve ungenerated sets [013] and [023], which are discussed below in connection with Fig. 6.3.

Since six is the smallest number with two distinct divisors, C6 is the smallest universe to have two distinct *perfectly even* transposition classes. Realized as rhythms, the classes model the two meters available in a bar with six beats. Setting the beat to ♪, [03] suggests a bar of $\frac{6}{8}$ meter ♫♪ ♫♪, and [024] a bar of $\frac{3}{4}$ meter ♫ ♫ ♫ with duple subdivisions. Juxtaposed, these meters model the Baroque pre-cadential hemiola. Superposed as $\{03\} \cup \{024\} = \{0234\}$, they convey the polymetric tug of a waltz, as well as the 3-against-2 cross-rhythms of West African and Afro-Caribbean repertories. The relation of these two perfectly even sets is thus the simplest instance of a situation that arises, in more complex form, in larger universes where c is

Fig. 6.3. Beethoven, String Quartet no. 8, Op. 59 no. 2, Allegretto, bars 1–8. The violin attacks from mm. 2–7 are class [023]; the complementary attacks in the remaining parts are class [013].

a multiple of two or more distinct primes, notably C12, C18, and C36 [8].

The complementary T-classes [013] and [023] introduce many new features that do not arise in smaller-cardinality universes. Unlike all sets where $c < 6$, neither of these classes is inversionally symmetric. Instead a set of one class inverts into a set of the other, which is to say that the two classes are abstractly related by *inversion* as well as complementation. Accordingly, they have identical interval vectors: one instance of each interval; C6 is the smallest universe that hosts non-trivial all-interval sets. These sets' uniform distribution of intervals is related to their ungenerability, as noted above.

Figure 6.3, the opening phrase of a Beethoven scherzo, demonstrates that the interaction of these two set classes has rich musical ramifications, and raises significant issues about the relation between structure and perception. After the initial chord, the texture splits into three registral streams: low bass, high melody, and mid-register harmony. These three streams partition the six beat classes as follows: BASS = $\{0\}$; HARMONY = $\{3, 4\}$; MELODY = $\{1, 2, 5\}$.

Although these three streams preserve some measure of registral autonomy, the bass and harmony also fuse to some degree, by virtue of their shared intermittency (in contrast to the legato melody), creating the combined stream OOM-PAH = BASS ∪ HARMONY = $\{0, 3, 4\}$. Both the OOM-PAH stream, of transposition class [013], and the complementary MELODY stream, of class [023], are all-interval. They relate to each other by inversion around a mid-bar axis, and also around a bar-line axis. Remarkably, despite this close structural relation, the two streams project quite different meters, creating a strong sense of metric disorientation that is (briefly) resolved at the end of the phrase (Fig. 6.4).

The OOM-PAH stream ♩ 𝄾♪♪ 𝄾 induces a strong sense of 3/4 meter, consistent with the meter signature. While the cello provides each measure's downbeat anchor $\{0\}$, the inner voices $\{3, 4\}$ throws accentual weight onto the later of its two paired attacks, $\{4\}$. This is consistent with two principles: that consecutive onsets cannot both participate in a slower pulse [17], and that (all else equal) an isolated

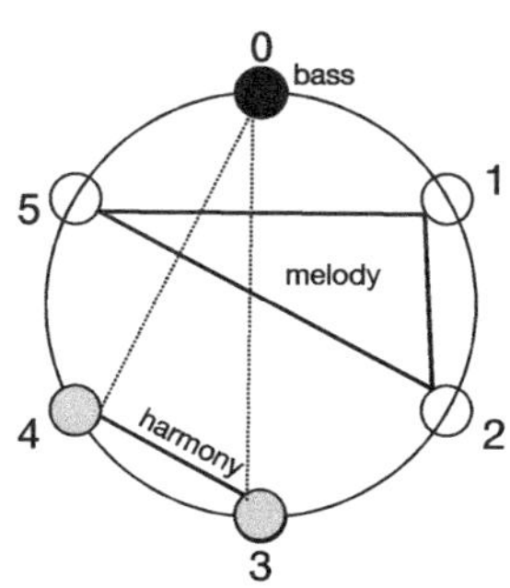

Fig. 6.4. Graphic portrait of beat-class sets in Beethoven scherzo (cf. Fig. 6.3). The rhythms of the three registral streams are shown by differently colored discs. The dotted lines connect the harmony and bass streams to form the oom-pah stream. OOM-PAH and MELODY sets have identically shaped triangles, which are related by inversion (reflection) about 2/3 and 0/5, but not by transposition (rotation).

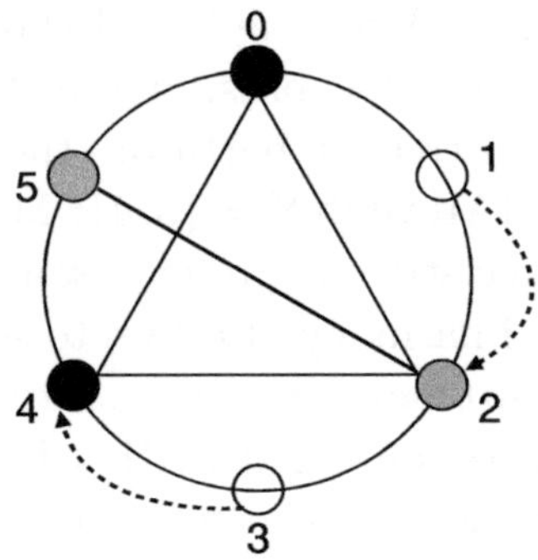

Fig. 6.5. Competing meters in the Beethoven Scherzo, Fig. 6.3. Adjacent onsets cannot both participate in slower pulses, so one must be reduced out at the next level of meter. Arrows indicate the iambic interpretation of isolated adjacent onsets, reducing out the earlier onset. The diameter represents the ♩. pulse projected by the remaining $\{2,5\}$ onsets in the violin, projecting a $\frac{6}{8}$ meter that is displaced from the downbeat. The triangle represents the ♩ pulse subjectively induced by the remaining $\{0,4\}$ oom-pah onsets, projecting a $\frac{3}{4}$ meter.

pair of onsets is interpreted iambically, i.e., throws its accentual weight onto the later of the pair [22]. Time point 3, an offbeat, is reduced out of the metric grid, leaving $\{0,4\}$. This rhythm 𝅗𝅥♩ projects a subjective ♩ pulse that is reinforced by the durational accent in the violin (Fig. 6.5).

The $\{1,2,5\}$ melody also has a pair of adjacent attacks $\{1,2\}$, whose iambic interpretation reduces time point 1 out of the slower pulse, leaving $\{2,5\}$, which projects a $\frac{6}{8}$ meter anchored on time point 2. Thus, the meter of the scherzo is doubly disoriented. The OOM-PAH stream is in $\frac{3}{4}$ meter while the melody in $\frac{6}{8}$ meter; and the OOM-PAH stream is anchored on downbeat $\{0\}$, the melody at time point $\{2\}$. This provides a vivid illustration of the potential disjunction between structure and percept: not every statement of mathematical equivalence corresponds to a judgment of perceptual equivalence.

Scaling up to the next rung, from C6 to C7, we move to an adjacent terrain with a dramatically different landscape. C7 also

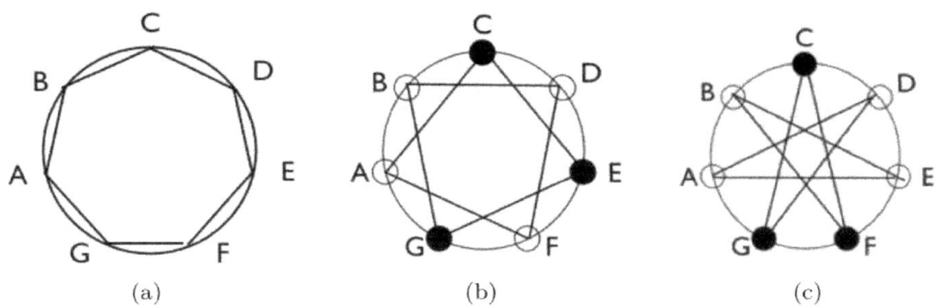

Fig. 6.6. Three generators for C7. (a) $g = 1$ produces a scale; (b) $g = 2$ produces chords such as triads (filled circles) and seventh chords (open circles). (c) $g = 3$ produces a cycle of diatonic fifths, connecting each modal tonic to its dominant and subdominant.

has three distinct intervals, and hence three distinct generators. But whereas in C6, $g > 1$ are idempotent divisors, in C7 each g generates the entire universe. This distinction is a direct consequence of their respective composite and prime cardinalities. So near, and yet so far! The three generators have distinct roles to play in the system of diatonic tonality that underlies historical European and contemporary global repertories: they respectively organize melody, harmony, and harmonic progression.

The three cyclic graphs of Fig. 6.6 show the action of these generators on the diatonic collection. The *step* interval ($g = 1$) generates scalar fragments, which are the basis of melodies. The *skip* interval ($g = 2$) generates "third-stacked" harmonies: [024] triads and [0135] seventh chords. The quasi-diametric *leap* interval ($g = 3$) generates the diatonic cycle of fifths, and thus its generated sets are the basis of progressions between successive harmonies. Most intermediate-cardinality set classes are generated by exactly one of these intervals, and thus can be seen to perform one of the three jobs. The exceptions are the four ungenerated, inversionally asymmetric classes, [013], [023], [0124], and [0234], all of which distribute their intervals uniformly across step, skip, and leap classes.

C7 is also an appropriate universe for introducing inclusion, *maximal evenness* (ME) and *maximal intersection* (MI), and the graphs that represent them [4, 27]. Inclusion follows naturally from interval generation, since the sets from a single generator form an inclusion network. The building blocks of classical tonality, fifths, triads, and seventh chords, are maximally even. And adjacent triads on a Tonnetz maximally intersect [7]. These properties and relations have significant ramifications in the C12 chromatic universe.

C8 and C9 can be studied in order, but also in tandem, as both are powers of small primes. They are the smallest universes that have both divisor and non-unit prime generators. The interaction of these two generator-classes is rich with dynamic potential in the context of metric cycles. The divisor generators for these universes (for C8, $g = (\pm 2, 4)$; for C9, $g = \pm 3$) underlie the isochronous meters of the Western European tradition ($\begin{smallmatrix}2\\4\end{smallmatrix}$, $\begin{smallmatrix}4\\4\end{smallmatrix}$, and $\begin{smallmatrix}9\\8\end{smallmatrix}$ meter respectively). Non-unit prime intervals (for C8, $g = \pm 3$; for C9, $g = \pm 2$) generate the non-isochronous meters of many popular, folk and world-music repertories (also referred to as additive, *aksak*, mixed, or quasi-meters) [19, 23]. The dialectic of high-art and vernacular meters is artfully exploited in a number of repertories beginning in the middle of the nineteenth century. In $\begin{smallmatrix}4\\4\end{smallmatrix}$ meter, Western pure-duple isochrony ($g = 2$) is juxtaposed with the Afro-Caribbean tresillo ($g = 3$) (Gottschalk, Joplin) or paradiddle (Reich) [6, 11]. A similar juxtaposition is available in $\begin{smallmatrix}9\\8\end{smallmatrix}$ meter, where pure-triple isochrony ($g = 3$) is juxtaposed with characteristic Balkan/Turkish rhythms ($g = 2$) (Bartók; see [9]). Analysis Assignment 1, at the end of this paper, presents a prompt for an analytical assignment focusing on a well-known Scott Joplin rag.

6.3. To the Summit: C12

In the course for undergraduate music majors at Yale University, the progression to nine elements takes about six 75-minute classes, or three weeks of a 13-week semester. Since C10 and C11 have no familiar applications, in the fourth week I begin the study of atonality proper, introducing the C12 chromatic pitch-class universe. Students are by now familiar with all of the foundational terms, concepts, and protocols of atonal theory. They can quickly generate a table of the 19 trichord classes, indicate which ones are inversionally symmetric, which two are inversionally paired, and recognize the special properties of the augmented triad; place trichord classes into a maximal-intersection network; and identify abstract inclusion and complement relations involving larger-cardinality sets.

Students also are in a position to appreciate what is special about living in a musical universe that has exactly twelve elements, and how different their world would be if that number were incrementally smaller or larger. Students who have studied the interaction of divisor generators 3×2 in C6 are primed to understand C12 as a cross-product of C4 $\times$ C3, realized respectively as [048] augmented triads and [0369] diminished-seventh chords, and to appreciate the ways that atonal composers compound these generated cycles to create interactions between hexatonic, whole-tone, and octatonic scales [29]. Because they have studied how prime and divisor generators interact in C8 and C9, they are in a position to understand how prime-generated diatonic sets ($g = \pm 5$) can be placed into opposition with divisor-generated ones in C12 ($g = \pm 2, 3, 4, 6$). Having studied transpositional invariance and maximal evenness in small-cardinality universes, they can more easily identify sets with those properties in C12, and recognize their musical significance. There are also significant applications of C12 in the beat-class domain. For example, the relations of the divisor-generated perfectly even sets underlies the interaction of $\binom{12}{8}$, $\binom{6}{4}$, and $\binom{3}{2}$ meters, as different ways to structure the interaction of incommensurate divisor generators [18, 21].

Along the way to C12, students have picked up intimate knowledge of pentatonic, diatonic, and time-cycle universes, and this knowledge has its own value for musicians. Much of the music that they perform, listen to, improvise, or compose is both diatonic and deeply metric. Students who have pursued this pedagogical path to atonality will have, along the way, acquired a model that helps them explore familiar repertories, the systems that underlie them, and the abstract relations those systems instantiate.

Bibliography

[1] M. Babbitt, Twelve-tone rhythmic structure and the electronic medium, *Perspect. New Music* **1** (1962) 49–79.

[2] M. J. Butler, *Unlocking the Groove: Rhythm, Meter, and Musical Design in Electronic Dance Music* (Indiana University Press, Bloomington, IN, 2006).

[3] J. Clough, Aspects of diatonic sets, *J. Music Theory* **23** (1979) 45–61.

[4] J. Clough and J. Douthett, Maximally even sets, *J. Music Theory* **35** (1991) 93–173.

[5] J. Clough and G. Myerson, Variety and multiplicity in diatonic systems, *J. Music Theory* **28** (1985) 249–270.

[6] R. Cohn, Transpositional combination of beat-class sets in Steve Reich's phase-shifting music, *Perspect. New Music* **30** (1992) 146–177.

[7] R. Cohn, Neo-Riemannian operations, parsimonious trichords, and their Tonnetz representations, *J. Music Theory* **41** (1997) 1–66.

[8] R. Cohn, Complex hemiolas, ski-hill graphs and metric spaces, *Music Anal.* **20** (2001) 295–326.

[9] R. Cohn, Pitch-time analogies in Bartók's Sonata for Two Pianos and Percussion, in *Music Theory and Mathematics: Chords, Collections, and Transformations,* eds. J. Douthett *et al.* (University of Rochester Press, Rochester, NY, 2008), pp. 49–71.

[10] R. Cohn, Why we don't teach meter and why we should, *J. Music Theory Pedagogy* **29** (2015) 1–19.

[11] R. Cohn, A Platonic model of funky rhythms, *Music Theory Online* **22**(2) (2016).

[12] R. Cohn, Teaching atonal and beat-class theory, modulo small, *MusMat: Brazilian J. Music Math.* **1** (2016) 15–24.

[13] J. Day-O'Connell, *Pentatonicism from the Eighteenth Century to Debussy* (University of Rochester Press, Rochester, NY, 2007).

[14] J. Easley, A Japanese approach to arithmetic, *For Learn. Math.* **3**(3) (1983) 8–14.

[15] A. Forte, *The Structure of Atonal Music* (Yale University Press, New Haven, 1973).

[16] M. L. Friedmann, *Ear Training for Twentieth-Century Music* (Yale University Press, New Haven, 1990).

[17] F. Lerdahl and R. Jackendoff, *A Generative Theory of Tonal Music*, (MIT Press, Cambridge, MA, 1983).

[18] D. Lewin, On harmony and meter in Brahms's op. 76, no. 8, *Nineteenth-Century Music* **4** (1981) 261–265.

[19] J. London, *Hearing in Time: Psychological Aspects of Musical Meter*, 2nd edn. (Oxford University Press, New York, 2012).

[20] E. Marvin and J. Clendinning, *The Musician's Guide to Theory and Analysis*, 3rd edn. (W.W. Norton, New York, 2016).

[21] D. Maw, Trespasser mesure: Meter in Machaut's polyphonic songs, *J. Musicol.* **21** (2004) 46–126.

[22] D. Povel and P. Essens, Perception of temporal patterns, *Music Percept.* **2** (1985) 411–440.

[23] J. Pressing, Cognitive isomorphisms between pitch and rhythm in world musics: West Africa, the Balkans and Western tonality, *Studies Music* **17** (1983) 38–61.

[24] J. Rahn, Turning the analysis around: Africa-derived rhythms and Europe-derived music theory, *Black Music Res. J.* **16** (1996) 71–89.
[25] J. Roeder, Beat-class modulation in Steve Reich's Music, *Music Theory Spectrum* **25** (2003) 275–304.
[26] M. Roig-Francoli, *Understanding Post-Tonal Music* (McGraw-Hill, New York, 2007).
[27] J. Straus, Voice leading in set-class space, *J. Music Theory* **49** (2005) 45–108.
[28] J. Straus, *Introduction to Post-Tonal Theory*, 4th edn. (W. W. Norton, New York, 2016).
[29] D. Tymoczko, Scale networks and Debussy, *J. Music Theory* **48** (2004) 219–294.

Some Problem Sets

Problem Set 1. *The first problem set is distributed after students have explored C3 with the instructor in class. It forms the basis for the introduction of C4 during the following class.* U^n *is the universal set for Cn;* $P(U^n)$ *is the Power set of that universal set;* $T_n(X)$ *is a transposition (rotation) of set* X *by* n *units clockwise.*

$c = 4$ for all problems in this set:

(1) $U^4 =$
(2) $|P(U^4)| =$
(3) $P(U^4) =$
(4) Place the elements of $P(U^4)$ into a two-column table, modeled after the table for $c = 3$ in the second set of class notes.
(5) Portray each set as a cyclic graph for (4, 2) [i.e., where $c = 4$, $d = 2$]. Group the portraits (by placing a box around them) so that sets equivalent under transposition (rotation) are together.
(6a) The cyclic graphs created in response to the previous problem group into two distinct transposition classes. Let's provisionally call them "class number 1" and "class number 2"; it doesn't matter which is which. List the constituent sets of the two classes, in the form of unordered sets. (Since these are sets of sets, embed curly brackets within curly brackets.)
(6b) The provisional names are OK for book-keeping, but heuristically unhelpful. Propose two alternative names for these classes, that will help us distinguish them from each other.

(6c) Why do the two classes (whose elements are themselves sets) have different cardinalities? Can you formulate (define, provisionally name) a special property of one of these classes, that causes it to have a different cardinality than we would expect it to have? [If this question mystifies you, remind yourself that the cardinality of a set class refers to the number of sets that it contains. The constituent sets, which form the elements of this larger set, have their own cardinality, which in every case is 2.]

Questions 7–10 pertain to the score reproduced below, eight measures from Mozart's Variations on "ah, vous dirai je maman". The title loosely translates (at least in the American south) as "hey mama, I'm fixin' to tell you ...". The song on which the variations are based goes under three different names today, pertaining respectively to astronomy, animal husbandry, and orthographical ordering. To kinetically engrave this music into your body and aurally engrave it in your ears (which are two complementary routes to engraving it in your brain), perform it at the keyboard, or listen to a recording while tapping the rhythms with both hands on a surface.

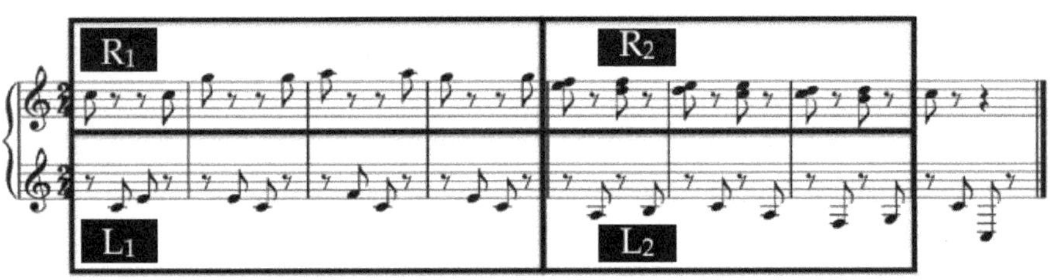

The boxes partition the score into four sections, with labels; R and L are abbreviations for right and left hand, respectively. All of the measures within a box have the same rhythm (= set of onset points).

(7) Number the quaver beats of each measure in order from 0 to 3. Then define sets R_1, R_2, L_1, and L_2 as the onset points for each measure within the corresponding box. Each of the four sets should thus be an element of $P(U^4)$.

$$R_1 = \quad R_2 = \quad L_1 = \quad L_2 =$$

(8) Indicate all of the ways to satisfy the following equations, if X and Y are both replaced by one of the four sets defined in problem (7). (Note: X and Y can be replaced by the same set, or by two different sets.)

$$(a)\ T_1(X) = Y; \quad (b)\ T_2(X) = Y; \quad (c)\ T_3(X) = Y.$$

(9) Again with reference to the same four time-point sets, solve the following equations, where the solution is some member of $P(U^4)$

(a) $R_1 \cup R_2 =$	$(b) R_1 \cup L_2 =$	$(c) L_1 \cup L_2 =$
(d) $L_1 \cup R_2 =$	$(e) R_1 \cap R_2 =$	$(f) R_1 \cap L_2 =$
(g) $L_1 \cap L_2 =$	$(h) L_1 \cap R_2 =$	

(10) Having responded to problems (7) and (9), you have now defined twelve of the sixteen sets in $P(U^4)$.

(a) Arrange these 12 sets into complementary pairs, representing each pairing using an expression of the form $U^4 \backslash X = Y$.

(b) Using union and intersection operations, and operands drawn from the four sets defined in problem (7), define the remaining four members of $P(U^4)$.

Problem Set 2. *This problem set follows a study of C6, and invites students to explore properties and applications of C7, C8 and C9, in preparation for classroom work on these topics.*

In exploring $c = 7$, I recommend that you draw a circle with seven elements, numbered from 0 to 6, and use it for reference. Then work through a few addition and subtraction problems using modulo-7 arithmetic, as a way of getting accustomed to its logic.

1. How large is the power set of a 7-element universe? Give two different methods for determining the response.
2. Consulting Pascal's triangle, determine
   (a) the number of sets for each value of d from 1 to 7.
   (b) the number of rotation (transposition) classes for each value of d, and
   (c) whether there are any rotationally invariant classes, and if so, at what value of d?

3. Create a rotation-class table for $c = 7$, placing prime forms of cardinality 0, 1, 2, and 3 down the left column, and their complements across from them in the right column.
4. For $d = 3$ and $d = 4$, which rotation classes are generated, and by what interval?
5. Interpreting the elements as diatonic degrees, T_1 generates a rising scale. What familiar musical patterns arise from T_2, T_3, and T_6?

And, looking ahead to our work of next week, consider the following questions about $c = 8$ and 9, which pertain to the distinction between prime and divisor generators. First, we put to the side the *unit* generators, which are of little musical interest; these include $g = \pm 1$. Recall we defined a *prime* generator as some value of g that shares no divisors (factors) with c, and generates the entire universe of elements. A *divisor* is a value of g that shares divisors with c, and generates only a part of the universe.

6. For $c = 8$, which of the non-unit generators are divisors, and which are prime?
7. Same question for $c = 9$.
8. Give prime forms for rotationally invariant rotation classes, for $c = 8$ and 9.
9. Thinking about repertory that you are familiar with, find a piece (or identify generic properties of a musical style) whose rhythms are based on the following generators:

   (a) $c = 8$, $g = 2$; (b) $c = 8$, $g = 3$; (c) a juxtaposition of (a) and (b)
   (d) $c = 9$, $g = 3$; (e) $c = 9$, $g = 2$; (f) a juxtaposition of (d) and (e)

Analysis Assignment 1. *This assignment comes after C8 and C9 and before the study of atonal pitch-class theory. For a more ambitious version of this assignment, I have sometimes paired it with an analysis of segments from Bartók's Sonata for Two Pianos and Percussion, first movement, which juxtaposes Balkan and Western interpretations of* 9/8 *meter.*

Scott Joplin, *The Entertainer* (1902), measures 1–36. Write an essay applying modulo-8 set theory to analyze the rhythmic structure, with a focus on the right hand/treble part. A non-exclusive list of topics likely to be of particular relevance are: rotational equivalence, transposition, prime and divisor generation, complementation, and inclusion (subset/superset).

There are several meaningful ways that the right-hand patterns could be interpreted as modulo-8 sets, depending on how one focused one's hearing and/or entrained one's body to the music. The obvious way — i.e., the one that involves the least amount of interpretation — would be to select the set of beats that are attacked in a given measure; on that ground, the first measure would be interpreted as set {012356} of class [012356], which is the complement of [03]. But one may also be inclined to hear a subset of those attacks as forming a musically salient stream, on the basis of register (e.g., all the highest notes), agogic accent (the longest notes), texture (all of the attacks that feature octave doubling), primacy (first note after a rest or silence), harmonic stability (all of those attacks whose tones are consonant with the underlying harmony), or some combination thereof. To ascertain what musical streams achieve salience in your hearing, you will need to listen, play, and apply your musical judgment. In your essay, be explicit about the criteria that make a rhythmic pattern salient for you.

Section III

Chapter 7

Matherhythm: Lessons on Divisibility and Rhythm

Francisco Gómez

Department of Applied Mathematics, Technical University of Madrid, carretera de Valencia, km. 7, s/n, 28031, Madrid, Spain
fmartin@etsisi.upm.es

7.1. The Divide

Arts and humanities along with sciences are said to be the two faces of the same coin: culture. We strongly disagree; the image of a coin suggests a sharp divide. If we look at one side, we won't see the other side. The coin itself, when looked at its edge, visually suggests a divide. Instead, we visualize arts, humanities, and sciences all together as a compact, vivid, iridescent ball that, when turned around, shows multiple angles, all of them enriching and complementing each other. However, in society in general and in education in particular, we again encounter a divide. Arts and humanities are sadly and inexplicably separated from science and vice versa. Sciences are taught turning their back on arts and humanities as if their knowledge, methods and open problems couldn't spark a smidgen of interest, while arts and humanities look at sciences with indifference and incomprehension. Surprisingly enough, the greatest artists, humanity authors and scholars, and scientists deeply appreciate what the other fields of knowledge have to offer. They understand that the more diverse the perspective is, the better the analysis of the subject is. British novelist and scientist Charles

Percy Snow condemned the divide between arts and humanities and sciences in a famous 1959 Rede Lecture [14]. The title of the lecture was *The Two Cultures* and on p. 3 we find one of the most cited paragraphs of his essay.

> *A good many times I have been present at gatherings of people who, by the standards of the traditional culture, are thought highly educated and who have with considerable gusto been expressing their incredulity at the illiteracy of scientists. Once or twice I have been provoked and have asked the company how many of them could describe the Second Law of Thermodynamics. The response was cold: it was also negative. Yet I was asking something which is the scientific equivalent of: Have you read a work of Shakespeare's?*
>
> *I now believe that if I had asked an even simpler question — such as, What do you mean by mass, or acceleration, which is the scientific equivalent of saying, Can you read? — not more than one in ten of the highly educated would have felt that I was speaking the same language. So the great edifice of modern physics goes up, and the majority of the cleverest people in the western world have about as much insight into it as their neolithic ancestors would have had.*

How can we then tear down the wall of that divide? The answer presents itself with clarity: through an all-round education. Only education will bring about a sincere and effective change of attitude toward this nefarious divide. Teachers should be the first to change their attitude toward the divide. Unfortunately, a good many science teachers don't believe arts and humanities have anything of interest to contribute to their lessons, in spite of the many applications of sciences to the domains of arts and humanities (computational linguistics, mathematical sociology, mathematical models in criminal justice, algorithmic art). A good many arts and humanities teachers hold the same beliefs about science, again regardless of the inspiration arts and humanities have drawn from sciences, the use of the same set of higher order thinking skills, or the tools that sciences have built to solve some of their problems.

However, often the problem is not that teachers of both sides don't desire teaching material inspired in other fields of knowledge. Many do, many crave for it, but they don't always have the appropriate material available to them. Certainly, most text books and manuals don't make connections to other disciplines, especially if the content is presented in a traditional way or is oriented to train the student to pass an exam. The aim of this volume is to provide teachers with material of quality to encourage them to teach lessons imbued with knowledge from other fields. Specifically, in this chapter we will establish connections between mathematics and music, more specifically between number theory (theory of division and modular arithmetic) and music theory (theory of rhythm). We will provide the reader with material to prepare a lesson that intertwines math and music. In terms of level the lesson ranges from high school students to college students.

7.2. Matherhythm or Rhythm is a Killer

The lesson we present here is based on the mathematical, musical show that Giovanna Farigu, Gutxi Céspedes and the author of these notes did for the event *Maths Week Ireland* [4]. This event is a celebration of math, where it is sought to promote awareness, appreciation and understanding of maths through a huge variety of activities. Many of these activities include connections to other fields; for example, they organize mathematical activities involving art, music, juggling, magic, or literature, among others, and bring the best math popularizers such as Andrew Jeffrey [10], Steve Humble [9] (the famous Doctor Math), Colm Mulcahy [12], Fernando Blasco [3], Colin Wright [15] or Kjartan Poskitt [13]. Our show is called *Matherhythm* [7] and it is a mixture of a serious conference, physical humor, and a music show; it is close to the concept of *concerférences* developed by Emmanuel Amiot in Chapter 8 of this volume.

We have two versions of the show. The simplest version is just the show suited to a general audience. This version requires the audience to be familiar with the concepts of division and greatest common divisor, although the content of the show is quite self-contained. The other version consists of a show plus a workshop and is suited to work with high school and college students. On some occasions, we give the teachers material to work with the students before the day of the show. On other occasions, we don't give previous information and after the show a workshop is held; in it, the ideas put forward during the show are explored. These explorations combine math and music activities and finishes by having the students composing music that Giovanna and myself play for them. All these ideas are developed in the next few sections.

The three next sections (Sections 7.3–7.5) contained the lesson. It is structured as follows: the first part is the mathematical section, where the concepts of division and greatest common divisor are introduced as well as Euclid's algorithm. The second part is the musical part and there a few basic rhythm concepts, such as time span or rhythm, are introduced. In the last part, the matherhythm part, math and music are combined by applying Euclid's algorithm to the formation of rhythms. The material will be unfolded as it were the script of the show, although not in the form of a dialogue. The exercises associated to each section are shown just right after it. They are presented in increasing order of difficulty so that the last few exercises can be left out for high school audiences. These exercises constitute the material for the workshop.

7.3. The Mathematics

7.3.1. *Division*

This is a talk about mathematics and music, and in particular, about rhythm. It's made up of three sections; the first is about mathematics, the second about music, and in the third we'll mix both. Let's see, do you all know how to divide? [*The audience do.*]

We will start by reviewing the concept of division. Division consists of forming groups. In a division you are given two terms, the **dividend** and the **divisor**. Thus, dividing the dividend by the divisor is to see how many groups of the size of the divisor can be formed with the dividend. Division is a way of grouping objects. For example, if we have 12 as dividend and 3 as divisor, the division $12 \div 3$ is equivalent to find how many groups of size 3 can be formed with 12 objects (see Fig. 7.1). In this case, the answer is 4. The number of

$$\boxed{1\,1\,1\,1\,1\,1\,1\,1\,1\,1\,1\,1} \quad \rightarrow \quad \boxed{1\,1\,1 \,\|\, 1\,1\,1 \,\|\, 1\,1\,1 \,\|\, 1\,1\,1}$$

Fig. 7.1. Exact division as formation of groups.

$$\boxed{1\,1\,1\,1\,1\,1\,1\,1\,1\,1\,1\,1\,1\,1\,1\,1\,1} \rightarrow \boxed{\begin{array}{l|l} 1\,1\,1 & 1\,1 \\ 1\,1\,1 & \\ 1\,1\,1 & \\ 1\,1\,1 & \\ 1\,1\,1 & \end{array}}$$

Fig. 7.2. Division with remainder as formation of groups.

groups is called the **quotient**. This kind of division is called **exact division**.

Is this clear to you? [*The audience give an affirmative nod.*]

However, sometimes it is not possible to form an integer number of groups, and then we speak of **division with remainder**. Indeed, sometimes after forming all the groups we see that there are elements left over. Those elements are called the **remainder**. In the previous example, $12 \div 3$ is an exact division. We can write

$$12 \div 3 \Longrightarrow 12 = 3 \times 4.$$

If we want to divide 17 by 5 we find it is a division with remainder.

$$\begin{array}{r|r} & 5 \\ \hline 3 & 17 \\ & -15 \\ \hline & 2 \end{array}$$

Here 2 is the remainder and 5 is the quotient. In this case we can write

$$17 \div 5 \Longrightarrow 17 = 5 \times 3 + 2.$$

Performing this division as formation of groups as shown in Fig. 7.2.

Groups have been formed by rows. The number of columns is the size of each group.

We made this a little bit more complicated. Is this still clear to you? [*The audience again give an affirmative nod; some of them seem to feign understanding.*]

Let's think a little bit more abstract. [*Sighs of fear come from the audience. Awkward pause. We carry on.*]

Let a be the dividend, b the divisor, q the quotient, and r the remainder of a division. The relation among those numbers through division is given by the following equation:

$$\boxed{a = b \cdot q + r} \tag{7.1}$$

There is a point to make here. When dividing two numbers, we form as many groups as we can. That implies that the remainder is always less than the divisor. In terms of our equation, that means $0 \leq r < b$.

Does everybody understand so far? [*The audience have paid attention and there is again a general affirmative nod; those who seemed to have feigned are now certain.*]

7.3.2. *Exercises in division*

(1) Classify the following divisions as exact or with remainder: $1 \div 1$, $3 \div 2$, $121 \div 11$, $0 \div 7$, $1089 \div 33$, $1405782039 \div 2$, $1405782039 \div 3$.
(2) Perform the division $20 \div 4$ by forming groups.
(3) Perform the division $21 \div 4$ by forming groups. Specify the dividend, divisor, quotient and remainder in terms of the groups formed.
(4) We are given 19 objects. We want to divide 19 by 3. After performing the division we obtain 5 groups of 3 elements each plus a remainder of 4. Is this division correct? If not, explain why.
(5) If we have two positive quantities, x and y, each of them measured in certain units, what is the meaning of the quotient $\frac{x}{y}$? Apply your explanation to the case where x is the distance traveled by an object over a period of time y. Measure x in inches and y in seconds.

7.3.3. *Greatest common divisor*

The greatest common divisor is a concept easy to understand. Given two numbers, each has a set of **divisors**, also called **factors** (both terms will be used interchangeably). The greatest common divisor (gcd from now on) is just the greatest common divisor found in both numbers. [*Some members of the audience crack a smile at the self-definition of the concept.*] The gcd always exists because 1 is a divisor of any number.

Here we have an example of the gcd. Take numbers 45 and 75. The divisors of those numbers are:

- Divisors of 45: $\{1, 3, 5, 9, 15, 45\}$.
- Divisors of 75: $\{1, 3, 5, 15, 25, 75\}$.

We easily see that the set of common divisors is $\{1, 3, 5, 15\}$, the greatest being 15. Therefore, the $\gcd(45, 75) = 15$.

This method of calculating the gcd consists of enumerating all divisors of both numbers. This is a good way of practicing division because you have to perform many divisions to find those divisors. [*"But we don't want to do divisions, but more fun stuff", we hear this as a whisper from the audience; we smile knowingly.*] If the numbers are small, it will be all right. If they are large, it will become cumbersome.

We pose the following question: How do we find the list of divisors of a number? First, we have to find its prime factors. By the way, what is a prime factor? A **prime number**, we may recall you, is a number only divisible by 1 and itself. Examples of prime numbers are 3, 5, 7, or 749027409284729381. Every number is the product of a series of prime factors. Normally, you find the prime factors of a number by trial and error. You check if your number is divisible by 2; if not, you carry on with 3, the next prime number, and so on. When a division is exact, you obtain a smaller number, and you continue trying with more, bigger prime numbers. For the number of our example, their decomposition in prime factors is

$$45 = 3^2 \cdot 5,$$
$$75 = 3 \cdot 5^2.$$

In view of that decomposition, it is easy to realize that the gcd is formed by the common factors raised to the least exponent. In our case the common factors are 3 and 5, and the least exponents are 1 in all cases. Therefore, $\gcd(45, 75) = 3 \cdot 5 = 15$. This idea relates the gcd with the decomposition in prime factors. However, it is not a good method for calculating the gcd in general. Again, when the numbers are big, finding the prime factorization is a very hard process. [*"And boring", we hear a few members of the audience utter it firmly and clearly.*]

7.3.4. *Exercises in the greatest common divisor*

(1) Calculate the gcd of the following pair of numbers by finding their prime factors: 33 and 11; 144 and 60; 121 and 275; 1089 and 924.
(2) With the ideas presented above, how would you calculate the gcd of three numbers? Use your ideas to calculate the $\gcd(35, 49, 77)$ and $\gcd(60, 84, 132)$.
(3) What is the maximum number of divisions you have to do obtain the prime factorization of a number?
(4) We define the least common multiple of two numbers as, well, the least common multiple of both numbers. What is the relationship between the greatest common divisor and the least common multiple?

7.3.5. *Euclid's algorithm*

How can we calculate the gcd in a better way? Euclid, a Greek mathematician who lived 400 years B.C., invented a way to do it. Euclid wrote down the equation of the division:

$$a = b \cdot q + r.$$

Every common factor of a and b — Euclid observed — must be a common factor of the remainder r. Let d be such a common factor. Then:

$$\frac{a}{d} = \frac{b}{d} \cdot q + \frac{r}{d}.$$

If numbers $\frac{a}{d}$ and $\frac{b}{d}$ are natural numbers, so will $\frac{r}{d}$ be. In particular, if d is the gcd of both numbers, this property will still be true. Therefore, gcd(a, b)=gcd(b, r). However, we should not stop here. We can carry on applying this idea until the remainder is 0. At that moment, the last quotient obtained is the gcd (or, equivalently, the last non-null remainder). [*The audience is now in utter silence, struck by the beauty of the idea. The speaker stares at the audience, grateful to be the means of conveying beauty of this kind.*]

Let's see how this **algorithm** works. Take $a = 75$ and $b = 45$, as before. We start off by dividing both numbers:

$$75 = 45 \cdot 1 + 30.$$

Here the remainder is 30. Is the remainder equal to 0? No. In that case, we continue doing divisions:

$$45 = 30 \cdot 1 + 15.$$

Again, is the remainder null? No. We proceed to the next division.

$$30 = 15 \cdot 2 + 0.$$

Is the remainder null now? Yes. We are done. The gcd is the quotient of this division, namely, 15.

Again, this process can be thought through formation of groups. Let's illustrate this by calculating the gcd of 16 and 12; see Fig. 7.3. We start by writing 12 ones followed by four zeros. This is equivalent to performing the first successive division 16 by 12.

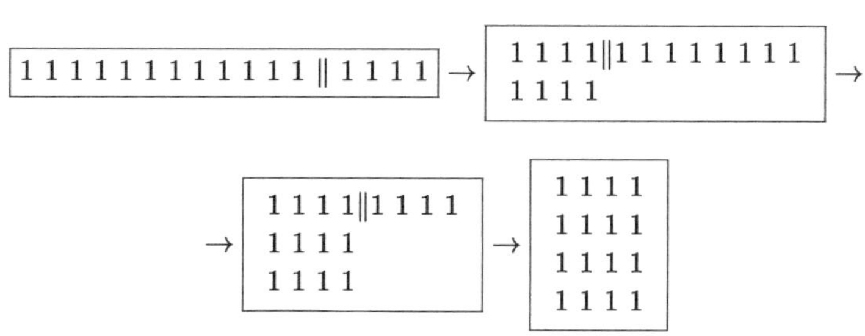

Fig. 7.3. Calculating the gcd through Euclid's algorithm and formation of groups.

The remainder is 4. Then, we make groups of four elements each and put them below the ones. Therefore, we have made three groups and no element has been left. Now, the division is over. Since the groups were formed by putting elements one below another, the gcd is the number of columns in the final box, that is, 4.

Here ends the mathematical section [*some breathed a sigh of relief*] and now starts the musical section [*expressions of enthusiasm are heard*].

7.3.6. *Exercises in the greatest common divisor*

(1) Calculate the gcd of the following pair of numbers by using Euclid's algorithm: 33 and 11; 144 and 60; 121 and 275; 1089 and 924. Compare how long it took you to the method of finding the primer factors. Which one is the fastest?
(2) Calculate the gcd of 24 and 18 by applying Euclid's algorithm and formation of groups.

7.4. Music

7.4.1. *Basic concepts of music*

We go down to the basics of music language. In order to do so, we first become familiar with concepts such as notes, rests, and rhythm. We start by defining **time span**, which is simply a fixed amount of time. It can be represented by a rectangle (see Fig. 7.4).

That time span can be divided in equal parts. Those parts are called **pulses**.

Each little box in the figure is a pulse (see Fig. 7.5). Pulses have the same length in time. [*Easy, isn't it?, we asked the audience. They all concur.*]

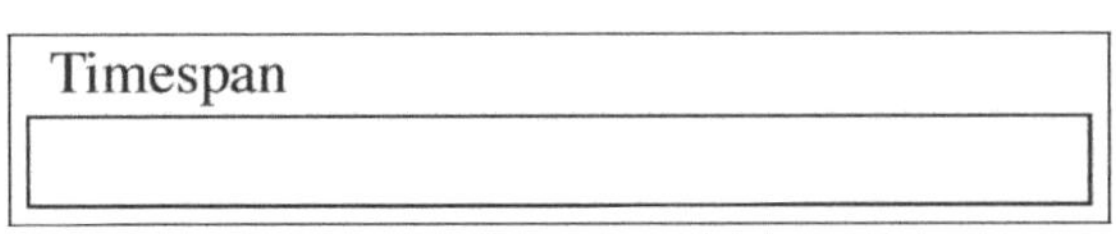

Fig. 7.4. The timespan.

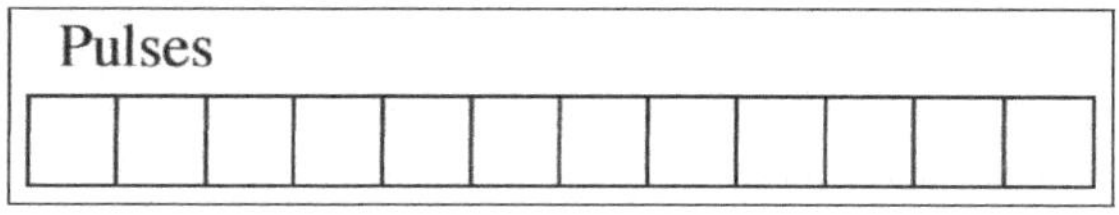

Fig. 7.5. Pulses in music.

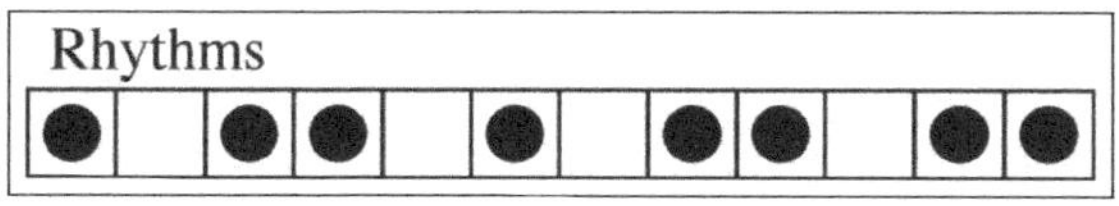

Fig. 7.6. The rhythm.

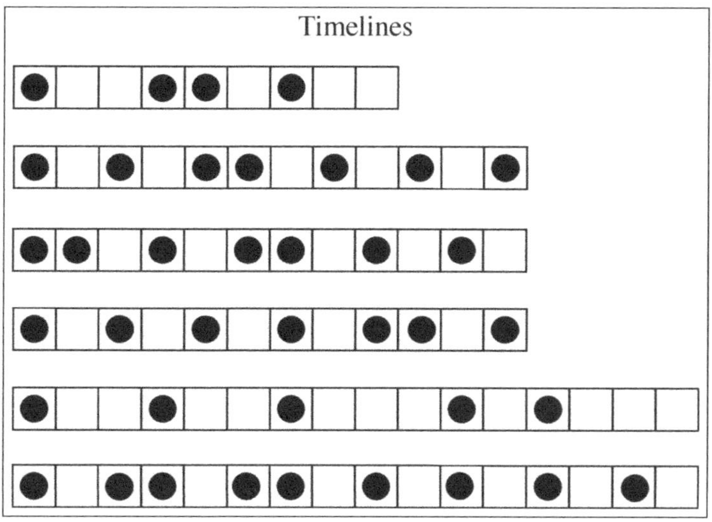

Fig. 7.7. Timelines of different lengths.

A **rhythm** is formed by combination of notes and rests played on the pulses.

The boxes with a dot are notes, the empty boxes are rests. Rests are not played, but have to be counted (see Fig. 7.6).

Here we are going to study a particular type of rhythm: **timelines**. A timeline is a rhythm design played throughout a piece with no variations. It is the leading temporal and structural reference within a piece. In Fig. 7.7 there are several timelines. Notice that these timelines have different length in terms of number of pulses.

The first timeline can be heard in many musical traditions, but we can find in the tango music (especially starting on the second onset). The second time is very common in the music in Africa; it's called the *standard pattern.* The third timeline is a rotation of the second. The rest of the rhythms are well-known timelines found in different world music traditions.

The musical section finishes here [*sighs of disappointment*]. Those are all the musical concepts needed for the last part, matherhythm, where we will mix mathematics and music. [*Dramatic pause here. We run our eyes over the audience, left to right, slowly; we even stare at some of the members of the audience.*] We will compose music by using mathematics. [*We let our words to sink in the audience. Sighs of incredulity. Grins of challenge. Another dramatic pause. There we go.*]

7.4.2. *Exercises in rhythm*

(1) Play the timelines given in Fig. 7.7 four times each. Play them by clapping your hands. Increase speed/tempo gradually, but keep a steady beat all along your practicing.
(2) Compose your own timelines using time spans of 10, 14, and 16 pulses. Practice them as suggested above.
(3) Compose your own timelines of arbitrary time spans. Practice them as suggested above.
(4) Compose two timelines of times span 16 to be played at the same time. Find a peer to play them.

7.5. Matherhythm

7.5.1. *Composing easy rhythms*

Let's now play with maths and music *together.* [*We perceive anxious anticipation in the audience.*] Let's fix a 12-pulse time span. If we want to play a 12-note rhythm, then we have to divide 12 (number of pulses) by 1 [*We don't show the answer on the screen. We challenge the audience. Soon we hear the right answer being shouted at us.*]:

$$\frac{12}{1} = 12,$$

and the resulting rhythm would be [*We don't show the answer. This time the audience is not that fast. After a few seconds, a young girl says: "tee-tee-tee-tee-tee-tee-tee-tee-tee-tee-tee-tee". We smile at the girl and show the answer, which coincides with hers.*]

x x x x x x x x x x x x

Here an x denotes a note. This is very easy since it is clear that every note must go on one pulse.

If we want to play four notes, then we have to divide 12 by 3 [*We hold the answer, but the audience understands the game. "Four, four, four", we hear all over the place.*]:

$$\frac{12}{3} = 4,$$

and the resulting rhythm would be [*We don't show the answer, but several voices sing the rhythm below. Some other voices sing a rotation of that rhythm, this one in particular:* [. . x . . x . . x . . x]. *We look at the audience feigning confusion. We announce that both rhythms are correct and that we will address that question later.*]

x . . x . . x . . x . .

Here a "." (a dot) denotes a rest. If we want to obtain this rhythm through division, all we have to do is divide 12 by 3 with ones (notes) and zeros (rests) as shown in Fig 7.8.

Again, since the groups were formed vertically, we produce the rhythm by reading the groups by columns. The resulting rhythm is [x . . x . . x . . x . .].

If we want to play six notes, then we have to divide 12 by 2 [*We hold the answer, but by this point the audience fully grasped the idea*

1 1 1 1 0 0 0 0 0 0 0 0	→	1 1 1 1‖ 0 0 0 0 0 0 0 0	→	1 1 1 1 0 0 0 0 0 0 0 0

Fig. 7.8. Making rhythms through division.

and everybody shouts, " Six, six, six!"]:

$$\frac{12}{2} = 6,$$

and the resulting rhythm would be [*The audience in unison sing the rhythm below.*]

x . x . x . x . x . x .

7.5.2. Composing more complicated rhythms

If we want to play eight notes, then we have to divide 12 by...[*Dramatic pause. The audience is in silence for a few seconds. Their words fight to escape their mouths. Still silence. Someone, an intrepid person, shyly says, "one point five?" Let's assume we don't want to divide our pulses, I wittily reply. More silence. Expectation. Some say, as if in a revelation, "It can't be done!" I smile and carry on with my explanation.*]

$$\frac{12}{X} = 8.$$

Oops! It turns out that 8 is greater than 6. No divisor of 12 can be greater than 6.

I CAN'T DO IT... THEN, HOW?

[*I mischievously stare at the audience. Time to reveal the secret.*] We'll use the so-called evenness principle, which reads as follows:

Evenness Principle: Distribute the notes among the pulses as evenly as possible.

Let's see how this principle works. If we have this rhythm:

x x x x x x x x . . . .

it is clear that its notes are not evenly distributed. However, if we move a few notes here and there, then this new rhythm

. x x . x x . x x . x x

does have its notes evenly distributed. How did we do it? By calculating the gcd with Euclid's algorithm and formation of groups. [*The audience is in awe. Sights of joy are heard from different points of the room.*]

The resulting rhythm here is [x . x x . x x . x x . x], which is not the rhythm we obtained above. This interesting fact has to do with rotations of rhythms. The evenness of a rhythm depends on the distances between its notes. Therefore, the rotation of an even rhythm is still even. In our case, both rhythms are the same up to a rotation.

Since the gcd of 12 and 8 is 4, our rhythm is formed by a small rhythmic cell, [. x x], repeated four times (Fig. 7.9).

Finally, notice that when the number of notes is a divisor of the number of pulses, applying the evenness principle is the same as performing a division. In that sense the evenness principle is a generalization of division.

If we want to play seven notes..., well, we already know we have to apply the evenness principle again [*The audience follow our explanation without missing a word.*] The resulting rhythm would be

x . x . x x . x . x . x

Let's see how we obtained this rhythm.

```
1 1 1 1 1 1 1 1 0 0 0 0  →  1 1 1 1|| 1 1 1 1  →
                            0 0 0 0

1 1 1 1
1 1 1 1  →  1 0 1 1 0 1 1 0 1 1 0 1
0 0 0 0
```

Fig. 7.9. Making rhythms through the gcd and formation of groups (12 pulses and 8 notes).

1 1 1 1 1 1 1 0 0 0 0 0	→	1 1 1 1 1 1 1 0 0 0 0 0	→	1 1 1 1 1 0 0 0 0 0 1 1	→

1 1 1 0 0 0 1 1 1 1 0 0	→	1 0 1 1 0 1 0 1 1 0 1 0

Fig. 7.10. Making rhythms through the gcd and formation of groups (12 pulses and 7 notes).

7-note rhythm:	x	.	x	.	x	x	.	x	.	x	.	x
4-note rhythm:	x	.	.	x	.	.	x	.	.	x	.	.
8-note rhythm:	.	x	x	.	x	x	.	x	x	.	x	x
6-note rhythm:	.	x	.	x	.	x	.	x	.	x	.	x
12-note rhythm:	x	x	x	x	x	x	x	x	x	x	x	x

Fig. 7.11. The four timelines.

This rhythm, as already mentioned, is a rotation of [x . x . x x . x . x . x]. In particular, it is a rotation by three positions to the right.

Rhythms produced by using the evenness principle are called **Euclidean rhythms** or **even rhythms** (Figs. 7.10 and 7.11). Finally, here we have the five timelines we obtained by considering the divisors of 12 and applying the evenness principle. [*The awe of the audience still lingers.*]

7.5.3. *Euclidean rhythms in actual music*

Although these rhythms admit a mathematical explanation, they actually exist. They come from an ancient, rich rhythmic tradition, the Ghana tradition. In particular these rhythms are the timelines for a piece of music called **gamamla**. They are played on a double bell called **gankogui** (see Fig. 7.12).

The gankogui produces two sounds, a low-pitched sound and a high-pitched one. The notes of the timelines are distributed among

Fig. 7.12. *Gankogui*, an African bell.

the two bells. Written in musical notation, the final score for the gamamla is given below; notes below the line mean low bell, whereas notes above the line means high bell (see Fig. 7.13).

To end this section let's play these rhythms for you. [*We play them on a set of bells. Round of rapturous applause.*]

7.5.4. *Composing Euclidean rhythms*

(1) Explore and practice the rotations of the 6-note and 8-note timelines.
(2) Explore and practice the rotations of the 7-note timeline [x . x . x x . x . x . x]. Which are the most interesting ones? Do you have an explanation?
(3) Create your own four timelines following the ideas in the text. Use a 16-pulse timeline. Play the piece by clapping your hands. Make the necessary adjustments in terms of rotations of rhythms.
(4) Take your favorite timeline and try all the rotations of it. Explain why you like more some rotations than others. Use your own arguments, but also analyze the rotations in terms of rhythmic tension, metrical contradiction, syncopation, and listener's expectations.

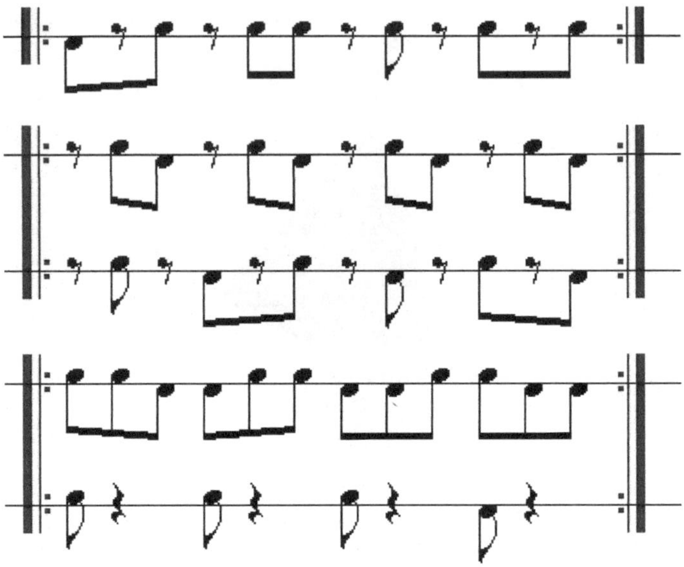

Fig. 7.13. Gamamla.

7.6. Euclidean Rhythms in Depth

7.6.1. *Euclid's algorithm*

Let us first describe how to modify Euclid's algorithm so that it outputs even rhythms instead of outputting the greatest common divisor of two integers. It was implicit in the content presented in the lesson, but we will next give a more formal description. This description will serve for the algorithm to be applied in more general contexts. Essentially, the modification consists of treating numbers as objects; those objects will be here notes and rests. Although he did not make the connection, Bjorklund [2] presented a very nice modification of Euclid's algorithm to distribute objects in boxes as evenly as possible. A Euclidean rhythm is a rhythm produced through the application of Euclid's algorithm (explained right below). We denote the Euclidean rhythm of k notes and n pulses by $E(k, n)$. The description of Bjorklund's algorithm below follows that of Gómez *et al.* [8]. Bjorklund's algorithm consists of two steps: **initialization step**, performed once at the beginning; and, a **subtraction step**, performed repeatedly until the **stopping condition** is satisfied. At all times Bjorklund's algorithm maintains two lists A and B of strings of bits, where a and b contain the number of strings in each list, respectively. In the description of this algorithm the ones represent notes, the zeros represent rests, and $\lfloor x \rfloor$ is the floor of x.

(1) **Initialization step**. In this step the algorithm builds the string $\{1, \overset{k}{\ldots\ldots}, 1, 0, \overset{n-k}{\ldots\ldots}, 0\}$, and sets A as the first $a = \min\{k, n-k\}$ bits of that string, and B as the remaining $b = \max\{k, n-k\}$ bits. Next the algorithm removes $\lfloor b/a \rfloor$ strings of a consecutive bits from B, starting with the rightmost bit, and places them under the a-bit strings in A one below the other (see Fig. 7.14, steps (1) and (2)). Lists A and B are then redefined: A is now composed of a strings (the a columns in A), each having $\lfloor b/a \rfloor + 1$ bits, and B is composed of $b \mod a$ strings of 0-bits. Finally, the algorithm sets $b = b \mod a$.

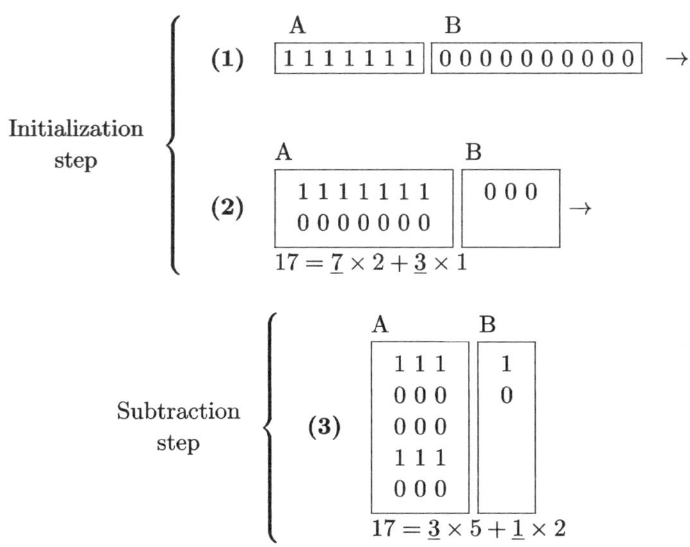

Output: **(4)** $E(7, 17) = \{1\ 0\ 0\ 1\ 0\ 1\ 0\ 0\ 1\ 0\ 1\ 0\ 0\ 1\ 0\ 1\ 0\}$

Fig. 7.14. Bjorklund's algorithm for generating Euclidean rhythms.

(2) **Subtraction step.** At a subtraction step, the algorithm removes $\lfloor a/b \rfloor$ strings of b consecutive bits (or columns) from B and A, starting with the rightmost bit of B and continuing with the rightmost bit of A, and places them at the bottom-left of the strings in A one below the other. Lists A and B are then redefined as follows: A is composed of the first b strings (starting with the leftmost bit), while B is composed of the remaining $a \mod b$ strings. Finally, the algorithm sets $b = a \mod b$ and $a = b$ (before b was redefined). See Fig. 7.14, step (3).

(3) **Stopping condition and output**. The algorithm stops when, after the end of a subtraction step list B is empty or consists of one string. The output then is produced by concatenating the strings of A from left to right and the strings of B, if not empty; see Fig. 7.14, step (4).

Demain *et al.* [6] proved that the rhythm output by this algorithm is unique up to a rotation. Here arises a fascinating music question. Their result states that Euclidean rhythms are invariant under rotations. However, musically, the rotation of a rhythm — equivalently, starting to play it on another onset — can dramatically change it up to the point to be perceptually and musically hardly recognizable. This due to cognitive and musical reasons.

Another algorithm that produces Euclidean rhythms is that of Clough and Douthett [5]. Its output is just the note positions in the rhythm. Those positions are given by the following formula:

$$E_{\mathrm{CD}}(k,n) = \left\{ \left\lfloor \frac{in}{k} \right\rfloor : i = 0, 1, \ldots, k-1 \right\}. \tag{7.2}$$

The rhythm is notated as $E_{\mathrm{CD}}(k,n)$ to distinguish it from $E(k,n)$, the output of Bjorklund's algorithm; as a matter of fact, one is a rotation of the other. Let us compute $E_{\mathrm{CD}}(7,17)$ by employing the formula above:

$$E_{\mathrm{CD}}(7,17) = \left\{ \left\lfloor \frac{0}{7} \right\rfloor = 0, \left\lfloor \frac{17}{7} \right\rfloor = 2, \left\lfloor \frac{34}{7} \right\rfloor = 4, \left\lfloor \frac{51}{7} \right\rfloor = 7, \right.$$
$$\left. \times \left\lfloor \frac{68}{7} \right\rfloor = 9, \left\lfloor \frac{85}{7} \right\rfloor = 12, \left\lfloor \frac{102}{7} \right\rfloor = 14 \right\}.$$

Written in box notation, this rhythm reads as $E_{\text{CD}}(7,17) = $[x . x . x . . x . x . . x . x . . x . x . .], which is a rotation of $E(7,17)$ by four positions to the right (or start playing it on the third onset). This algorithm is concise and wisely inspired in the same nature of integer division. The elegant, beautiful formula of Clough and Douthett is eloquently stating that division is the perfect way of distributing objects in boxes with maximum evenness.

A close observation of how Bjorklund's algorithm works reveals its internal structure. At the last step we watch the algorithm concatenating a certain pattern P a few times, and next appending another pattern T (an empty one in some cases). Gómez *et al.* [8] proved that P and T are both Euclidean, which endows Euclidean rhythms with a self-similarity structure. Rhythm $E(7,17) = $[x . . x . |x . . x . |x . . x . |x .] is formed by the concatenation of $P = $[x . . x .] three times followed by $T = $[x .] (vertical lines were added to depict it more clearly). Rhythm P is in fact $E(2,5)$ and T is $E(1,3)$ up to rotations.

7.6.2. *Euclidean rhythms in non-Western musical traditions*

One of the most paradigmatic examples of Euclidean rhythms in world music is gamamla [11]. It is a musical piece played in Ghana, often to celebrate the harvest. The piece is essentially rhythmic and is composed of five parts, each played on a double bell called gankogui. One is high-pitched and the other acts as bass bell (see again Fig. 7.12) and they are joined together at the head.

The gamamla has 12 pulses, a number that is often found in world rhythms because it allows both ternary and binary even divisions of the timespan. The rhythms of this piece are the Euclidean rhythms $E(12,12)$, $E(4,12)$, $E(6,12)$, $E(8,12)$, and $E(7,12)$. The five parts are displayed in Fig. 7.13. Rhythm $E(12,12)$ is a rhythmic density. Rhythm $E(4,12)$ provides a ternary feeling as it divides the timespan into four parts of duration three each (one note and two rests). On the contrary, rhythm $E(6,12)$ conveys a binary sense as a note is played on every other pulse. At this moment, it is noticeable that the gamamla is strongly polyrhythmic. Up to this point all numbers of notes were even divisors of 12 and therefore the rhythms were formed by a repeated motif. Next is rhythm $E(8,12)$. In spite of 8 not being an even divisor of 12, since the greatest common divisor of 8 and 12 is 4, it is still composed of the repetition of a rhythmic motif ([. x x] in this case). Finally, the last rhythm is really irregular, syncopated, with no repeated motifs. One reason for that is that the number of notes and pulses are relatively primes; another reason is the chosen rotation of the rhythm.

There is another powerful musical parameter that comes into play in the gamamla: timbre. If we examine Fig. 7.13, we will notice that the rhythms are written by using two positions, above and below the staff line. Notes below the line correspond to the bass bell, whereas notes above to the high-pitched bell. The choice of the timbre here is quite significant. The 12-, 6- and 8-note parts alternate between high and low notes. Rhythm $E(4,12)$, which would apparently provide great rhythmic stabilization, has the lowest sound on the fourth note, thus defying the listener's perceptual expectations. In sharp contrast, the most irregular and vital rhythm of all, $E(7,12)$ possess a resounding first note played on the low bell, which certainly contributes to determine where the cycle starts. Although not annotated in the score, another characteristic of the gamamla music is dynamics; in actual performances, players change the volume, often to destroy the natural grouping of the rhythm.

For purposes of illustration, here follows a very abridged list of Euclidean rhythms found in world music. For a longer, comprehensive list, consult the appendix of Demain *et al.* [6]. Comments on the particular rotation of the rhythms have been included. The distance sequence of the rhythms is also listed.

- $E(4,15)$ = [x . . . x . . . x . . . x . .] = (4443) is the metric pattern of the pañcam savārī tāl of North Indian music.
- $E(5,8)$ = [x . x x . x x .] = (21212) is the Cuban cinquillo pattern; it appears in important genres as the danzón. It is also the pattern of the Malfuf rhythm, found in Egypt, as well as the Korean Nong

P'yŏn drum pattern. Started on the second onset, it is a very popular Middle Eastern rhythm, the Timini rhythm of Senegal, the Adzogbo dance rhythm of Benin, as well as the Spanish tango, among other rhythms. When it is started on the third onset it is the Msemmen rhythm of Turkey.

- $E(5,9)$ = [x . x . x . x . x] = (22221) is a popular Arabic rhythm called Agsag-Samai; notice how the distribution of the notes suggests a binary grouping in contrast with the ternary nature of the number of pulses. Started on the second onset, it is a drum pattern used by the Venda in South Africa, also a Rumanian folk-dance rhythm, and the Samai aktsak rhythm of Turkey, among other rhythms. Started on the third onset, it is the rhythmic pattern of the Nawahiid rhythm of Turkey.
- $E(5,12)$ = [x . . x . x . . x . x .] = (32322) is a common rhythm played in the Central African Republic by the Aka Pygmies; see [1]. It is also heard in the Venda clapping pattern of a South African children's song. Started on the second onset, it is the columbia bell pattern popular in Cuba and West Africa, as well as a drumming pattern used in the Chakacha dance of Kenya. Started on the third onset, it is the bemba bell pattern used in Northern Zimbabwe.
- $E(7,12)$ = [x . x x . x . x x . x .] = (2122122). This bell pattern is so common in West Africa that it is called the standard pattern. For example, it is used in the Mpre rhythm of the Ashanti people of Ghana and, of course, one of the clave rhythms of gamamla. Started on the seventh (last) onset, it is a Yoruba bell pattern of Nigeria, a Babenzele pattern of Central Africa, and a Mende pattern of Sierra Leone.
- $E(7,16)$ = [x . . x . x . x . . x . x . x .] = (3223222) is a samba rhythm necklace from Brazil. The actual samba rhythm is [x . x . . x . x . x . . x. x .], obtained by starting $E(7,16)$ on the last onset. When $E(7,16)$ is started on the fifth onset it is a clapping pattern from Ghana.
- $E(9,16)$ = [x . x x . x . x . x x . x . x .] = (212221222) is a rhythm necklace used in the Central African Republic. When it is started on the second onset it is a bell pattern of the Luba people

of Congo. When it is started on the fourth onset it is a rhythm played in West and Central Africa, as well as a cowbell pattern in the Brazilian samba.

7.7. Conclusion

In this chapter we have presented ideas to plan lessons about mathematical theory of rhythm. Our lessons include exercises that can be adapted to different audiences such as high school and college students, and teaching contexts such as class activities over several days, projects, or a show. The mathematical material will make students think about division from a special angle, the formation of groups, and how to generalize it when the divisor is greater than half of the dividend. Conceptually, the evenness principle is more powerful than just a generalization of division. It constitutes a general principle of organization, in our case, organization of the musical material. The musical material will show the students how some simple, effective composition principles — the sonification of evenly distributed onsets in a time span — leads to the creation of meaningful music.

The ideas developed here have been put into practice by the author of this chapter in numerous occasions such as workshops for both students and teachers, shows, conferences, mini-courses. In the event *Maths Week Ireland* [4] we did a version for an activity called math in the street, where mathematical activities are proposed to casual passers-by. This proves how versatile the material is.

As we stated at the outset, the divide between arts and humanities and science is inflicting considerable harm to culture and education. If arts, humanities, and sciences were taught as a whole, taking examples from one another, we would have a better understanding of the world. In this chapter we tried to make out the case for the integration of mathematics and music in their teaching. Tear down the divide. See the world. Or isn't the divide a wall?

Bibliography

[1] S. Arom, *African Polyphony and Polyrhythm* (Cambridge University Press, Cambridge, 1991).

[2] E. Bjorklund, The theory of rep-rate pattern generation in the SNS timing system, SNS ASD Technical Note SNS-NOTE-CNTRL-99, Los Alamos National Laboratory, Los Alamos, USA (2003).

[3] F. Blasco, Fernando Blasco, http://www.fblasco.com/ (2017).

[4] CALMAST, Maths Week Ireland, http://www.mathsweek.ie (2017).

[5] J. Clough and J. Douthett, Maximally even sets, *J. Music Theory* **35** (1991) 93–173.

[6] E. D. Demaine, F. Gomez-Martin, H. Meijer, D. Rappaport, P. Taslakian, G. T. Toussaint, T. Winograd and D. R. Wood, The distance geometry of music, *Comput. Geom.* **42** (2009) 429–454.

[7] F. Gómez, G. Farigu and G. Céspedes, Matherhythm or rhythm is a killer, http://webpgomez.com/artes/contrasteatro-contrastheatre/396-matherhythm-or-rhythm-is-a-killer-eng (2012).

[8] F. Gómez, T. P. and G. Toussaint, Structural properties of Euclidean rhythms, *J. Math. Music* **3** (2009) 1–14.

[9] S. Humble, Doctor Maths, https://drmaths.org/steve-humble-aka-drmaths/ (2017).

[10] A. Jeffrey, Andrew Jeffrey: the mathemagician, http://www.andrewjeffrey.co.uk/ (2017).

[11] T. Klőwer, *The Joy of Drumming: Drums and Percussion Instruments from Around the World* (Binkey Kok Publications, Diever, Holland, 1997).

[12] C. Mulcahy, Card Colm, http://cardcolm.org/ (2017).

[13] K. Poskitt, Murderous Maths, http://www.murderousmaths.co.uk/ (2017).

[14] C. P. Snow, *The Two Cultures* (Cambridge University Press, London, 2011 [1959]).

[15] C. Wright, Colin Wright, http://www.solipsys.co.uk/new/ColinWright,html (2017).

Chapter 8

"Concerférences": Addressing Different Publics for Mathemusical Popularization

Emmanuel Amiot

University of Perpignan, France
manu.amiot@free.fr

8.1. Introduction

This chapter addresses the specific question of popularization. It is a very important dimension, because 'Maths and Music', as an autonomous discipline, is mostly unknown by the general public. This is a little paradoxical, since most people will readily issue blunt statements such as 'Ah yes, music is a part of maths' or 'You need to be a mathematician to understand music theory', usually meaning that it is useful for a musician to know how to count (to 12). I used to answer such remarks curtly with 'shoemakers count to higher numbers', but there are more constructive alleys which we must explore in order to attain general and academic recognition.

In recent years, there have been a number of occurrences of *"concerférences"* by mathemusical researchers, myself among and sometimes along with others. Obviously this is a successful concept, rapidly developing.[a] Nobody could place the time of its invention, since its definition may be a matter of degree of mixing theoretical exposition with musical or artistic performance, but I may perhaps claim coining the name a few years back.

[a]See for instance Andreatta's page http://repmus.ircam.fr/moreno/music.

Quite a few artists like to put in a few words of explanation alongside with their performance: I remember for instance the pianist Miguel Angel Estrela telling about the influence of Habanera on Tango before following up Ravel's *Habanera* with his transcription of Piazzolla's *Grand Tango*. On the other hand, I also heard pianists 'explaining' that Debussy's *L'Isle Joyeuse* is constructed on the whole-tone scale (?!), and such debatable half-truths were certainly instrumental in provoking me (and other mathemusical actors) to provide sounder and more comprehensive arguments.

The interest of this specific form of talk is multifold:

- The alternance of music and theory enhances the perception of both, in the tradition of the 'good cop/bad cop' routine: theory enables a better appreciation and understanding of the music played, whereas the musical interludes alleviate the suffering otherwise inflicted by requiring intellectual efforts.
- The allure of an artistic show — the 'concert' part — is enticing enough for audiences who would not necessarily be interested in a dry, purely mathematical talk.
- This is true of course for non-specialized audiences, but also for specific ones, like corporate meetings (researchers, teachers, etc...), which could be less receptive to traditional conferences (even if the subject is actually the same).

This kind of manifestation, with its versatility and adaptability, is one of the best ways (though not the only one) to address general misconceptions and ignorance about our discipline: on the one hand, the general public often believes in a profound unity of maths and music but on wrong or shaky grounds (like 'music = numbers') while on the other, qualified scientists often dismiss the field as kindergarten mathematics mostly focused on rational approximations of $\log_2(3/2)$ and addition modulo 12. A multimedia show including video, graphics and of course music (recorded or performed), enables to hammer in the usefulness of group theory, categories, topology, graphs, polynomials, and so on, at an appropriate level. The only price to pay for such gratifying endeavors is the usual one in popularization, where one has to sacrifice a little of the rigor and exhaustiveness of a true scientific conference for the sake of understandability and the pleasure of the audience.

8.2. Concerférences for the General Public

8.2.1. *Choice of topics*

In this section I will not just mention 'concerférences' for the most general public but also for *specific though non-specialized audiences*, like school/college/university and those cultural associations that sometimes ask for an unfamiliar event concerning music and maths. The common denominator would be the absence of any prior bystander knowledge pertaining to the matter. It could be objected that interested spectators — interested sometimes to the point of buying a ticket for the conference — would be informed or at least cultivated. In my experience it can be quite the reverse: secondary school students may be more knowledgeable than educated grown-ups, who will have learned more but forgotten aplenty, but the former can be relied upon for some half-baked but still fresh notions. For instance, with 14-year-olds I draw on the notion of identical vectors between different couples of points to help understand the notion of interval mod 12 on the Kremer circle; pointing out 'strange parallelograms' (the *Pink Panther* theme is a favorite) is appealing to them, because it comes as a welcome change and a relief from the usual definition drilled into them at school, see Fig. 8.1.

This example shows that modular arithmetic can be a topic of choice for such publics, though it is not usually taught before pre-graduate (maths) level. However, with enough pictures and audio illustrations, the notion of pitch-class goes down quite well. Two of my favorite routines for demonstrating modulo octave equivalence are:

- a Shepard–Risset never-ending scale, played while a Penrose stair (or Escher fountain) is shown, and
- asking the audience to sing some popular song ('Brother John' or 'Black Sheep'), showing by example how voices spontaneously settle an octave apart.

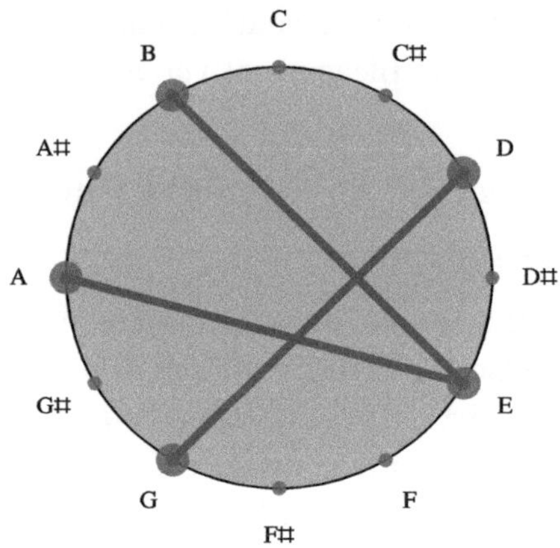

Fig. 8.1. Some parallel fifths in the circle model.

French poetry-minded audiences (like the aforementioned cultural associations) can also enjoy searching for the author of the following revealing verse:

"La treizième revient, c'est encor la première;"[b]

More generally, it is usually a good idea to establish unexpected connections — a romantic poet with modular algebra, Beethoven with graph theory as we will develop below — as it strikes the public's attention, mobilizes their personal knowledge as something that can help them tread unfamiliar ground, and establishes synaptic connections, which is the acknowledged way for memorizing new notions.

As usual in the case of specialists addressing laymen, it is a mandatory effort to remain modest in scope, and not to provide too technical or too detailed information: most of the 'obvious' stuff that researchers gloss over — say, set-theoretic notions like intersection or complementation, but also elementary musical notions like names of notes, keys, scales, triads,... — is new and even difficult for the

[b]"The thirteenth comes back, and is still the first": Gérard de Nerval, *Chimères.* Googleable questions like this should not be overused however, lest smartphones captivate the attention of the audience instead of the speaker.

audience. For instance, addition mod 12 is fine (adding up pitch-classes and intervals), multiplication is not (M5–M7 operations).[c]

I remember only of one occasion when we dared to venture a bit further with non-professionals, who were especially enthusiastic about browsing new knowledge: Pierre de Fermat's birthday is celebrated every year in the family manor in Beaumont de Lomagne (South-West of France) by a *Fête des Mathématiques*,[d] and in October 2014 we gave there a fairly thorough 'concerférence'.[e] Topics were: modular arithmetic in the cyclic model of pitch-classes and pc-sets, the *Tonnetz* with its cycles, among which Hamiltonian cycles with recent compositional applications in pop music (see below), geometrical musical spaces, Möbius strip in Bach's *Musical Offering*, rhythmical mosaic canons (tilings of periodic rhythms), Tom Johnson's square perfect tilings and their connections with Galois theory (with a wink at number theory aficionados in Fermat's own house!), maximally even sets (in scales and rhythms), ending with S. Reich's *Clapping Music* — a non-mosaic rhythmic canon with incrementation — performed by the audience. Quite a lot on their plate! Admittedly there may have been quite a few maths teachers or at least amateurs, and the younger part of the audience included many especially gifted pupils, so perhaps this should not count as a general-public occasion.

However, some notions that seem reserved for specialists can sometimes be adequate for general-public *concerférences*, if they lend themselves to nice, illustrative, graphical representations (even though the underlying mathematics is actually quite complicated). Most *geometrical musical spaces* are suitable, even orbifolds [11] (the Möbius strip of dyads is a nice one because part of the audience has some previous knowledge of the strip) or Baroin's 4D-Model [5]; but my favorite one is the *Tonnetz* (or its dual).

---

[c]It can be tried in high school however, because sentences like "$5 \times 5 = 7 \times 7 = 1$" jolt the young audience's attention, since it is close to their quotidian drilling but refreshingly different and even delightfully shocking.
[d]https://www.fermat-science.com/agenda-manifestations/.
[e]With Moreno Andreatta and Gilles Baroin.

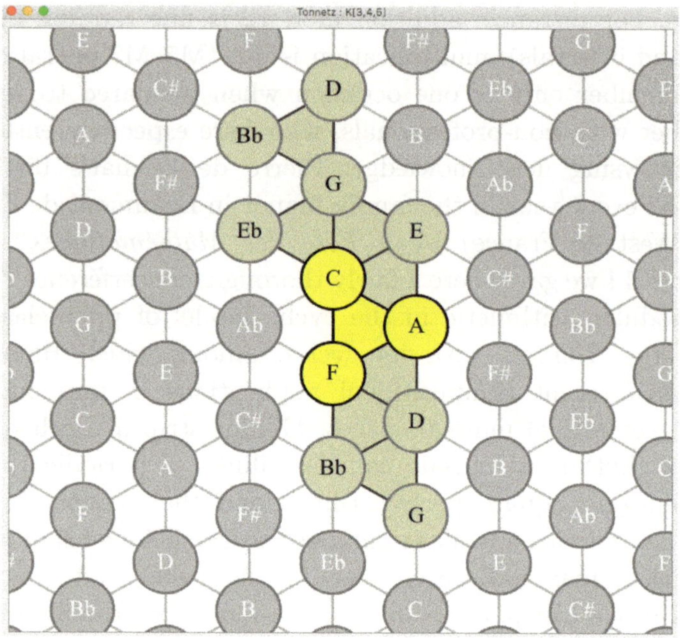

Fig. 8.2. Cycling triads in the *Tonnetz* with HexaChord.

Its topological structure is quite easy to grab when the audience follows a sequence of chords/notes going through one side and turning up on the opposite one, and there is a wealth of interesting videos using this model. A fantastic pedagogical tool is Louis Bigo's software HexaChord,[f] which enables to follow chord progressions in real time as we can see in Fig. 8.2.

8.2.2. *The epic saga of Hamiltonian cycles on the* Tonnetz

This makes a great story for any concerférencer, which spans almost three centuries[g]: Leonhard Euler invents the *Tonnetz* (and graph theory!) in his *Tentamen* in 1739. The edges of the graph are the

[f] Available at: http://www.lacl.fr/~lbigo/hexachord.

[g] The adventure goes on, with current research on the graph of seventh chords recently studied in [7]. It is known to be Hamiltonian, but the exhaustive search for cycles stumbles on exponential complexity.

consonant pure intervals of fifth and thirds, as per Euler's own theory of consonance based on simple rational ratios between sound frequencies. The *dual* graph is made of the centers of the triangles, connected to their neighbors. These triangles are major or minor triads, and moving to one neighbor triads involves changing one note only, a 'parsimonious' operation with maximal simplicity. These operations are the fundamental bricks of Öttingen's and Riemann's renewed theory of *Tonnetz* (1856): R (Relative) exchanges, say, C major and A minor (moving only the G to A); P (Parallel) exchanges C minor and C major and L (Leittonwächsel) downs the C major tonic, changing the chord to E minor — or the reverse. This grammar of transformations is taught nowadays as a powerful (and fashionable) tool for analysis of tonal music, much simpler than traditional and often ambiguous labelings of degrees in local tonalities.

But much had been done with P, L and R even before they were even named. For instance, Beethoven wrote a suggestive sequence of triads in the third movement of his Ninth Symphony (1824). The middle section of this cycle is shown in Fig. 8.3; the operations are LRLRLR.... This was recognized as a cyclic sequence of parsimonious operations much later, by R. Cohn in 1996 who defined general P-cycles between pc-sets [9].

But Beethoven's cycle has one additional and remarkable quality: it passes through each of the 24 triads once and exactly once.[h] Such a

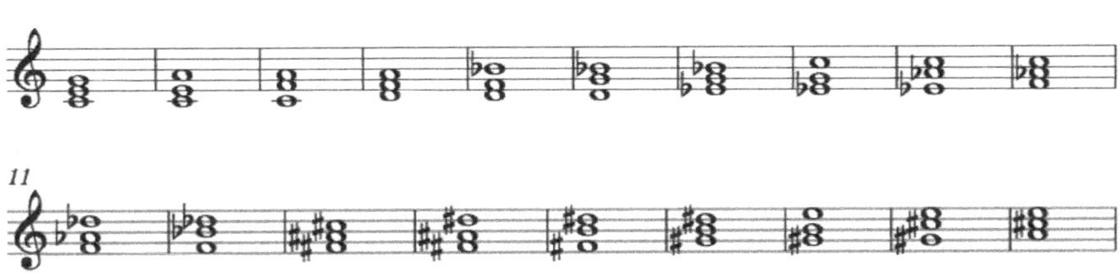

Fig. 8.3. Cycling triads in Beethoven's Ninth Symphony.

[h]Actually Beethoven went from C major to A major only, leaving out the six last triads what would have completed the cycle. But carrying on would have been straightforward.

cycle in a graph, crossing each vertex exactly once, is a Hamiltonian cycle; the notion emerged around 1856 — simultaneously with the resurgence of the *Tonnetz*.

However, it took again a century and a half for researchers to come to grips with the obvious question: what are the other possible Hamiltonian cycles in the *Tonnetz* of triads? It is certainly possible to find some solutions by hand, but an exhaustive search requires some raw computer power, since finding Hamiltonian cycles is now known to be an NP-complete problem. This was tackled and solved in 2009, by Albini and Antonioni [1] who found the 262 solutions. I was thrilled when I first encountered this result, which had just then become accessible with a personal computer (I checked on mine and it took a couple of hours at the time). The ultimate development of this exemplary sequence of mathemusical analysis was of course to use the new cycles for original compositions. In *concerférences*, we sometimes use G. Albini's seminal variant[i] of Bach's first cello Suite, *Corale #4* which shows beautifully the parsimonious character of chord transitions. However, when I am privileged to share the stage with Gilles Baroin and Moreno Andreatta, the latter plays and sings live one of his own 'Hamiltonian songs' while the former projects his stunning graphics renderings in diverse geometrical models, for instance *Aprile* [4] on a moving poem by Gabriele d'Annunzio. The three Hamiltonian cycle of triads used in *Aprile* appears in Fig. 8.4.

Not anecdotically, journeying in the *Tonnetz* (or similar spaces) widens the musical repertoire to pop/rock music, which is mandatory both for general and youthful audiences. Other examples illustrated similarly in the *Tonnetz* (or alternative spaces) include Paolo Conte or Frank Zappa and can be visited at http://www.mathemusic4d.net/.

More generally, besides appropriate choices of topics, there are ways to ensure the audience's continued attention and satisfaction.

[i]Cf. https://youtube/rXR64vFcf-Q.

8.2.3. *Meeting and involving the audience*

8.2.3.1. *Simple acts*

If one wants to involve the audience, the most natural way to do so must be to have them sing, since anybody can do it (or believes so). I already mentioned how this can help grasp the notion of octave equivalence, for example. Also — barring special environments — one cannot expect to find many songs or tunes known to a whole audience, because of cultural and generational differences. The point is that clapping hands is the cheapest and most readily available musical instrument, and that the capacity for playing regular rhythmic cells is fairly well shared among the human genus.

Invoking yet another muse, Terpsichore, may not cross the mind of many Mathematical Music theory experts, but dancing is a very evocative and powerful expression of music, notably but not exclusively because of its rhythmic component. In *La Chapelle Gély* in Montpellier I had an unexpected *impromptu* experience: I was learnedly explaining why the *tresillo* rhythm 10010010, i.e., 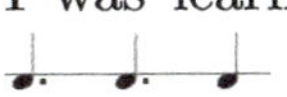 , was a maximally even division of 8, showing its two different steps and generator, when M. Andreatta sat at the piano

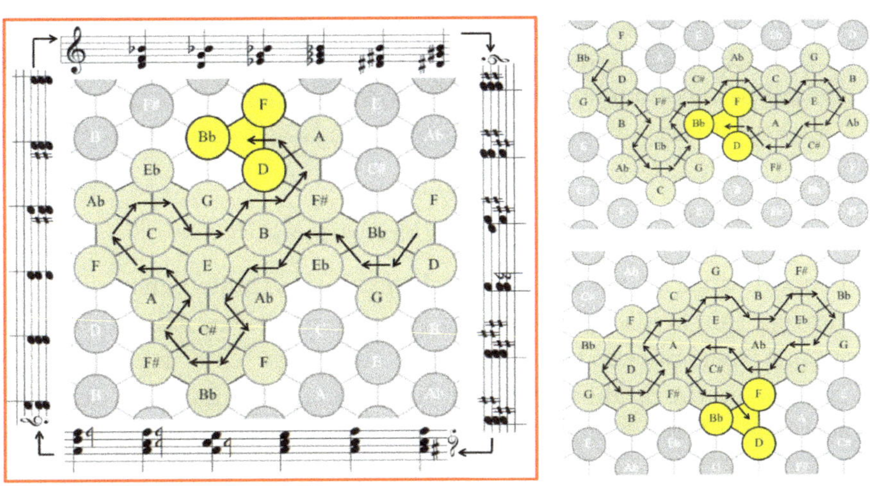

Fig. 8.4. Hamiltonian cycles in the *Tonnetz* (*Aprile*, d'Annunzio/Andreatta).

Fig. 8.5. A simple rhythmic canon.

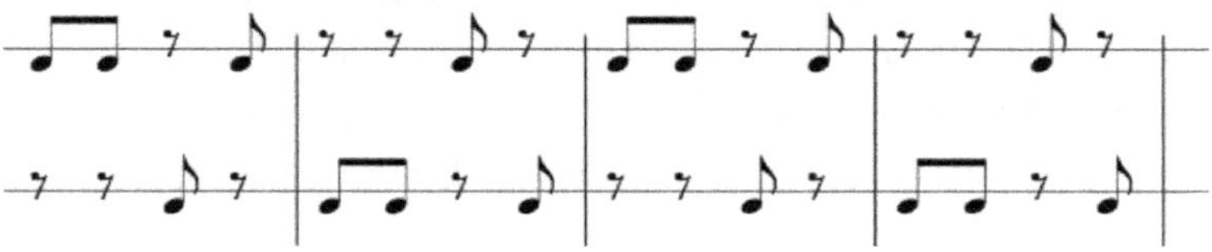

Fig. 8.6. A more challenging rhythmic canon.

and attacked Piazzolla's *Libertango*; feet itching, I had no option but to invite a member of the audience to dance it, for what was generally considered as the best moment of the *concerférence*.[j]

In the same (long) *concerférence*, we had enough time to introduce the notion of rhythmic canons and tilings. This is a lovely topic for involving the public yet another way: most human beings can clap their hands to a beat, and indeed we were surprised at how well the audience managed Steve Reich's *Clapping Music*. I would nonetheless recommend simpler motives, like the one in Fig. 8.5.

More difficult but with less voices is the classic motif 0136 modulo 8, i.e., `1101001`: (see Fig. 8.6).

8.2.3.2. *Getting involved with rhythmic canons*

Still more difficult is the general theory of rhythmic canons, cf. [2]. However, this is a very nice topic for concerférences since the basic principle can be experimented and felt from experience by the members of the audience: a rhythmic canon is made of different voices playing the same rhythm but with different onsets. Variants

[j]https://www.youtube.com/watch?v=eUe1Ddkv2M4&t=1108s.

include modifying the motif not only by changing the onset, but also inverting it in time [no pitch inversion since pitch is ignored here] or playing it at different tempi (augmentation). A *tiling rhythmic canon* has exactly one, and only one, note for each beat. Producing tiling rhythmic canons is a real challenge: as of today there is no general rule for deciding whether a given rhythm can generated a canon (be it by translation, with retrogradation, or augmentation). For instance, motif 1001101  looks very similar to 1101001 just above, but it cannot tile by translation (try it); however, it tiles with its retrograde, as shown in Fig. 8.7.

Partial results are known: for instance, any three-note rhythm does tile with retrogradation, but one has better start with the form of the motif which is balanced on the right as can be seen on Fig. 8.8, with a more abstract/pictural presentation where the motives appear on each line.

Similarly, motif 11011 cannot tile either by translation or retrogradation (irrelevant here since the motif is symmetric), because there is no way to fill the small hole in it without overlapping; but it can tile with augmentations. The smallest solutions appear on Fig. 8.9 (I used them in a choral composition).

At times, I play *Noli me Tanguero*, a tango of mine whose rhythmic structure stems from retrogradation tilings of the motif 100100101, cf. Fig. 8.10.

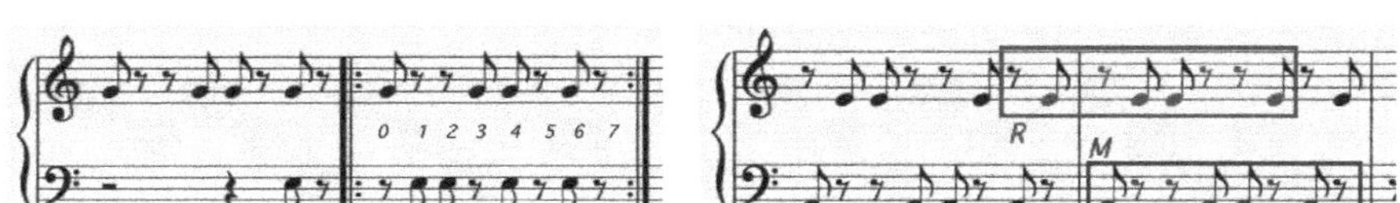

Fig. 8.7. The habanera motif does not tile by translation but does by retrogradation.

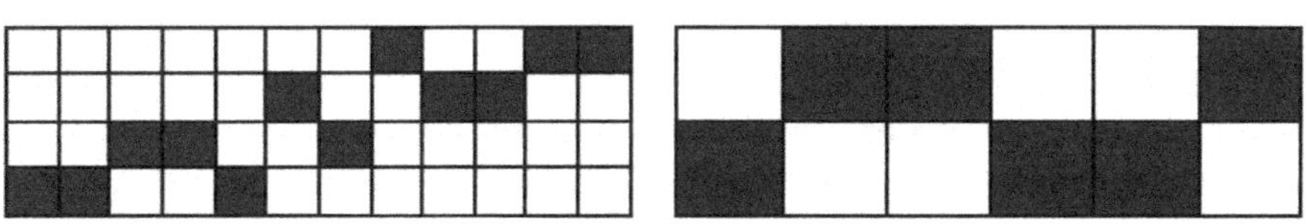

Fig. 8.8. Tiling with 11001 and 10011.

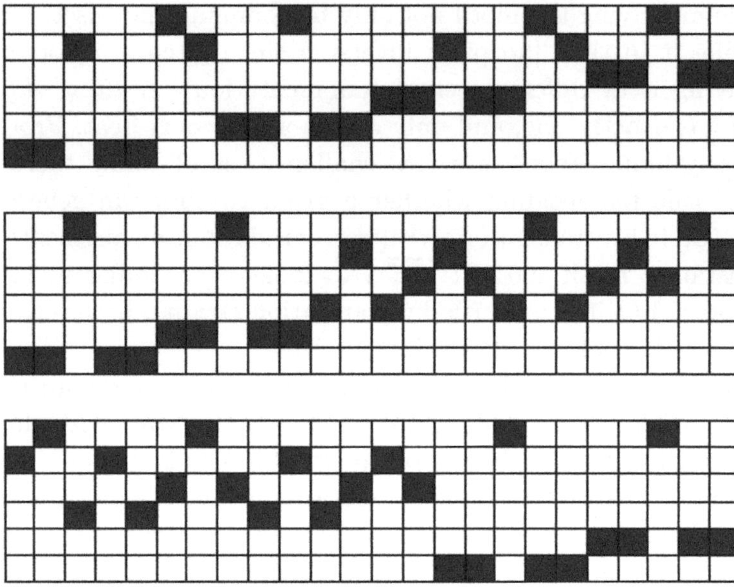

Fig. 8.9. Tiling with augmentations of 11011.

Fig. 8.10. A six voice tiling by retrogradation.

I used to mention Vuza canons a lot — tiling rhythmic canons by translation which are not concatenations of smaller canons — but nowadays I prefer to discuss simpler problems. For instance, composer Tom Johnson tried to tile with augmentations of the simplest three-notes motif 111, i.e., 10101, 1001001 and so on. He

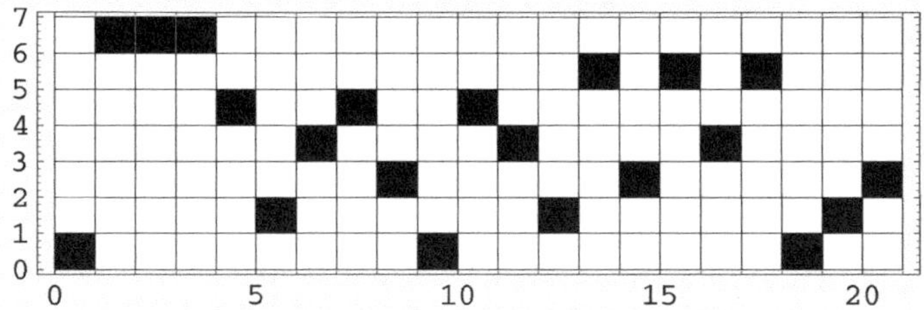

Fig. 8.11. Tiling with $3k$-augmentations of 111.

was puzzled to discover that one has to use all of ratios 3, 6 and 9, as happens in lines 1, 4 and 5 in Fig. 8.11, or none of them. Why cannot one use, say, the 3-augmented motif 1001001 without the two other ones?

This is easily solved if each voice is interpreted as a polynomial: for instance, 111 is $1 + x + x^2$ and 0010101 is $x^2 + x^4 + x^6$; the different voices in Fig. 8.11 are $1 + x^9 + x^{18}, x^5 + x^{12} + x^{19}, x^8 + x^{14} + x^{20}$ and so on, adding up to

$$1 + x + x^2 + \cdots + x^{19} + x^{20} = \frac{x^{21} - 1}{x - 1}.$$

In general, one has to combine several voices with ratio k and offset m and associated polynomial $x^m(1+x^k+x^{2k})$. Setting $x = j = e^{2i\pi/3}$ will make this polynomial vanish whenever k is *not* a multiple of 3. So does their sum which is $\frac{x^{3n}-1}{x-1}$ if n is the number of voices. This means that voices where the ratio *is* a multiple of 3 must have their polynomials cancel out for $x = j$. Since their values are $3j^m$, one must have three (or 6, or 9) of them, with appropriate values for the offsets m. This is a nice illustration of the power of polynomials and roots of unity.

Another of Johnson's problem about tilings by augmentation was solved with polynomials: why do tilings by augmentations of 11001 (with *binary* ratios: $2, 4, 8, \ldots$) all have a number of notes which is a multiple of 15? The smallest such tiling is shown on Fig. 8.12.

However, this problem involves surprisingly advanced algebraic tools — Galois groups on finite fields, see [2] —, as the value 15

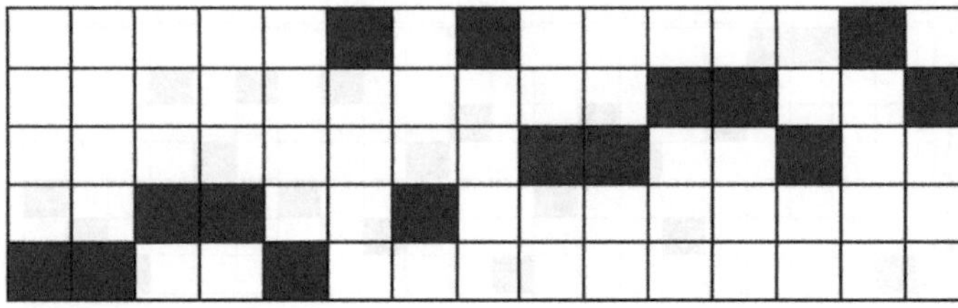

Fig. 8.12. A tiling with five binary augmentations of 11001.

finally happens to be the number of invertible elements of $\mathbb{GF}_{16}$, which is the decomposition field of polynomial $1 + x + x^4$ in $\mathbb{GF}_2[x]$! This is perhaps best left for audiences with strong mathematical capabilities — I use it to convince these specific audiences that mathemusical research involves quite serious maths.

8.2.3.3. *Further involvement*

As mentioned above, in some cases a *concerférence* can be given at the invitation of some institution (high school, private association, university). In this case, there are interesting possibilities of interaction, before or after the talk. Besides the obvious dimension of communication (advertisement, articulation with previous events harbored by the institution, discussion of specific needs or interests), there may be some follow-up of the *concerférence* in classes: for instance, if the concepts of musical inversions and retrogradations have been shown, students can be enticed to try them on their own musical compositions, for instance with synthesizers online like http://www.audiosauna.com/studio/. A former student of mine, G. Baixas, did precisely that for 12 year olds: they had to create a melody and apply the transformations. In the process, most of them will have grasped (hopefully for the rest of their lives) that the composition of two planar axial symmetries is a central symmetry, cf. Fig. 8.13.

This can easily lead to the installation of maths and music workshops, taken over by inspired local teachers, with the kind of curricula that are developed in other parts of this book.

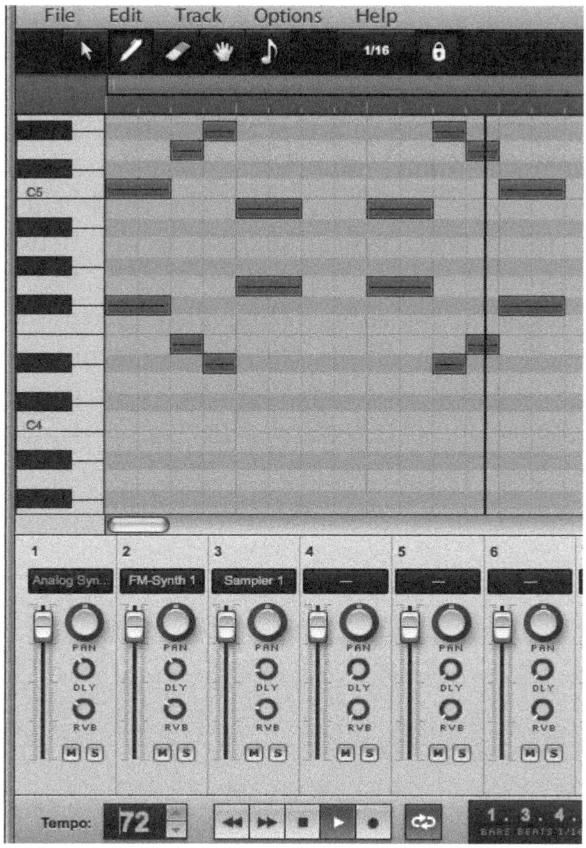

Fig. 8.13. Composing symmetries with Audiosauna.

8.3. Concerférences for Specialists

Owing to the double heading of the discipline, the mathemusictalker can meet specialists in either music or sciences (not necessarily/only mathematicians). This can change the deal substantially.

For instance, again with Andreatta and Baroin we held a Bach evening, in November 2014 at *La Chapelle Gély* in Montpellier.[k] Most of the public was knowledgeable about some basic musical notions (who was J.S. Bach, what is a fugue, symmetries in

[k]http://images.math.cnrs.fr/+Bach-entre-nombre-et-geometrie+.html.

counterpoint, even some ideas about tunings). In this case, the talker's job was to provide better, unambiguous definitions of the required operations. For instance, it was instructive to show the audience why the 5th and 6th canons of the *Goldberg Variations* cannot properly be named *'Canon alla Quarta'* (respectively, *'alla Quinta'*) since they are canons by inversion and not simple transposition — hence there is no well defined, fixed interval, between a motif and its transformed version, as can be seen in Fig. 8.14. In the same vein, graphical renderings (simplified sonograms) of the 30 variations showed at a glance the kind of symmetries used by the composer, whereas Jos Leys' famous video animation of the *Canon cancrizans* in *The musical Offering*[1] exemplified a global symmetry curving the whole musical space into a Möbius strip,

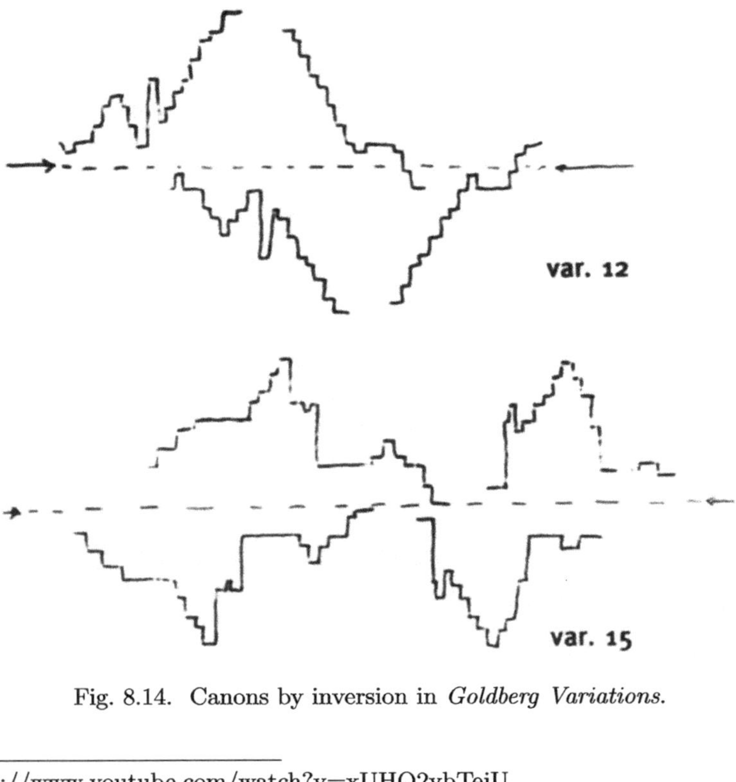

Fig. 8.14. Canons by inversion in *Goldberg Variations.*

[1]https://www.youtube.com/watch?v=xUHQ2ybTejU.

which was duly realized live, both in gluing a printed score (with a twist) in front of the audience, and playing the canon with two instrumentists (one pushing the other off the piano stool at the end of the loop).

With the help of IRCAM, I organized in Paris in May 2012 a seminar for professors in the 'Classes Préparatoires' system (wherein I work) which seemed to fulfill a need.[m] Besides, this homogeneous category of teachers was given the incentive to push their students towards projects in maths and music which they might not have considered before the talk made them aware of the interest of such topics. Indeed, I have received a significant number of requests from their students for their 'TIPE' or *Travaux d'Initiative Personnelle Encadrés*, which are research projects for CPGE students with a tremendous importance in their evaluations. One such student even went through TIPE and a master thesis all the way to a Ph.D.[n] on the topic of rhythmic canons modulo p, a notion that I had invented in 2005. Other topics at TIPE level included: rhythmic canons (several times), spectral analysis for identification of bird's songs, variation of spectrum of a clarinet sound according to pitch, comparison of frets on a guitar with equal 12-TeT and its influence on production of harmonic notes, autosimilar melodies, maximally even sets, defining metrics on chord (or melody) spaces taking into account intervallic content, perception of 'pure' (sinusoidal) sound, Markovian analysis and synthesis of chord progressions in a *Tonnetz*, Polya enumeration in combinatorics of rhythms, etc.

The scientific competence of such an audience[o] enables the speakers to indulge in discussing cutting-edge research in some depth. However, extra care has to be taken in explaining the musical fundamentals (pitch-classes, parameters/time spaces, etc.) and providing simple, even basic, musical illustrations. It is easy, seeing their

[m]http://repmus.ircam.fr/mamux/saisons/saison10-2010-2011/stage-math-musique. Though not properly a *concerférence*, I mention it in this chapter because there was a fair amount of musical content, like the Hamiltonian songs mentioned above.
[n]See [8].
[o]CPGE professors teach students around pre-graduate level, but typically hold a Ph.D. themselves, in Maths, Physics, Chemistry or Computer Science.

quickness in grasping subtle concepts, to forget that such publics can be extremely naïve on comparatively trivial musical questions, like octave identification, the distribution of white and black keys on a keyboard, the existence of microtonal systems, etc.

On the other hand, every so often scientists have some good amateur knowledge of music, or better. In the latter case, the mathemusictalker has to make his audience aware that music as a science has developed far, far beyond the old chestnuts of Pythagorean tuning and division of the octave, and involves much more modern tools than logarithms and Diophantine approximation. It usually comes as a considerable surprise for such sophisticated audiences to discover that we use group theory, category theory, differential calculus, advanced algebra (like Galois theory on finite or continuous fields) and so on.

Whereas it is better to select a simple topic and gravitate around it when addressing non-specialists, it may be a good idea to take advantage of a knowledgeable audience in order to cover more *extensive* ground. In the present case, the four conferences (respectively by M. Andreatta, C. Agon, G. Assayag and myself) were about:

- A panorama of the discipline, with musical interpretations of mathematical problems (such as tilings) [10].
- The diversity of appropriate curricula in *Mathemusic* as exemplified by the ATIAM master formation in IRCAM.[p]
- Top notch computer and AI interaction with musicians and improvisers, with the OMax software [5].
- The extremely wide field of application of Discrete Fourier Transform in Music Theory (actually too wide by now to be presented here, see [3]).

One can go for even more technical presentations in the case of specialists associations, like professional mathematicians or math

[p]http://www.atiam.ircam.fr/fr/.

teachers. We encountered both with M. Andreatta and G. Baroin, respectively in Firenze[q] and Laon.[r]

In both occurrences we developed a presentation of sophisticated musical spaces — generalized *Tonnetze* — from a triple angle:

- Musical creation, through execution of pop songs composed by Andreatta using Hamiltonian cycles on the standard *Tonnetz* (cf. Section 8.2.1).
- Graphical renderings, video animations in diverse geometrical projections of the *Tonnetz*, allowing to follow the moves around the 24 triads.
- At some point, a rather thorough theoretical explanation of the definition of the graphs and musical spaces involved, including the other *Tonnetze*.

The last point is the gratifying difference between a general popularization talk/show and one before an enlightened audience, that enables to provide sense and comprehensive meaning to an elsewise mainly decorative illustration of concepts: providing actual precise, scientific definitions in terms intelligible to the audience, and mathematical results stated in unambiguous terms more akin to a scientific paper presentation. However, such contexts are a luxury for a mathemusictalker.

8.4. Conclusion

It is an onerous task to break the ice between specialists of Maths and Music and the general public, but also an urgent one. The know-how of popularization events is immediately transposable to encounters with more knowledgeable publics, like maths or music or science teachers, that need to be reached too. Though scientists generally have no quarrel with a determinedly mathematical approach to musical questions, the reverse applies to some publics less familiar

[q]18 April 2016, Conferenza-concerto "Matematica e musica" for *Festa della Mathematica*: http://roma.institutfrancais-italia.com/fr/node/7492.
[r]Journées APMEP, "Les mathématiques, quelle histoire?", http://www.jnlaon 2015.fr/programme/programme.php?item=10.

with 'the unreasonable efficiency of mathematics' who harbor a more romantic approach to the ineffability of music (which is a polite way of forbidding rational discourse on the topic), a point of view unfortunately still well shared by many composers, analysts and practitioners — late French composer André Riotte once told me how much he was stung by Olivier Messiaen's violent reaction when he told him that limited transposition modes are readily obtained as orbits of a group action. My usual answer to the teleological argument that Music, being the breath of Gods, is best left respectfully unstained by maths, is: "the better you know the person you love, the better you love him/her", a fairly convincing metaphor if the public's reactions to it are anything to judge by.

It is our duty to go meet these people and help them correct these misinterpretations. The 'concerférences' described *supra* are a privileged means to this end, and one that I hope will develop and bloom in coming years. I have tried to help in this direction with the present contribution.

However, it may well be that newer ways of reaching large publics, like blogging and YouTubing, will prove best. Already these are more efficient in reaching younger publics who would not dream of getting away from their computer screen and walk all the way to a conference hall; already, some stunning scientific videos and blogs are seen by millions[s] and (even considering the high percentage of people it is wasted on) dispatch knowledge to many more than could ever be reached by traditional channels of information. So probably when we engineer concerférences, we should at least record them and upload the videos, thus stepping in the future in quiet assertion of the worth of our centuries-old discipline.

Bibliography

[1] G. Albini and S. Antonini, Hamiltonian cycles in the topological dual of the Tonnetz. in eds. E. Chew, A. Childs and C. H. Chuan, *Mathematics*

[s]See for instance 3Blue1Brown on https://www.youtube.com/channel/UCYO_jab_esuFRV4b17AJtAw.

and Computation in Music. MCM 2009, Communications in Computer and Information Science, Vol. 38 (Springer, Berlin, 2009).
[2] E. Amiot, New perspectives on rhythmic canons and the spectral conjecture, *J. Mathe. Music* **2** (2009) (Special Issue Tiling Problems in Music).
[3] E. Amiot, *Music through Fourier Space*, CSM Series (Springer, 2016).
[4] M. Andreatta, https://www.youtube.com/watch?v=AB8By7ghTkU.
[5] G. Assayag, *et al.* http://omax.ircam.fr/.
[6] G. Baroin, The planet-4D model: an original hypersymmetric music space based on graph theory, in *Mathematics and Computation in Music. MCM 2011*, Paris (2011).
[7] S. Canas, S. Antonini and L. Pernazza, On the group of transformations of classical types of seventh chords, in *Mathematics and Computation in Music. MCM 2017, Mexico City* (2007), https://www.researchgate.net/publication/317218582_On_the_group_of_transformations_of_classical_types_of_seventh_chords.
[8] H. Caure, Outils algébriques pour l'étude des canons rythmiques mosaqïues et du pavage modulo p, Master thesis, (2013), http://www.atiam.ircam.fr/Archives/Stages1213/CAURE_Helianthe.pdf.
[9] R. Cohn, Maximally smooth cycles, hexatonic systems, and the analysis of late-romantic triadic progressions, *Music Anal.* **15**(1) (1996) 9–40.
[10] M. Andreatta, Mathematica est exercitium musicae: La recherche mathé-musicale et ses interactions avec les autres disciplines, Habilitation à diriger des recherches, Strasbourg (2010), http://recherche.ircam.fr/equipes/repmus/moreno/TexteHDR.pdf.
[11] D. Tymoczko, The geometry of musical chords, *Science* **313** (2006) 72–74.

Chapter 9

Visualizing and Sonifying Mathematical Music Theory with Software Applications: Implications of Computer-Based Models for Practice and Education

Courtney Hilton[*,†], **Andrea Calilhanna**[‡,§] **and Andrew J. Milne**[¶]

[*]*Centre for Research on Learning and Innovation, The University of Sydney, Australia*

[†]*School of Psychology, The University of Sydney, Australia*

[‡]*Sydney Conservatorium of Music, The University of Sydney, Australia*

[§]*Cherrybrook Music Studio, Sydney, Australia*

[¶]*The MARCS Institute for Brain, Behaviour and Development, Western Sydney University, Australia*

9.1. Introduction

This chapter discusses what software applications offer to the practice of mathematical music theory and, more broadly, to music education. Traditionally, mathematical music theory uses the formalisms of mathematics (such as equations and graphs) to represent and produce models of musical phenomena that serve explanatory, predictive, or generative purposes. By contrast, computer-based models use interactive elements to represent and model musical phenomena within a software environment.

These two approaches support quite distinct ways of working, thinking, and learning. The former entails a slow analytic process, constrained by step-wise workings and calculations, and the latter allows for faster and more intuitive experimentation and hypothesis testing. While for most learners, learning to model musical phenomena in purely mathematical terms is cumbersome and challenging, well-designed software may enable such model-based learning to become more accessible and fluent. Thus, we argue that software can uniquely help visualize and sonify challenging concepts in mathematical music theory, helping students learn them more intuitively, and in ways that are more likely to support transfer to real musical situations.

It has been argued that computer-based modeling has constituted a major revolution in how people do science [36, 82] and how people learn challenging concepts in science and mathematics [25, 65, 66, 81]. A computer-based model, broadly defined, is a software application that allows the exploration of a mathematical or agent-based model computationally. This allows the computer to do the hard work on aspects of the modeling that are not directly relevant to learning or the conceptual domain in question (in our case: music theory). In other words, a computer is good at *scaffolding* our thinking and learning [71]. Another advantage is that computers are able to output real-time visualizations and sonifications of the model. For example, in science, one can run models on and visualize the dynamics of phenomena that are otherwise invisible, and thus difficult to learn and reason about, such as nanoparticles [43]. And so too in music, a computer-based model can output sonifications and visualizations of the musical structures we are modeling, which sometimes might be challenging to get a perceptual handle on.

How we represent musical information — whether it be with conventional notation, solfege, or mathematical formalisms — can have a significant effect on learning and practice [81]. Consider, for example, the historical shift from Roman numerals to the Hindu–Arabic numerals we use today. This change, far from being arbitrary, resulted in more people being able to understand and use mathematical ideas [6, 41, 81]. Similarly, we would like to propose that certain mathematical models and their instantiation in well-designed software are in a similar position to help more people learn and understand music: a democratization of mathematical music theory.

In the next section, we consider some recent mathematical models of musical structure that can be usefully incorporated into interactive software applications and modeling activities such as those outlined above. We briefly summarize these theories and suggest some of the educational and creative affordances they provide. In the final section, Andrea Calilhanna — a practicing music teacher — will give a qualitative account of how introducing software based on mathematical representations positively influenced her teaching practice and her students' learning.

9.2. Mathematical Models of Musical Structure and Their Software Representations

Many recent mathematical models of musical structure are applicable to both the tonal and the metrical domains. This makes them particularly appealing in an educational context because any single such model has application across music's two most fundamental dimensions: pitch and time. Unlike conventional notation, which has different ways of representing pitch and time, mathematics provides a common vocabulary that invites learners to make connections between musical dimensions. And indeed there is a rich source of isomorphisms between pitch and time (e.g., Pressing [69], Monahan [60], though London [47] provides caution about extending the parallels too far). For example, both rhythms and scales are typically:

- periodic — for example, the diatonic scale repeats every octave; the clave rhythm repeats every two measures;
- subsets of a regular universe — for example, the diatonic scale is a 7-pitch subset of the 12-chromatic pitches; the clave rhythm is a 5-beat subset of 16 isochronous pulses;
- hierarchical — for example, the pentatonic scale is embedded in the diatonic which is embedded in the chromatic; a meter often

comprises numerous metrical levels each of which have differing groupings.

As subsequently detailed, notable recent mathematical music theories relevant to time, meter, pitch, and tonality include *maximal evenness* [14], *well-formedness* [11], *perfect balance* [51], *the discrete Fourier transform* [2], and *spatial isomorphisms* [19, 59]. This list is far from complete because the subsequent focus will be on mathematical models that are practical to visualize; for example, the unavoidably high dimensionality of voice-leading spaces (e.g., Tymoczko's voice-leading orbifolds) make them impractical unless restricted to two or, at most, three voices (David Bulger's useful interactive visualizations and sonifications of voice-leading spaces for two and three-part harmony, using Shepard tones, can be found at http://science.mq.edu.au/~dbulger/).

9.2.1. *Maximal evenness*

The property of *maximal evenness* [14] applies to periodic scales or rhythms where all pitches or beats fall at some regular division of the period (e.g., the octave or measure). For example, consider 7-tone scales in the familiar 12-tone equally tempered tuning; or 5-beat rhythms that fit into a grid of 16 *isochronous* (equally-spaced in time) pulses. When the number K of pitches in the scale divides into the number N of equally-spaced chromatic pitches, the maximally even scale is itself equally spaced, hence of limited interest (analogous results hold for rhythms).

But, when K does not divide N, the maximally even scale (or rhythm) always comprises no more than two step sizes (interonset intervals) and has a number of interesting properties: their complement is also maximally even; the two steps sizes are distributed as evenly as possible; every *generic* interval — e.g., second, third, fourth, etc. — comes in two *specific* sizes — e.g., m2 and M2, m3 and M3, P4 and Aug4; the distribution of sequences of specific sizes of seconds within larger generic intervals have the lowest possible entropy [54], which may confer cognitive advantages.

Furthermore, maximally even scales and rhythms are common in real-world music; for instance, the maximally even seven-pitch scale in 12-TET is the diatonic scale; its rhythmic analog is an archetypal West African timeline. The maximally even five-pitch scale in 12-TET is the anhemitonic pentatonic; perhaps the commonest of scales across the world. Numerous analogous examples of maximally even rhythms in world music are provided in [78].

The method to calculate maximally even scales (rhythms) is straightforward: Clough and Douthett [14] introduced a simple algorithm: for a K-pitch scale in an N-tone equal temperament, the octave is first divided into K equally-spaced pitches that are expressed in semitone units; then all these values are truncated to the nearest integer. But, performing calculations like this by hand, or with a spreadsheet, is tedious. Far better to allow users simply to choose an N and a K, and have the maximally even pattern automatically calculated, displayed and sonified (as in SequenceApp and Rhythm Necklace). Furthermore, multiple maximally even rhythms can be simultaneously sounded, each with differing rotations, allowing for maximally even polyrhythms.

Such maximally even structures, either expressed in pitch or time, are conducive to pedagogical treatments that teach mathematics with music and music with mathematics. Maximally even rhythms in cyclical graphs can be a grounding concept that can help children embody fundamental mathematical concepts and processes, including division and remainder, prime numbers, set inclusion, and modular arithmetic. Our research group is exploring such ideas in ongoing experiments, and we suggest that such cases present exciting opportunities for future work.

9.2.2. *Well-formedness*

There are many formal definitions of well-formedness [11, 83], all of which lead to the same end result. One way of understanding this principle is to consider it as a generalization of maximal evenness: a generalization that extends it from scales or rhythms with discrete values (i.e., subsets of a regular and finite universe of chromatic pitches or isochronous pulses) to scales or rhythms that are subsets of a smooth continuum. This generalization allows scales whose pitches do not fall at some equal division of the octave (e.g., the historically important quarter-comma meantone and Pythagorean tunings [9]; or rhythms, such as swung jazz rhythms, that use consistent microtimings to impart "groove" [28]).

In a smooth continuum, the maximally even scale or rhythm will always be equal-stepped (isochronous) because, unlike in the discrete context, the pitches (beats) are no longer constrained to fall at a specific Nth subdivision of the octave or metrical period. But, a well-formed scale (rhythm) works with an alternative constraint: it is the maximally even scale or rhythm comprising a given number of *large* and *small* steps. For example, the well-formed scale with five large steps and two small steps is the diatonic scale. But, unlike the maximally even version, the precise sizes of these scale steps are now flexible.

This means that the diatonic scale is well-formed regardless of its precise tuning — it could be in 12-TET, it could be in 17-TET, or 31-TET, or 19-TET, or it could be in a tuning with no equal steps at all, such as the previously mentioned meantone and Pythagorean tunings. All of these well-formed diatonic scales have the same pattern of large (L) and small (s) steps ($LLsLLLs$), but the ratio of the sizes of L and s differs. For example, in the 12-TET diatonic, $L/s = 2$; that is, the large steps (major seconds) are twice the size of the small steps (minor seconds); in the 19-TET diatonic, $L/s = 3/2$; in the quarter-comma meantone diatonic scale, $L/s = \log(25/16)/\log(4096/3125) \approx 1.649$.

A similar generality across scale-step ratios (or interonset interval ratios) holds for scales and rhythms with any pair of numbers of large and small steps; for example, 4 large steps and 3 small, or 3 large steps and 5 small. Each possible coprime pair of these numbers produces a unique family of new scales and rhythms. And all of them have properties analogous to those of maximally even scales or rhythms: their interval size distribution minimizes entropy, every generic interval comes in no more than two specific sizes, and so forth.

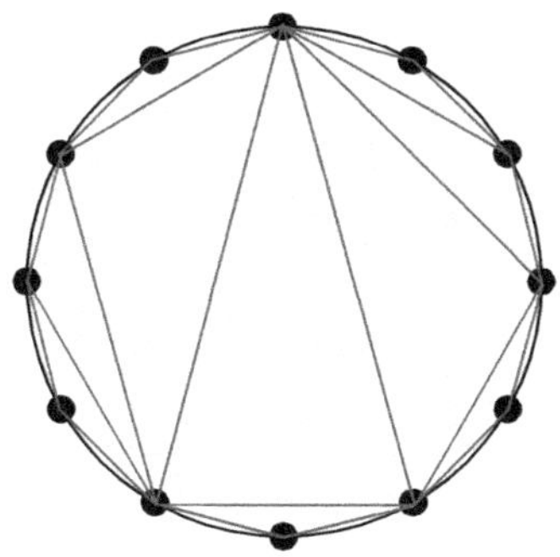

Fig. 9.1. The well-formed hierarchy of perfect fifth, tetractys, pentatonic, diatonic, chromatic (detailed in the main text).

But, well-formed scales (rhythms) also possess a number of additional useful properties, as detailed in Milne *et al.* [53], and Milne and Dean [54]. Notable amongst these being their hierarchical nature; for example, the principal scales in Western music are all well-formed and all hierarchically "nested" sets: the well-formed perfect fifth (D, A) is a subset of the well-formed tetractys (D, G, A), which is a subset of the well-formed pentatonic (C, D, E, G, A), which is a subset of the well-formed diatonic (C, D, E, F, G, A, B), which is a subset of the 12-pitch class chromatic set (see Fig. 9.1, for a visualization of this hierarchy). Hierarchical embeddings such as these are particularly useful for rhythms and meters, which are commonly hierarchical in structure.

The broad generality of this model of scale and rhythm construction has been exploited in the Dynamic Tonality software developed by Milne and colleagues (http://www.dynamictonality.com). In terms of pitch, the MIDI sequencer Hex [68] allows music to be composed in arbitrary well-formed scales that can be smoothly changed in tuning, and a suite of synthesizers can sonify these musical scales and produce matched timbres to maximize perceived consonance [55, 57, 58, 74]. In terms of rhythm, the Dynamic Tonality loop generator XronoMorph facilitates the creation and manipulation, in real time, of hierarchical well-formed rhythms and melodic hockets [55, 57]. This produces rhythms that, while remarkably complex, are still groovy; furthermore, different rhythms can be smoothly morphed between — a novel and striking musical effect. Video demonstrations of XronoMorph can be viewed at https://www.youtube.com/c/xronomorph.

The above applications, and enthusiastic responses to them from musicians and music producers, have demonstrated their potential for facilitating creative engagement with, at times, unorthodox musical structures that break conventional constraints on tuning or timing. In terms of music education, they can provide effective examples of how extracting features from traditional systems — such as the pentatonic–diatonic–chromatic hierarchy — and recasting them into different, but analogous, forms can generate interesting and novel variations.

9.2.3. *Perfect balance*

Perfect balance [51, 52] is a recently developed organizational principle for periodic scales and rhythms. It is conceptually simple: if pitch classes or beat classes are represented by point masses on a circle, the resulting scale or rhythm is perfectly balanced if their centre of mass (mean position) is at the centre of the circle. More generally, the *balance* of a scale or rhythm is the proximity of its centre of mass to the centre of the circle, normalized so that a balance of 1 implies perfect balance, and 0 implies perfect imbalance (which occurs only when all pitches are the same, or all beats occur simultaneously).

All isochronous rhythms are perfectly balanced and the sum of such isochronous rhythms is also perfectly balanced. This, therefore, includes most conventional metrical structures (like 3/4, 4/4, 5/4, 6/4,..., 3/8, 5/8, 6/8, 7/8,...) as well as familiar polyrhythms — common in African musical traditions — where a period is divided into both 2 and 3, or into both 3 and 4, or into both 3 and 5, and so on. Furthermore, it also includes polyrhythms where the different cycles are out of phase so they never coincide (a musical possibility perhaps first identified by Hofstadter [33]); perfectly balanced *interweaving polyrhythms* [4], such as these, are also found in African musical traditions [51] (Fig. 9.2).

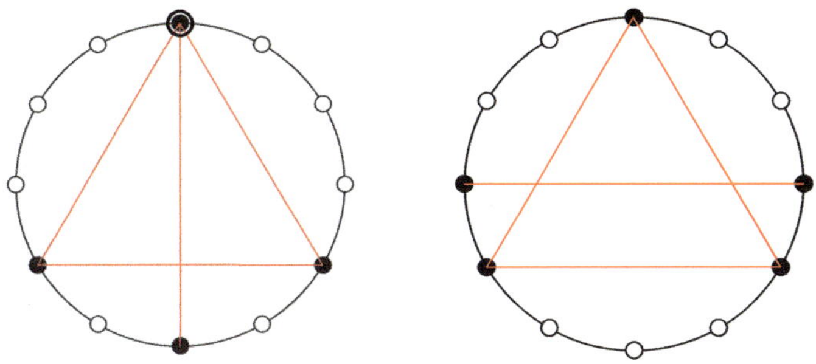

Fig. 9.2. Two against three polyrhythms: the first is the classical hemiola, the second is an interesting variant where the two rhythms are out of phase and never coincide. Both are perfectly balanced.

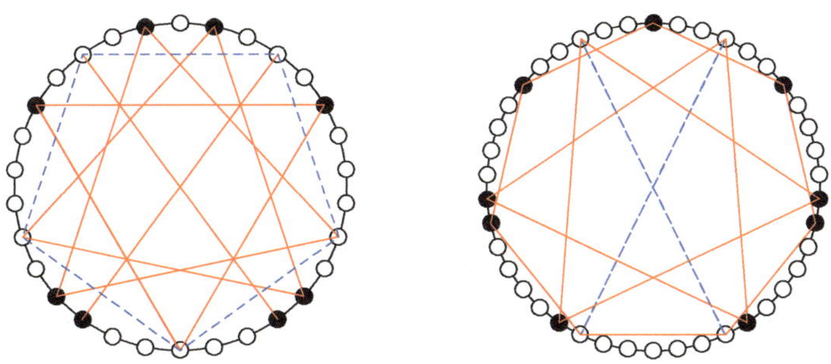

Fig. 9.3. Two minimal perfectly balanced primitive rhythms. The regular polygons with dashed lines are negatively-weighted; the regular polygons with solid lines are positively-weighted. When vertices of a positive and negative polygon coincide, they cancel each other out. Minimal perfectly balanced primitive patterns, such as these, cannot be constructed solely from positively-weighted regular polygons [51]. Perfectly balanced rhythms such as these can be explored — visualized and sonified — in XronoMorph (see also https://youtube/uKcOOBGxzJc).

Intriguingly, there are further generalizations of polyrhythms opened up by the mathematical definition of perfect balance (Fig. 9.3). Instead of simply *adding* isochronous beats, it is also possible to *subtract* isochronous beats. This results in meaningful rhythms so long as the result has no negatively-weighted beats. In this way, "ghostly" polyrhythms can be created where the impact of the subtracted rhythms is the absence rather than the presence of a sounded beat. Figure 9.3 shows the construction of two of these *minimal primitive perfectly balanced* rhythms.

From the perspective of teaching music, these visualizations with regular polygons make the construction of polyrhythms clear and easy to understand. This is important because representing polyrhythmic structures either with conventional notation or on a MIDI pianoroll, obfuscates their underlying simplicity. The generalizations of perfect balance, also allow for unusual, but musically interesting, polyrhythms to be explored. From the perspective of teaching mathematics, these patterns can help learning the concept of coprimeness: any number of regular polygons with coprime vertices can only ever all meet (visually and sonically) at one point in the period; when the numbers of vertices are not coprime, they can intersect at multiple points. One might imagine a group of students — guided by the animated visualization in the software — tapping out polyrhythms to fully embody this understanding.

9.2.4. *DFT coefficients*

A discrete scale can be conveniently represented by an *indicator vector*; for instance, the diatonic scale can be represented by the 12-entry indicator vector $(1, 0, 1, 0, 1, 1, 0, 1, 0, 1, 0, 1)$, where the ones represent the presence of a pitch in the scale and a zero represents the absence of a pitch in the scale. The discrete Fourier transform of this vector is another vector of 12 elements, each of which is a complex number. The magnitudes and phases of the first seven coefficients (more, generally $\lceil N/2 \rceil$, where N is the number of chromatic pitches or isochronous pulses) can be used to identify and manipulate interesting properties of the scale. This use of the discrete Fourier transform was introduced by Lewin [46], and exploration of the meanings of these coefficients has been a hot topic in recent music theory [1, 2, 10, 27, 70].

Indeed, the magnitude of the first coefficient is proportional to balance (as defined above). In the 12-TET context, the magnitude of the fifth coefficient has been characterized as the "diatonicity" of the scale; the magnitude of the fourth coefficient as its "octatonicity"; the magnitude of its sixth coefficient as its "whole-tone quality". Clearly, with different N, such as in a microtonal scale system or in many rhythms, the musical meanings of the coefficients (with the exception of the first) differs.

One utility of the discrete Fourier transform is that it transforms the common musical — but mathematically difficult — operation of convolution into the simpler operation of multiplication (indeed it is the only linear transformation that can do this [2, Theorem 1.11]). Convolution in the pitch domain corresponds to the musical operation Cohn [17] termed *transpositional combination*: it is the process by which a pitch class set is transposed and then added. Such scales are *rotationally symmetric* (they are also known as transpositionally invariant or TINV pitch class sets) and have found frequent use and been met with much theoretical interest; for example, all of Messiaen's modes of limited transposition [49] are rotationally symmetric [16]. Temporal analogs for rhythm also occur [17]. Amiot [2, p. 7] suggests that the discrete Fourier transform is "unreasonably efficient" in music theory.

From the creative perspective, *Fourier scratching* is a technique developed by Amiot, Noll, Andreatta, Agon, and Carlé [3, 12, 53] where musical outputs can be controlled directly by manipulating the coefficients of a scale's discrete Fourier transform. It seems likely that useful software interfaces and realtime visualizations will also be developed for educational and analytical purposes. The musical illustrations may also provide motivation for more advanced students to better understand the Fourier transform.

9.2.5. *Interactive spatial isomorphisms of musical structures*

Spatial isomorphisms help to make visualizations of pitch and tonality, time and meter, and their underlying mathematical constructions, easy to understand and to manipulate. In a musical context, the term "isomorphism" is usually applied to two-dimensional layouts of pitches in musical interfaces; but, as shown subsequently, it also applies to higher order musical structures such as tonality and meter.

The definition of isomorphism relevant here (this is not a strict mathematical definition) is a one-to-one and invertible (structure-preserving) map between two domains. Here, the domains are some musical feature (such as pitch, metrical level, chord) and space (one, two, or three-dimensional). The focus, here, will be on two-dimensional space, because this affords more interaction possibilities than a sole dimension, and because it is more practical to implement than three dimensions. And, because isomorphic spatial representations of musical structures are structure-preserving and consistent, it is often implied that they are intuitive and easier to understand than non-isomorphic representations.

The importance of considering spatial information and the extent of its isomorphism, or congruity, with musical information is emphasized by a growing body of cognitive and neuroscientific research showing that the way we process space is closely connected with how we process the musical dimensions of both pitch [22, 26] and time [37]. And, more generally, similar patterns are found in other domains such as mathematics [40, 44, 45, 50] and scientific reasoning [24]. Some go as far as to say that space is at the very heart of human thought [42].

The interactivity of representations also matters. If we accept that space can be meaningful, we interface with and manipulate this meaning through action. For example, Goldstone, Landy and Son [29] studied how experts in algebra solved equations such as $2x + 5 = 13$. Rather than abstractly computing the correct answer, like a computer would, they found evidence to support the idea that experts mentally visualize the mathematical symbols in their mind's-eye and interact and manipulate the symbols with imagined gestures, such as dragging the '5' to the other side of the equation. Based on this, they designed a software application called Graspable Math [30, 62] that supports the development of this dynamically embodied way of thinking about algebra — https://graspablemath.com/. The software supported this by having the symbolic representations of mathematics dynamically respond to gestures such as dragging.

We will now provide an overview of representations in music that are spatially isomorphic with musical structures and offer affordances for meaningful interaction and gesture.

9.2.5.1. *Pitch layouts*

Physical isomorphic pitch layouts (also known as *generalized keyboards*) date back to the nineteenth century, with numerous examples detailed by Helmholtz and Ellis [32] (see also Keislar [39]). These were designed to make conventional music easier to play than on the conventional piano keyboard by ensuring that the same musical interval always has the same "shape" (i.e., angle and distance) regardless of transposition. For example, the major third between C and E has the same shape as the major third between D and F♯ (something that is not true of the piano keyboard). They were also designed to facilitate the use of musical tunings that more closely approximate just intonation than does 12-TET (e.g., 53-TET and 31-TET). Numerous recent hardware musical controllers have also utilized isomorphic layouts: Array Mbira [5], Thummer [63], AXiS-49 [23], LinnStrument [72], Lightpad Block [73], and Terpstra [77].

An advantage of software interfaces combined with multitouch screens is that they easily allow for a variety of such layouts to be explored; for example, the iOS app Musix Pro [67] provides a range of isomorphic layouts for 12-TET, while Hex [68] uses such layouts for MIDI sequencing.

It has been argued that isomorphic layouts have important benefits for elucidating the structure of tonality. For example, they make explicit the invariance of intervallic structure when transposing to a different key. They also clearly expose the structure of well-formed scales (defined below) such as the pentatonic and diatonic, because these are always spatially represented as notes arranged on successive lines at different heights — see the "$3 + 2$" pattern of rows made by the pentatonic scale and the "$3 + 4$" pattern made by the diatonic scale in Fig. 9.4.

Furthermore, every isomorphic layout has two *axes* that indicate two important musical dimensions: *pitch height* and *perfect fifth*

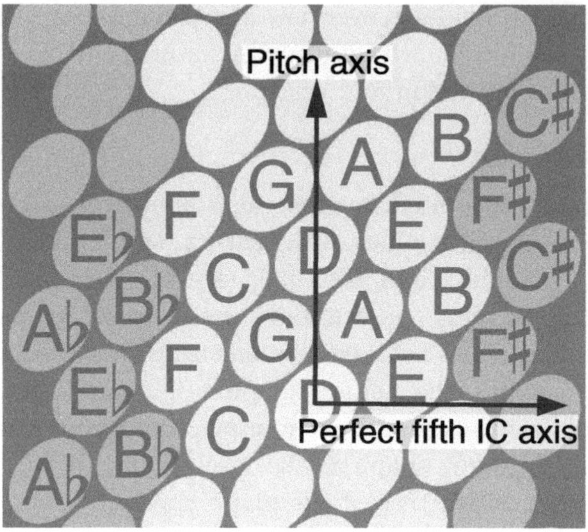

Fig. 9.4. A pitch layout where the pitch axis is vertical and the perfect fifth interval class axis is horizontal, making both of these important dimensions of pitch distance easy to see or to sense by proprioception. The well-formed pentatonic scale follows a $3 + 2$ pattern of rows, the well-formed diatonic scale follows a $3 + 4$ pattern of rows. In microtonal tunings, related patterns occur for all possible well-formed scales.

interval class "width" (*IC5 width*, for short). The *pitch axis* is any line angled so that, along this line, the position of every pitch-playing button-centre is proportional to its pitch height; for instance, the pitch layout in Fig. 9.4 has a vertical pitch axis, hence the vertical height of every pitch-playing button corresponds to its pitch height. The *IC5 axis* (termed the *generator span axis* in [68]) is any line angled so that, along this line, the position of every pitch-playing button-centre is proportional to its position in the chain of perfect fifth interval classes (IC5s); for example, the pitch layout in Fig. 9.4 has a perfectly horizontal IC5 axis, hence the left–right position of any button is proportional to its position in the chain-of-fifths. These two aspects of tonal relations — pitch height and the chain-of-fifths (or circle-of-fifths, depending on the precise tuning used) — are salient features of Western music and its theory [13, 31].

This makes the precise pitch layout shown in Fig. 9.4 interesting because its pitch axis and its IC5 axis are orthogonal and perfectly vertical/horizontal (this orthogonality is achieved by geometrically shearing a standard Wicki layout [79]). In recent experiments, we have established that having a perfectly vertical pitch axis strongly facilitates the learning and playing of new melodies (the impact of the angle of the IC5 axis has not yet been tested) [48].

9.2.5.2. *Chord/key Tonnetz*

When considering relationships between chords or keys (as represented by their tonic triad), a different isomorphic representation — based on pitch classes rather than pitches — has proved useful: the *chord Tonnetz*. Although commonly represented in a regular hexagonal form (see Fig. 9.5(a)), experiments obtaining ratings of the fits of different pitches and chords have shown that a linear

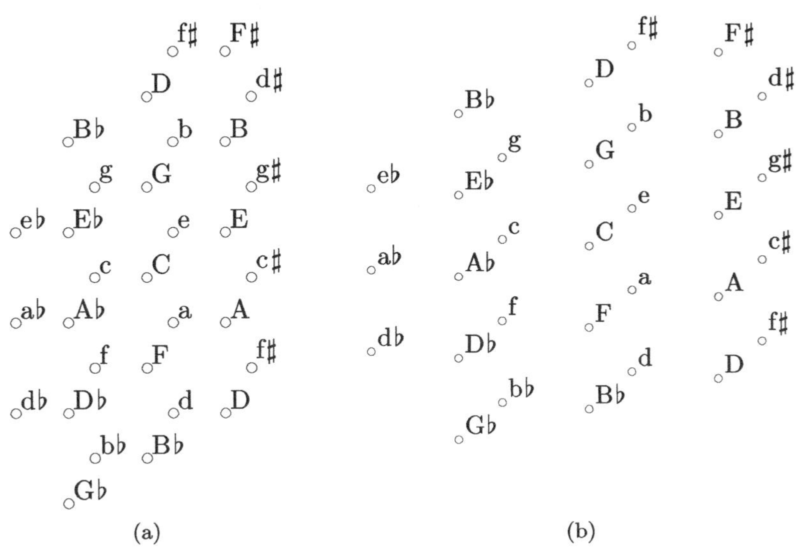

Fig. 9.5. The chord *Tonnetz* on the left is in the classical regular hexagonal form (major triads are in upper case, minor triads in lower case). The chord *Tonnetz* on the right has been sheared and scaled to optimize the correlation between spatial distances and ratings given by 42 participants of the similarity and fit of all 26 possible pairs of root position major and minor triads (the resulting correlation is a substantial $r = 0.92$ [56]).

transformation (involving a shear and a one-dimensional scaling) of the regular form provides a substantially better fit of spatial distances to perceptual distances [56] — as shown in Fig. 9.5(b).

It seems clear that the chord *Tonnetz* has potential for allowing music students to quickly visualize not just the relationships between chords, but also the degree of fit between pairs of such chords — the manipulation of fit and tension being, perhaps, one of the principal devices used in tonal composition for the expression of emotions.

The power this brings, like with pitch layouts, is afforded by the cognitively congruent use of spatial information. Just as displaying algebra in spatially congruent ways facilitates mathematical thinking [45], it can be said here that displaying tonal information in spatially congruent ways supports musical thinking. The effectiveness of such a representation may be further extended by rendering it in software. A computer-based model of this could sonify the tonal relationships that are expressed spatially. This would enable a qualitatively different modeling process involving intuitive back-and-forth interaction between ideas suggested by the spatial information and their auditory consequences. One such application is Harmony Space, which is a tool designed to facilitate rapid learning about the practical use and theory of tonal harmony [34, 35]. Such software has applications for both teaching and creative composition.

9.2.5.3. *Circles, polygons and periodicity*

A natural isomorphic representation of the periodicity found in musical scales and rhythms is a circular form (as in Figs. 9.6–9.8).[a] The software applications XronoMorph (see Fig. 9.6), Rhythm Necklace, SequenceApp, and Euclidean Pattern Generator all represent

[a]Having said that, in many situations (particularly melodic), pitches an octave apart are not perceived as identical. A common model of pitch perception is as a helix, where pitch class (chroma) is the circular dimension and pitch height is the orthogonal linear dimension [75]. Using Shepard tones, which comprise partials that are only in octave relationships, makes it possible to seamlessly sonify just this circular dimension. For rhythms, the circularity is easier to make concrete because special sounds are not required.

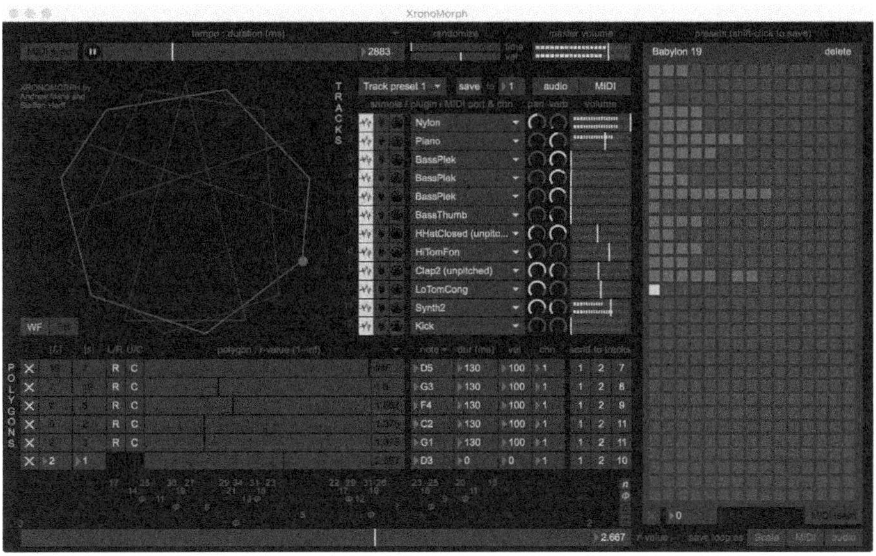

Fig. 9.6. The user interface of XronoMorph showing, on the left, a circular representation of a multilayered (hierarchical well-formed) rhythm. Each rhythmic level is distinguished through the use of inscribed polygons. One advantage of keeping all rhythmic levels on the same periodic circle is that the temporal and geometrical relationships between them can be easily seen.

rhythmic loops in a circular format, with periodic time mapped to angle. XronoMorph and some of the others also use polygons created by connecting together the rhythmic points on the circle (i.e., the polygons are inscribed in a circle). These cyclical graphs can be a useful way of visually differentiating between multiple voices — such as may be found in a polyrhythm — on the same circle.

Rendering a cyclical graph in software can also enable meaningful embodied interactions such as those supported for algebra in Graspable Math. For example, consider the concept of transpositional equivalence in set theory: to obtain a transposition by 2 of the pitch-class set $\{0, 4, 7\}$ (a major triad), one may follow the canonical algorithm of adding 2 to each member to reach $\{2, 6, 9\}$. However, a more cognitively informed approach would be to conceive of the transpositional relationship as 'rotational equivalence'; that is, as a perception–action routine. The polygons represented

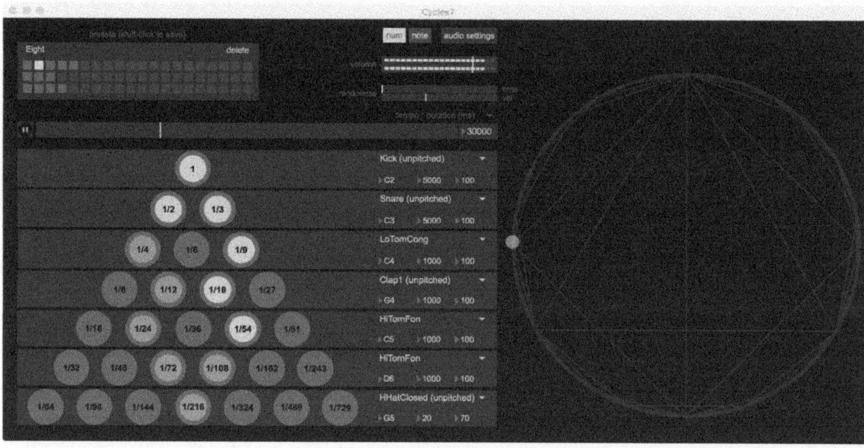

Fig. 9.7. A prototype of the SkiHill software application — discussed, later, by Andrea Calilhanna. A user can select any node to make its corresponding pulsation sound — a selected node is highlighted and it flashes green while actually sounding. Each row (metrical level) can be assigned to an instrumental sound, so that the whole metrical structure can be sonified by a virtual percussion ensemble. Like XronoMorph, the rhythm is also illustrated with polygons inscribed in a circle.

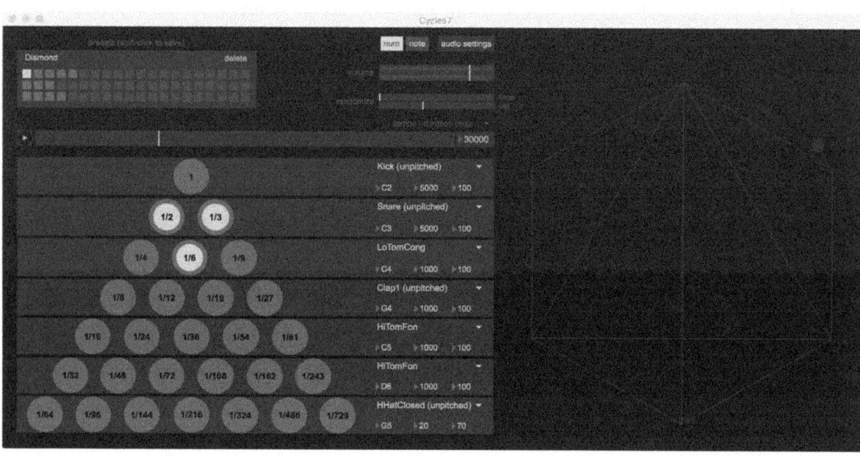

Fig. 9.8. Ski-hill graph (left) with the nodes mapped as fractions and a mod-6 cycle (right) illustrating a 3:2 hemiola; e.g., dotted semibreve and semibreve, or dotted minim and minim.

in XronoMorph, which are representations of a subset, can be interactively rotated. Getting students to engage and internalize these perception–action routines for transforming a subset may help them develop a more grounded understanding of the concept of equivalence. This form of interaction is supported in a computational domain and, in educational settings, may be best supported by touchscreen or free-form interfaces.

9.2.5.4. *Meter and ski-hill graphs*

Cohn [19] proposed an interesting representation of metrical structure designed to elucidate the multiple hierarchical levels that are inherent to meter in the common practice tradition, as illustrated in the triangular section of the software in Fig. 9.7.

The ski-hill graph is an isomorphic representation of meter. Each node represents a given pulse speed. The next node "South West" has a pulse that is doubled in speed; the next node "South East" has a pulse that is tripled in speed. This creates a hierarchy of possible relationships, where every metrical level (node on a row) can be subdivided into two beats and/or three beats. The pulse speed ratios between any two nodes is always invariant to translation: for example, two horizontal adjacent nodes are always in a 2:3 relationship; two nodes that are in a WSW relationship are always in a 3:4 relationship; and so forth.

This isomorphic structure (invariance with respect to translation) clearly represents the way that musical notation of meter is somewhat arbitrary (e.g., a given pulse level could be notated with a quarter note, an eight note, or a half note, so long as all other levels make a corresponding change). It also emphasizes that metrical structures are "deeper" than is implied by standard time-signatures. For example, a time signature of 3/4 tells us that each measure is divided into three quarter notes (crotchets), each of which is divided into two eighth notes (quavers). But it gives no information about longer metrical groupings (are measures grouped in twos or threes) nor about finer metrical subdivisions (are the eighth notes divided into two or three)? This information is all explicitly — and isomorphically — visualized by the ski-hill graph.

The visualizations and sonifications provided by software such as XronoMorph and the SkiHill app offer numerous advantages over static versions of the same thing. One of these advantages is quite simple and intuitive: when reasoning about musical structures and ideas, one cares about how these more abstract relations translate into sonorous experience and how this makes one feel.

In a sense, learning music theory is about developing intuitive mappings between musical experiences and formal representations and operations. However, helping learners develop this connection between the formal and the experiential is challenging in the traditional classroom. In an ideal world, one would juxtapose the musical experience and the theoretical idea in close succession, and offer the learner opportunities to change an aspect of the model and see how this manifests in the musical experience. The ability to fluently make this transformation, however, is beyond the abilities of all but the most advanced students. One would either have to have very developed internal audiation abilities (to imagine in one's mind the resulting music accurately) or to have to perform this musical material on an instrument. These options are less immediate and, beyond a certain complexity of content, impossible.

Computer-based models allow one to simulate musical systems in a perceptually immediate way. This immediacy allows one to rapidly iterate between various settings of the model, facilitating hypothesis testing and creative explorations. Such ways of learning with computer-based models have become central to learning complex science concepts [38, 76, 80–82] and similar gains, we argue, are to be found for mathematical music theory.

9.2.6. *Summary*

Despite their wide utility as models of musical structure, mathematical music theories can be challenging for non-mathematicians and, importantly in an educational context, children. However, when these theories are instantiated in software applications with attractive visualizations and sonifications, with well-chosen parameterizations, the mathematics can be brought to life: made beautiful, relevant, and memorable. In the same way that computer-based models help children gain intuitions about challenging concepts such as calculus and complex systems [81], computer-based models of music may help children gain intuitions about concepts in mathematical music theory.

In summary, software visualizations and sonifications of mathematical music theory have at least three key benefits. First, they facilitate a deeper and broader understanding of music because they identify commonalities between different musical domains (e.g., pitch and time) and between different musical traditions (they are relevant to pop, rock, and non-Western musical traditions, as well as to common practice classical music); in this way, we can teach music with mathematics. Secondly, these mathematical principles act as high-level descriptors and manipulators of musical structure, which means they can serve as excellent tools to foster musical creativity and novelty. Thirdly, the musical realizations produced by the software can help to embody, visualize and sonify otherwise complicated mathematical ideas; in this way, we can also teach mathematics with music.

In the following section, music teacher Andrea Calilhanna gives us some invaluable "real world" insight into how software embodying two of the mathematical representations described above — the ski-hill graph and cyclical graphs of rhythm — have impacted on her teaching practice and on her students' learning experiences.

9.3. From the Perspective of Andrea's Teaching Studio

In 2015, I studied a semester of musical meter theory classes taught by Richard Cohn in Sydney, Australia (see Chapter 6). To begin, I wondered what I could possibly learn about meter after teaching for 30 years. Isn't meter telling the student, for example, the piece is in

3/4, it's simple triple and to focus on the "strong, weak, weak" of the three crotchet beats per measure? This was what I had been taught, it was the information supplied by the secondary music classroom textbooks and theory books for exam preparation, and this is what would gain my students the marks they needed on their music examinations (my music studio work involves preparing students for piano and music theory examinations, tutoring for secondary high school Music 1 and 2, university auditions and preparation for tertiary music analysis and aural skills). By the end of the course, I had completely shifted in my understanding and teaching about meter and I experienced the realization that I had been teaching only a superficial understanding of meter. One of the main reasons for this leap in my thinking and practice was my introduction to visualizations of meter: the ski-hill and cyclical graph. In this section, I describe how I have used these visualizations to teach musical meter and rhythm, and how software animations and sonifications of these visualizations helped engage my learners.

Although Cohn [19] had originally intended the ski-hill graph as a way of graphically representing complex hemiolas in Beethoven's music, in 2015 I adapted it for teaching much younger students from primary and high school through to young adults. I find the ski-hill graph to be the most compact and efficient way for my students to graphically represent their hearing of the hierarchical relations between adjacent pulses that form meters. As discussed in the previous sections, this is because the ski-hill graph effectively uses spatial information to reflect the hierarchical organization of meter into pulses grouped in either 2s or 3s.

In a lesson, my approach is to ask students to map pulses they hear in the music to nodes on the ski-hill graph. Students map pulses in a relation of inclusion[b] they hear forming duple relationships (duple meter) on the left pathways and pulses in a relation of

[b] *Inclusion relations* refers here to sets of pulses which form meter through inclusion. The condition of inclusion requires that "each time point of the slower pulse is also a time point of the faster one". [20, class notes. Sydney].

inclusion they hear forming triple relationships (triple meter) on the right pathways. This is done first without traditional notation so as to build a foundation of metric equivalence — the same metrical structure could be expressed in multiple redundant notations. From here, I prompt them to consider pulses at multiple levels to discuss how certain pulses are related to each other by either duple or triple inclusion relations. During this process, students are encouraged to articulate reasons why they choose to map pulses in the way they did and only look to the score for clues if necessary. Another appealing aspect of the ski-hill graph pedagogically is the ease with which the pulses can then be mapped onto other forms of metrical representation such as cyclical graphs. Cyclical graphs [21] then bring their own strengths in helping to demonstrate the cyclical and isochronous characteristics of meter — why repeat a pattern (meter) in a straight line if it can be represented once in a circle?

Aside from my frequent use of the ski-hill graph as a handwritten graphic representation of meter I introduced the SkiHill app (the prototype version discussed above) into my studio in 2017.[c] The SkiHill app allows students to instantly produce sound and animations of the pulses they hear on nodes.

As an instrument for analyzing meter, the software version of the ski-hill graph allows a far more interactive and immediate experience through processes of listening, moving their bodies, and tapping/clapping to the beat. This is quite different to the more passive process of sitting with pen and paper, analyzing a score, or being told what to hear by a teacher. The student graphically represents their own hearing and temporal experience of meter from their own understanding.

[c]This occurred because, in 2015, I began to wonder if such an app existed but found nothing of its kind available. In 2016, I wrote to Richard Cohn and Andrew Milne and suggested the idea of developing a ski-hill graph app to help students learn more about meter. They both thought it was a good idea and thankfully for us we now have the world's first ski-hill graph app.

Analyzing meter through the SkiHill app means my students interact with the computer not as passive consumers of information [61, 64]; rather, they manipulate the computer so that their knowledge is transformed into symbolic representation. Thus, through this approach the computer becomes, in a sense, a "mediator" between information and knowledge [7]. To analyze meter in this way means students (and teachers) are then equipped to articulate their learning in many ways, such as through symbol, movement, language, and sound.

9.3.1. *Rohit conquers metric dissonance with ski-hill graphs*

One reason I started using ski-hill graphs was to help my students with musical performance through a deeper understanding of meter. For example, the Grade 3 piano examination piece "Abenddämmerung" (Evening Twilight) No. 3[d] proved tricky for my student Rohit[e] (13 years), who found he never performed measures 17–20 with stable timing and was baffled as to why this was the case. Together we studied the meter in "Abenddämmerung" by listening and drawing a ski-hill graph (see Fig. 9.9) and afterwards examined the score for clues (see Fig. 9.10, mm. 14–20).

Figure 9.9 illustrates the ski-hill graph we workshopped from Rohit's hearing (reproduced here), which represents the pulses he heard forming two different meters in mm. 1–42. He then mapped it onto the ski-hill graph app to observe the sound, notation, fractions and mathematical proportions at work audibly and visually.

When mapping both meters together on the ski-hill graph (see Fig. 9.9) Rohit formed the hemiola he heard in mm. 17–20, which triggered indirect metric dissonance with the introduction of the

---

[d] "Abenddämmerung" (Evening Twilight) No. 3 from *Notenbuch für Klein und Groß* Op. 138 by Stephen Heller measures 17–20.
[e] Real names are not used.

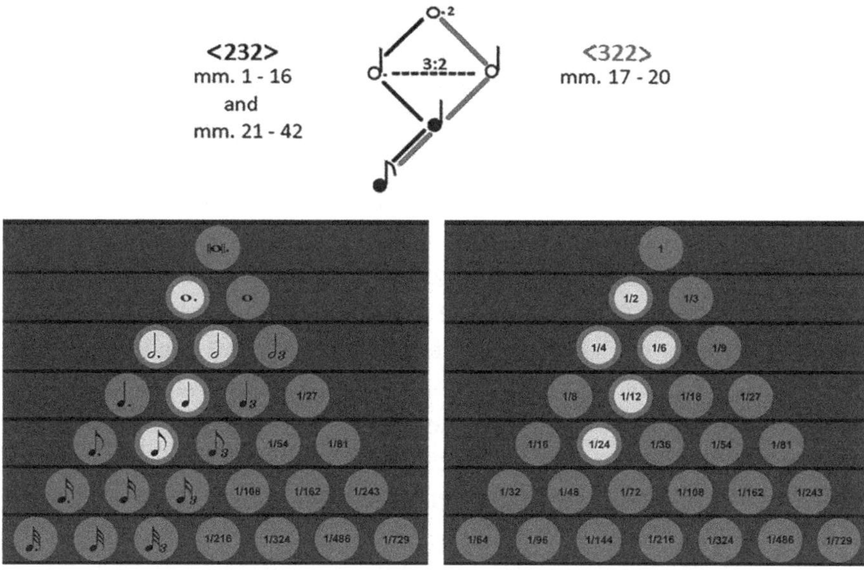

Fig. 9.9. The top figure illustrates a reproduction of my student's ski-hill graph graphically representing the meters ⟨232⟩ and ⟨322⟩[f] of "Abenddämmerung" (Evening Twilight) No. 3, which includes a hemiola. He then mapped it onto the SkiHill app to observe the sound, notation, fractions and mathematical proportions at work audibly and visually.

minim pulse (unlike direct metric dissonance, where the two pulses are heard simultaneously, here they are heard consecutively). He soon realized that this change in pulse was the cause of his timing problem. Through using the ski-hill graph, Rohit could easily hear and see how the two pulses (dotted minim and minim) form a ratio of 3:2 as shown by the horizontal dotted line (Fig. 9.9) and so were not in an inclusion relation (one pulse divides into the other by 2 or 3) hence the metric "conflict" or dissonance.

[f]These "deep meters" are parsimoniously represented with Cohn's *ordered set notation* [18], which show the inclusion relations of four metrical levels. For example, in ⟨322⟩ each pulse of the slowest metrical level contains 3 pulses of the next faster metrical level, which contains 2 pulses of the next faster level, which contains 2 pulses of the next faster level.

Rohit and I analyzed how the composer had achieved this metric shift from ⟨232⟩ to ⟨322⟩ (both, confusingly, notated in 3/4 in conventional notation). The composer introduced metric displacement (syncopation) in measure 17 by subtracting a crotchet pulse (−1 ♩) and placing harmonic changes one unit early using restless V7 and I chords at onsets, which my student noticed led him to regroup the crotchets from sets of 3's to sets of 2's (notably, the crotchets were largely imagined rather than real to the hearing prior to measure 16). To subtract a crotchet pulse, the notated crotchet chord is placed a beat prior to the downbeat of measure 18 and tied over with the addition of the emphatic dynamic change ***fp***, followed by two crotchet chords and a minim on the downbeat at measure 19; another set of tied crotchet chords (which to the hearing is effectively a minim pulse over mm. 19–20 with the dynamic ***fp*** followed by two crotchet chords).

Through these observations Rohit soon realized that his performance glitch would be solved if he shifted the set of pulses he entrained to from one set of pulses to another, as captured by his ski-hill graph. From our workshop, Rohit learned that there was more to meter in a piece than what was symbolically expressed in the notated time signature: the reality was far more dynamic and interesting. Figure 9.10 illustrates the evidence we gathered from listening, analyzing the notation and from pulses mapped on Rohit's ski-hill graph: the solid black arrows illustrate the dotted

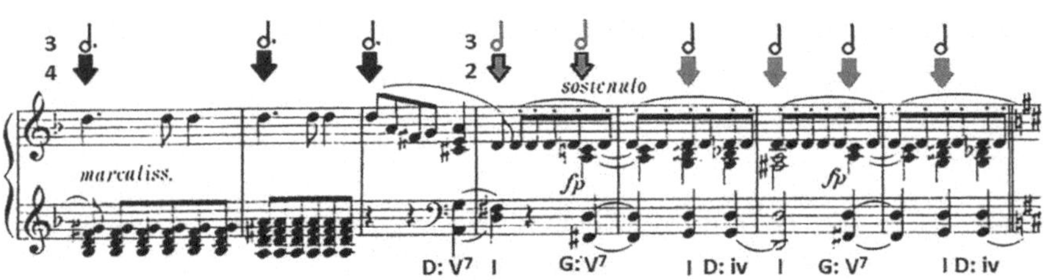

Fig. 9.10. "Abenddämmerung" (Evening Twilight) No. 3 from *Notenbuch für Klein und Groß* Op. 138 by Stephen Heller mm 14–20.

minim downbeat and grey arrows illustrate the minim pulse (the new "downbeat"). The grey arrows with black outlines are the pulses we labeled as metrically ambiguous (the pulses could be considered as either 3/4 or 3/2 at this point in the music). Since this realization, Rohit has never had a problem with the timing of these measures. It is always pleasing when students volunteer statements like, "Oh yeah! I get it!" and "I never thought about that before!"

Figure 9.11 shows Rohit listening to and mapping all of the pulses he hears in a new piece he is preparing for a Grade 4 piano exam "Bolero".[g] Like before, he mapped the pulses he heard onto duple and triple pathways on the SkiHill app. From his previous lessons, he remembered that we often perceive pulses even when they don't exist in the physical sound. For example, he "heard" crotchet and

Fig. 9.11. Rohit mapping his hand-written ski-hill graph onto the SkiHill app. Photo credit: Andrea Calilhanna.

[g] "Bolero" No. 4 *11 Pezzi Infantile* Op. 35 by Alfredo Casella.

hypermetric pulses although there are no crotchet pulses and 2 or 4 measure hyperpulses notated. Through choosing adjacent pulses in inclusion relation on the SkiHill app, and in receiving instantaneous feedback of sound, Rohit gained a deeper understanding of the meter, including pulses which are not explicitly notated.

9.3.2. *Stella discovers mathematics helps her performances through understanding more about meter*

Like most children I've taught, Stella hadn't explicitly connected music with mathematics; yet, every time Stella works out the duple and/or triple relationships between the pulses that make up meter(s) she intuitively engages mathematical principles such as ratio, measurement, pattern, shape, multiplication, division, fractions, proportion, addition and maximal evenness. In my studio, we work through each of these principles as they arise relevant to the materials. I then encourage my students to familiarize themselves with the mathematics in the music, the music in the mathematics, and their embodiment of both music and mathematics, in order to learn more deeply about musical meter [8]. Stella is now quite at home identifying and demonstrating the hypermetric pulse in her piano pieces, which is a logical outcome of her understanding of meter as a hierarchy.

Stella's piece "The Banjo"[h] is in pure duple meter and uses a repetitive pattern of quavers and minims to reflect the plucking of banjo strings. In measure 7, the pattern begins to change and, in measure 8, Stella repeatedly played the minims as crotchets. This was surprising considering no crotchets were notated on the score and no amount of counting and clapping seemed to help. I introduced Stella to the SkiHill app and asked her to map all of the pulses she could hear. She soon understood that the pulses she chose were related to

[h]The "Banjo" by Jennifer Trynes.

Fig. 9.12. Stella (aged 7) mapping all of the metrical pulses she hears in a piano piece she is preparing for an examination. Photo credit: Andrea Calilhanna.

each other in duple divisions and, when she related this to her difficult measure, she started to entrain to two or more pulses at a time, "filling in" the missing crotchet pulse and minim pulse. For Stella, this meant she stopped skipping a pulse causing the destabilizing effect on the performance of her preliminary exam piece. I asked Stella if this helped her in that one measure and she seemed pleased to say, "Yes it did!" (Figs. 9.12 and 9.13).

9.3.3. *Max the music turtle — more than meets the eye*

Max, see Fig. 9.14, is a toy turtle whose "job" it is to remind my very young students to curve their fingers and who occasionally spends a week with a student who isn't well or who has worked hard at their lessons. Recently, I realized Max had another important message to

Fig. 9.13. The interactive ski-hill graph can also be used as a multi-pulse metronome, which helps students relate their theoretical understandings of meter to their playing and practice of music. Stella playing her piece as the SkiHill app sounds all of the pulses she is hearing. Photo credit: Andrea Calilhanna.

share with my students: the regular pattern of six sections on his shell could well serve as a mod-small cycle [21] to teach my students about cycles. I now use Max's shell to show my primary school students that they can place up to three pulses on Max's mod-6 cycle shell by placing colored discs to show pulses in inclusion relation making minimal and deep meters while listening to pulses in pieces in 3/4, 3/8 and 6/8. My hope is Max will one day become an app for children where they can add pulses in inclusion relation and make sounds on a touch screen to make meters. Using mod-small cycles in ways such as this, and especially through using Milne's SkiHill app, makes for a very early introduction to the principles of set theory and, in particular, Richard Cohn's beat class set theory using mod-small cycles to help students understand meter more deeply.

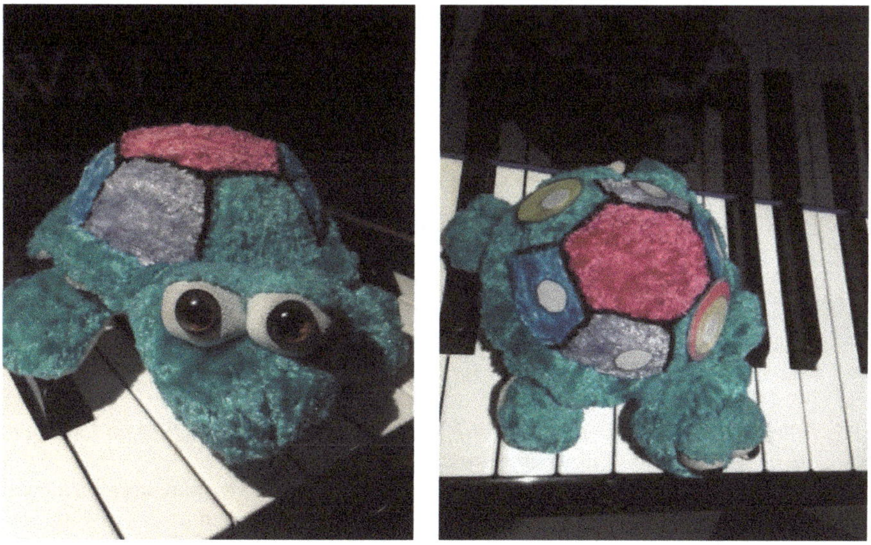

(a) (b)

Fig. 9.14. (a) "Max" with a "mod-6 shell"; (b) "Max" modeling three pulses in one mod 6 cycle (equivalent to one measure of 6/8): the dotted minim (the pink disc near Max's head); dotted crotchet (the yellow disks near Max's head and tail); quaver (the white disks on every segment of Max's shell). Photo credit: Andrea Calilhanna.

9.3.4. *Conclusion*

In summary, through my own teaching practice, I have found both ski-hill and cyclical graphs an effective way for students to learn about meter and rhythm in an intuitive and non-intimidating way. Students were able to construct their metrical interpretations of the music, supported by software that scaffolded their growing understandings. My students have benefitted in so many ways, by gaining: a deeper understanding of the importance of musical meter and where meter is located; an ability to solve many problems involving analyzing and applying note values; awareness and use of division, proportion and counting when practicing new pieces; informed ability to identify pulses and articulate their choices of pulses; awareness of all the pulses that make up the meters they hear, including "imagined" pulses; understanding of hemiolas; comprehension of the cyclical nature of meter; metric equivalence; set theory; maximal evenness;

awareness of notation as "quasi-arbitrary"; meter as independent of the bar-lines and meter signatures; and increased confidence to perform, given their more secure metrical and rhythmic grounding.

Bibliography

[1] E. Amiot, David Lewin and maximally even sets, *J. Math. Music* **1**(3) (2007) 157–172.

[2] E. Amiot, *Music Through Fourier Space: Discrete Fourier Transform in Music Theory* (Springer, Cham, 2016).

[3] E. Amiot, T. Noll, M. Andreatta and C. Agon, Fourier oracles for computer-aided improvisation, in *Proc. Int. Computer Music Conf.* New Orleans, LA, USA (2006), pp. 99–103.

[4] S. Arom, *African Polyphony and Polyrhythm: Musical Structure and Methodology* (Cambridge University Press, Cambridge, 1991).

[5] Array Instruments. The Array Mbira, (2017), http://www.arraymbira.com.

[6] W. W. R. Ball, *A Short Account of the History of Mathematics* (Dover, New York, 1960).

[7] J. Bamberger, The computer as mediator, in *High Technology and Low-Income Communities: Prospects for the Positive Use of Advanced Information Technology*, eds. D. A. Schön, B. Sanyal and W. J. Mitchell (MIT Press, Cambridge, MA, 1999), pp. 235–263.

[8] J. Bamberger, Music as embodied mathematics: A study of a mutually informing affinity, *Int. J. Comput. Math. Learning* **8**(2) (2003) 123–160.

[9] J. M. Barbour, *Tuning and Temperament: A Historical Survey* (Michigan State College Press, East Lansing, MI, 1951).

[10] C. Callender, Continuous harmonic spaces, *J. Music Theory* **51**(2) (2007) 277–332.

[11] N. Carey and D. Clampitt, Aspects of well-formed scales, *Music Theory Spectrum* **11**(2) (1989) 187–206.

[12] M. Carlé and T. Noll, Fourier-scratching, in {*SOUNDINGCODE*} *SuperCollider Symposium* 2010, Berlin (2010).

[13] D. Clampitt and T. Noll, Modes, the height-width duality, and Handschin's tone character, *Music Theory Online* **17**(1) (2011).

[14] J. Clough and J. Douthett, Maximally even sets, *J. Music Theory* **35**(1/2) (1991) 93–173.

[15] R. Cohn, Inversional symmetry and transpositional combination in Bartók, *Music Theory Spectrum* **10** (1988) 19–42.

[16] R. Cohn, Properties and generability of transpositionally invariant sets, *J. Music Theory* **35**(1/2) (1991) 1–32.

[17] R. Cohn, Transpositional combination of beat-class sets in Steve Reich's phase-shifting music, *Perspect. New Music* **30**(2) (1992) 146–177.

[18] R. Cohn, Dramatization of hypermetric conflicts in the scherzo of Beethoven's Ninth Symphony, *Nineteenth-Century Music* **15**(3) (1992) 22–40.

[19] R. Cohn, Complex hemiolas, ski-hill graphs and metric spaces, *Music Anal.* **20**(3) (2001) 295–326.
[20] R. Cohn, Why we don't teach meter, and why we should, *J. Music Theory Pedagogy* **29** (2015) 1–19.
[21] R. Cohn, Teaching atonal and beat-class theory, modulo small, *MusMat: Brazilian J. Music Math.* **1**(1) (2016) 15–24.
[22] L. Connell, Z. G. Cai and J. Holler, Do you see what I'm singing? Visuospatial movement biases pitch perception, *Brain Cognition* **81**(1) (2013) 124–130.
[23] C-Thru Music, *The AXiS-49 USB music interface*, (2017), http://www.c-thru-music.com/cgi/?page=prod_axis-49.
[24] S. B. Day and R. L. Goldstone, Analogical transfer from a simulated physical system, *J. Exp. Psychol. Learn. Mem. Cogn.* **37**(3) (2011) 551–567. https://doi.org/10.1037/a0022333.
[25] A. diSessa, *Changing Minds: Computers, Learning, and Literacy* (MIT Press, Cambridge, MA, 2001).
[26] K. M. Douglas and D. K. Bilkey, Amusia is associated with deficits in spatial processing, *Nat. Neurosc.* **10**(7) (2007) 915–921.
[27] T. Fiore and C. Callender, Perfect balance and the discrete Fourier transform, *J. Math. Music* **11**(2) (2017) [Special issue].
[28] A. Friberg and A. Sundström, Swing ratios and ensemble timing in jazz performance: Evidence for a common rhythmic pattern, *Music Percep.* **19**(3) (2002) 333–349.
[29] R. L. Goldstone, D. H. Landy and J. Y. Son, The education of perception, *Top. Cogn. Sci.* **2**(2) (2010) 265–284. https://doi.org/10.1111/j.1756-8765.2009.01055.x.
[30] R. L. Goldstone, T. Marghetis, E. Weitnauer, E. R. Ottmar and D. Landy, Adapting perception, action, and technology for mathematical reasoning, *Curr. Dir. Psychol. Sci.* **26**(5) (2017).
[31] J. Handschin, *Der Toncharakter: Eine Einführung in die Tonpsychologie* (Atlantis, Zurich, 1948).
[32] H. L. F. Helmholtz, *On the Sensations of Tone as a Physiological Basis for the Theory of Music* (Dover, New York, NY, 1877).
[33] D. R. Hofstadter, *Metamagical Themas: Questing for the Essence of Mind and Pattern* (Basic Books, New York, NY, 1985).
[34] S. Holland, Artificial intelligence, education and music Ph.D. thesis, The Open University, Milton Keynes, UK (1989).
[35] S. Holland, Harmony and technology enhanced learning, in *The Routledge Companion to Music, Technology and Education*, eds. A. King, E. Himonides and S. A. Ruthmann (Routledge, New York, NY, 2016), pp. 377–392.
[36] P. Humphreys, The philosophical novelty of computer simulation methods, *Synthese* **169** (2009) 615–626.
[37] M. Ishihara, P. E. Keller, Y. Rossetti and W. Prinz, Horizontal spatial representations of time: Evidence for the STEARC effect, *Cortex* **44**(4) (2008) 454–461.

[38] M. Jacobson, L. Markauskaite, A. Portolese, M. Kapur, P. Lai and G. Roberts, Designs for learning about climate change as a complex system, *Learn. Instr.* **52** (2017) 1–14.
[39] D. Keislar, History and principles of microtonal keyboards, *Comput. Music J.* **11**(1) (1987) 18–28.
[40] P. J. Kellman, C. M. Massey and J. Son, Perceptual learning modules in mathematics: Enhancing students' pattern recognition, structure extraction, and fluency, *Topics Cognitive Sci.* **2** (2010) 285–305.
[41] M. Kline, *Mathematical Thought from Ancient to Modern Times* (Oxford University Press, New York, NY, 1972).
[42] M. Knauff, *Space to Reason: A Spatial Theory of Human Thought* (MIT Press, Cambridge, MA, 2013).
[43] P. Lai, M. Jacobson and L. Markauskaite, Agent-based models versus video-based visualizations to learn nanoscience concepts: An embodied cognition perspective, in *American Educational Research Association (AERA) Annual Meeting*, AERA, Washington, DC, (2016).
[44] G. Lakoff and R. E. Nuñez, *Where Mathematics Comes From: How the Embodied Mind Brings Mathematics Into Being* (Basic Books, New York, NY, 2000).
[45] D. Landy and R. L. Goldstone, How abstract is symbolic thought? *J. Exp. Psychol. Learn. Mem. Cogn.* **33**(4) (2007) 720–733.
[46] D. Lewin, Re: Intervallic relations between two collections of notes, *J. Music Theory* **3**(2) (1959) 298–301.
[47] J. London, Some non-isomorphisms between pitch and time, *J. Music Theory* **46**(1/2) (2002) 127–151.
[48] J. MacRitchie and A. J. Milne, Exploring the effects of pitch layout on learning a new musical instrument, *Appl. Sci.* **7**(12) (2017) 12–18.
[49] O. Messiaen (1944). *Technique de mon Langage Musical.* Leduc, Paris.
[50] E. Mettler and P. J. Kellman, Adaptive response-time-based category sequencing in perceptual learning, *Vision Res.* **99** (2014) 111–123.
[51] A. J. Milne, D. Bulger and S. A. Herff, Exploring the space of perfectly balanced rhythms and scales, *J. Math. Music* **11**(2–3) (2017).
[52] A. J. Milne, D. Bulger, S. A. Herff and W. A. Sethares, Perfect balance: A novel organizational principle for musical scales and meters, in *Mathematics and Computation in Music*, eds. T. Collins, D. Meredith and A. Volk, Lecture Notes in Arificial Intelligence, Vol. 9110 (Springer, Berlin, 2015), pp. 97–108.
[53] A. J. Milne, M. Carlé, W. A. Sethares, T. Noll and S. Holland, Scratching the scale labyrinth, in *Mathematics and Computation in Music*, eds. C. Agon, E. Amiot, M. Andreatta, G. Assayag, J. Bresson and J. Mandereau, Lecture Notes in Artificial Intelligence, Vol. 6726 (Springer, Berlin, 2011), pp. 180–195.
[54] A. J. Milne and R. T. Dean, Computational creation and morphing of multilevel rhythms by control of evenness, *Comput. Music J.* **40**(1) (2016) 35–53.

[55] A. J. Milne, S. A. Herff, D. Bulger, W. A. Sethares and R. T. Dean, XronoMorph: Algorithmic generation of perfectly balanced and well-formed rhythms, in *Proc. 2016 Int. Conf. New Interfaces for Musical Expression (NIME 2016)*, Brisbane, Australia. Griffith University (2016), pp. 388–393.

[56] A. J. Milne and S. Holland, Empirically testing voice-leading, Tonnetz, and spectral models of perceived triadic distance, *J. Math. Music* **10**(1) (2016) 59–85.

[57] A. J. Milne, R. Laney and D. B. Sharp, Testing a spectral model of tonal affinity with microtonal melodies and inharmonic spectra, *Music. Sci.* **20**(4) (2016) 465–494.

[58] A. J. Milne and A. Prechtl, New tonalities with the Thummer and The Viking, in *Proc. 3rd Int. Haptic and Auditory Interaction Design Workshop*, Vol. 2, eds. A. Crossan and T. Kaaresoja, Jyväskylä, Finland (2008), pp. 20–22.

[59] A. J. Milne, W. A. Sethares and J. Plamondon, Tuning continua and keyboard layouts, *J. Math. and Music* **2**(1) (2008) 1–19.

[60] C. B. Monahan, Parallels between pitch and time and how they go together, in *Psychology and Music: The Understanding of Melody and Rhythm*, eds. W. J. Dowling and T. J. Tighe (Lawrence Erlbaum Associates, Hillsdale, NJ, 1993), pp. 121–154.

[61] D. Osberg, G. Biesta and P. Cilliers, From representation to emergence: Complexity's challenge to the epistemology of schooling, *Educ. Philos. Theory* **40**(1) (2008) 213–227.

[62] E. Ottmar and D. Landy, Concreteness fading of algebraic instruction: Effects on learning, *J. Learn. Sci.* **26**(1) (2017) 51–78.

[63] G. Paine, I. Stevenson and A. Pearce, Thummer mapping project (ThuMP) report, in *Proc. 2007 Int. Conf. New Interfaces for Musical Expression (NIME07)*, ed. L. Crawford, (2007), pp. 70–77.

[64] S. Papavlasopoulou, M. Giannakos and M. L. Jaccheri, Empirical studies on the maker movement, a promising approach to learning: A literature review, *Entertainment Comput.* **18** (2017) 57–78.

[65] S. Papert, *Mindstorms: Children, Computers, and Powerful Ideas* (Basic Books, New York, NY, 1980).

[66] S. Papert, *The Children's Machine: Rethinking School in the Age of the Computer* (Basic Books, New York, NY, 1993).

[67] B. Park and D. Gerhard, Rainboard and Musix: Building dynamic isomorphic interfaces, in *Proc. Int. Conf. Interfaces for Musical Expression*, Daejeon, Republic of Korea (2013), pp. 319–324.

[68] A. Prechtl, A. J. Milne, S. Holland, R. Laney and D. B. Sharp, A MIDI sequencer that widens access to the compositional possibilities of novel tunings, *Comput. Music J.* **36**(1), (2012) 42–54.

[69] J. Pressing, Cognitive isomorphisms between pitch and rhythm in world musics: West Africa, the Balkans and Western tonality, *Studies Music* **17** (1983) 38–61.

[70] I. Quinn, General equal-tempered harmony: Parts two and three. *Perspec. New Music* **45**(1) (2006) 4–63.

[71] B. Reiser and I. Tabak, Scaffolding in *The Cambridge Handbook of the Learning Sciences* (Cambridge University Press, Cambridge, 2014).

[72] Roger Linn Design, LinnStrument: A revolutionary expressive musical performance controller, (2017), http://www.rogerlinndesign.com/linnstrument.html.

[73] ROLI, *ROLI — BLOCKS*, (2017), https://roli.com/products/blocks.

[74] W. A. Sethares, A. J. Milne, S. Tiedje, A. Prechtl and J. Plamondon, Spectral tools for dynamic tonality and audio morphing, *Comput. Music J.* **33**(2) (2009) 71–84.

[75] R. N. Shepard, Circularity in judgements of relative pitch, *J. Acous. Soc. Amer.* **36**(12) (1964) 2346–2353.

[76] W. Stroup and U. Wilensky, On the embedded complementarity of agent-based and aggregate reasoning in students' developing understanding of dynamic systems, *Technol. Knowl. Learn.* **19**(1–2) (2014) 19–52.

[77] S. Terpstra and D. Horvath, Terpstra keyboard, (2017), http://terpstra keyboard.com.

[78] G. T. Toussaint, The Euclidean algorithm generates traditional musical rhythms, in *Proc. BRIDGES: Mathematical Connections in Art, Music, and Science* Banff, Alberta, Canada (2005), pp. 47–56.

[79] K. Wicki, (1896). *Tastatur für Musikinstrumente.* Patent, Neumatt (Münster, Luzern, Schweiz).

[80] U. Wilensky, Statistical mechanics for secondary school: The gaslab multi-agent modeling toolkit. *Int. J. Comput. Math. Learn.* **8**(1) (2003) 1–41. https://doi.org/10.1023/A:1025651502936.

[81] U. Wilensky, and S. Papert, Restructurations: Reformulating knowledge disciplines through new representational forms, in *Constructionism Conference Paris* (2010), pp. 1–14.

[82] U. Wilensky and W. Rand, *An Introduction to Agent-Based Modeling: Modeling Natural, Social and Engineered Complex Systems with NetLogo* (MIT Press, Cambridge, MA, 2015).

[83] E. Wilson, Letter to Chalmers pertaining to moments-of-symmetry/Tanabe cycle, (1975), PDF document Retrieved from: http://www.anaphoria.com/mos.pdf.

Chapter 10

Muthsics for Clueless: An Experiment with Euclidean Rhythms

Miguel R. Wilhelmi[*,‡] **and Mariana Montiel**[†,§]

[*]*Department of Mathematics, Public University of Navarre, 31011 Pamplona, Navarre, Spain*
[†]*Department of Mathematics and Statistics, Georgia State University, Atlanta, GA 30303, USA*
[‡]*miguelr.wilhelmi@unavarra.es*
[§]*mmontiel@gsu.edu*

10.1. Introduction

The search for novel ways to transmit mathematical concepts is a constant for pedagogues at all educational levels. In the context of mathematics education, *interdisciplinary experiences* are enjoying growing popularity, especially in terms of the "hard" sciences [7, 25, 26] although there are also reports of the use of the arts in the teaching of mathematics [2, 5, 6, 16, 17]. The use of music, in particular, as a context for mathematics education is not unknown and there is reference to it, especially in relation to primary education, on the one hand, and university mathematics, on the other [2, 14, 19, 21].

"Muthsics" is the intentional combination of "mu-sic" and "(ma)th-s". Music is not a pretext for learning mathematics; we do not try to describe music through mathematical modeling. At least not here, not in the experience that forms the core of the content of this chapter. In our case, music and mathematics walk together as twin brothers, each one contributing with his unique characteristics. The most visceral and intuitive brother (music) challenges the cerebral and Cartesian other (mathematics). The experience detailed in this chapter tried to assess the relations that people with a scientific background establish between mathematics and music, not from a perspective of knowledge or training, but from the intuition and aesthetics as perceived in Euclidean rhythms: *Muthsics* for clueless.

We will report on various study sessions concerning Euclidean rhythms for future mathematics teachers at the secondary level in Spain (FDMS) with a solid technical-scientific background but very little or no background in music. The training sessions relied on the musical intuition of the FDMS, latent and preexisting, and the objective was to model this informal intuition by using concepts, processes, and meanings in agreement with the official school standards that teachers need to comply with.

The chapter is organized in the following way. In Section 10.2 we will explain the musical and mathematical content of the sessions, as well as their interrelations. Section 10.3 describes the theoretical and methodological frameworks used. In Section 10.4 all aspects of the experiment are described, including the sample, the instruments employed and the explicit objectives; in Section 10.5, the results are presented and discussed. Finally, specific conclusions are established and some implications for teaching are offered. In Sections 10.2 and 10.4 specific exercises are put forward in detail, with the hope that they can serve as didactical material in future courses, as well as tools that will permit the repetition of the experiment, contributing to the establishment of *muthsics* content in the training of future secondary level teachers.

10.2. Mathematical and Musical Content

We will begin with a brief description of the mathematical content included and how the musical rhythms were employed to enhance teaching. It is worth underlining that much of the theoretical underpinnings and connections have been developed by academicians interested in this subject [4, 12, 29]. At the end of this section we will show how this content relates to the school standards.

The subjects included can be grouped into three general categories as follows:

(1) Euclid's lemma and Euclid's algorithm, maximal evenness and Euclidean rhythms.
(2) Clapping music and cyclic permutations.
(3) Automation of Euclidean rhythms and mathematical calculations such as the greatest common divisor of two natural numbers.

The first category revolves around the quotient–remainder theorem, also known as Euclid's division lemma. This theorem formalizes ideas and techniques that are learned during the first years of primary school, and recasts them at the secondary level, where they are generalized to polynomials. It goes without mention the importance role that this theorem plays in abstract algebra, for students who will study mathematics at the university level, or of its presence in the teaching of programming languages.

Euclid's lemma establishes the following: Given four integers a, b, q and r, such that $a = b \times q + r$, if an integer d is a divisor of a and b then it is also a divisor of r. To justify this proposition it can be observed that if d is a divisor of a and b, there exist two integers a' and b' such that $a = a' \times d$ and $b = b' \times d$, hence:

$$r = a - b \times q = a' \times d - b' \times d \times q = d \times (a' - b' \times q).$$

Euclid's algorithm, based on this lemma, determines the greatest common divisor of two numbers by means of a repeated application of Euclidean division, in which the remainder becomes the divisor in the following stage. When a remainder of zero is finally obtained, the greatest common divisor is seen to be the next to last remainder, that is, the remainder that appears immediately before the stage in which the remainder is zero. For example, to determine that the greatest common divisor of 30 and 8 is 2 ($\text{GCD}(30, 8) = 2$), one proceeds as indicated in Table 10.1.

This algorithm can repeat itself as many times as necessary and, in fact, it is easily programmed on a spreadsheet, which itself becomes a dynamical instrument where it is only necessary to define the

Table 10.1. Calculating the GCD(30,8) = 2.

Division		1st	2nd	3rd
Dividend/divisor	30	8	6	**2**
Quotient		3	1	3
Remainder		6	**2**	0

Table 10.2. Calculating the GCD(8670, 5440) = 170.

Division			1st	2nd	3rd	4th	5th
		A	B	C	D	E	**F**
Dividend/divisor	1	8670	5440	$3230^{(3)}$	$2210^{(6)}$	1020	**170**
Quotient	2		$1^{(1)}$	$1^{(4)}$	$1^{(6)}$	2	6
Remainder	3		$3230^{(2)}$	$2210^{(5)}$	$1020^{(6)}$	**170**	0

Key: (1) = INT(A1/B1); (2) = A1 − B2 ∗ B1; (3) = B3; (4) = INT(B1/C1); (5) = B1 − C2 ∗ C1; (6) To obtain the values of the columns D, E and F, one only needs to select and drag the cells C1, C2 and C3.

initial values "Dividend / divisor" to generate the result given in Table 10.2.

The notion of *maximal evenness* arose in mathematical music theory. The diatonic scale with seven notes (the white keys of the piano can serve as a prototype) is distributed as evenly as possible in the 12-note chromatic scale. Indeed, the concept of maximally even can address the question of why the black and white notes are distributed on the piano keyboard the way they are found. This same idea can be applied to rhythm. If there are twelve pulses, how can seven strong beats be distributed to mark the rhythm (Fig. 10.1). The rhythms in which the strong beats are distributed in a maximally even way are known as *Euclidean rhythms* [28].

The second general topic consists of the analysis of cyclic rhythms. The cyclic permutations were motivated by Steve Reich's Clapping Music [27]. There are a number of graphical attempts to

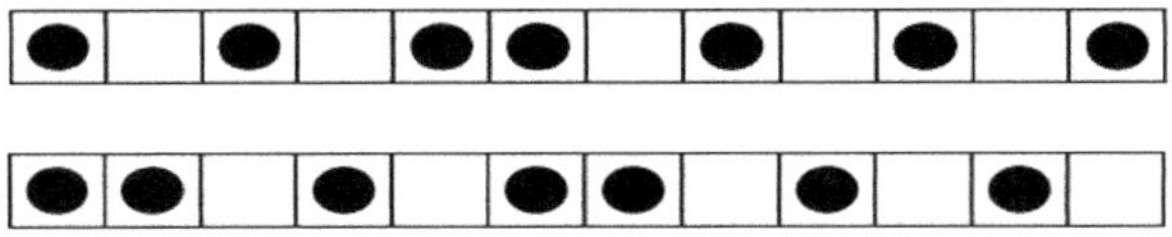

Fig. 10.1. Two rotations of the maximally even distribution of seven strong beats in twelve pulses.

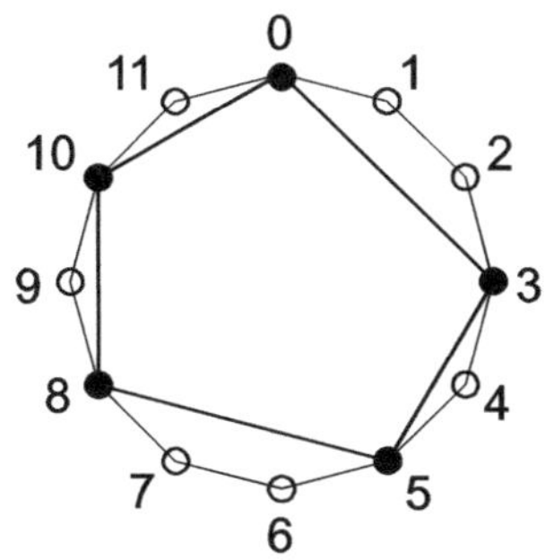

Fig. 10.2. A cyclic rhythm represented on the circumference of a circle.

visualize Clapping Music as well that include groups of people clapping (https://youtu.be/eu-tRXgOrdg), or electronic interpretation (https://youtu.be/45oY-rA9vvw).

As a rhythm can always be represented by points on the circumference of a circle (Fig. 10.2), the geometry of isometries was a perfect subject, together with combinatory concepts.

There are antecedents of the use of this piece in a pedagogical context [13] at the university level, given the notions of group theory and combinatory that can be illustrated with the pattern chosen to create the rhythm. In effect, as the pattern rotates and the phases change, a series of intertwined rhythms are created together with a great rhythmic variety. These variations create symmetries due the fact that once the pattern is defined the rules are very rigid; any other pattern chosen would not create the same aesthetic effect.

The third general topic consists of the automation of the Euclidean rhythms and calculations, such as the greatest common divisor of two natural numbers. For example, in the context of mathematical music theory, the idea was to generalize to other numbers of relatively prime sets and subsets, and to look for new scales that would maintain some of the best properties of the traditional scale. In terms of rhythm, it has been seen that the most common world rhythms are Euclidean rhythms [29] and, on the other hand, since their discovery as such in 2005, composers and improvising musicians have shown an interest in incorporating them in their production, and there has been a proliferation of software due to this motivation [15, Synthopia, http://www.synthtopia.com/content/tag/euclidean-rhythms/].

In the mathematical context, there is growing interest for the incorporation of automatized procedures that mimic classical calculations; this interest has encouraged a constant development of programming languages and software for numerical and symbolic calculations. Indeed, computation and programming have been incorporated into the classification of mathematical areas [1].

Along with the growing interest for computer science and programming, classical mathematical contents that were developed without information resources are substituted more and more for topics in mathematics that can be linked to the computer (*maths by computer*). This perspective covers the learning stages at all levels, not only the university. The six principles for School Mathematics according to the NCTM (http://www.nctm.org) are: Equity, Curriculum, Teaching, Learning, Assessment and Technology. Technology determines, whether we like it or not, not only how to teach, but what to teach. The relation of students with mathematics through technology, and the possibilities and limitations of this approach, modify the mathematical horizon and affects the cognitive development of the student.

> "Technology is essential in teaching and learning mathematics; it influences the mathematics that is taught and enhances students' learning". Furthermore, students can develop deeper understanding of mathematics with the appropriate use of technology. Technology can help support investigation by students in every area of mathematics and allow them to focus on decision-making, reflection, reasoning, and problem solving. The existence, versatility, and power of technology make it possible and necessary to reexamine

> what mathematics students should learn as well as how they can best learn it". [24, p. 3]

Indeed, the key position granted to technology in teaching and learning has motivated that programs such as Scratch (https://scratch.mit.edu/) or GeoGebra (https://www.geogebra.org/) be implemented from the preschool to the university levels. Another development in this vein is the extended use of spreadsheets in the teaching of statistics, in the analysis of data, and in the marking of tendencies or simulations, which has become more common every day.

10.3. Theoretical and Methodological Framework

It is interesting to take into account the two extreme philosophical positions towards mathematics, that is: new mathematics are created or they are discovered. It seems evident that there should be a middle ground in this debate but it would be out-of-place here to pursue it. Strangely enough, there are musicians who have proposed that music itself, together with mathematics, has its own existence. Johnson [18] remembers the warning that his professor, Morton Feldman, gave him time and again: "Let the music do what it wants to do".

Johnson [18] gives examples of musicians (John Cage, Morton Feldman, Steve Reich, Pauline Oliveros, Alvin Lucier, Paul Panhuyen, Jerry Hunt, Julius and Marcel Duchamps) that share his search for "available" music that "only" needs someone to notice it and make it flourish.

> "I must hasten to add that music which is 'found' is not usually found easily. I know from experience, and I suspect that all the people I have mentioned would agree, that it often takes much longer to find a good piece than to compose one". [18, p. 3]

This search, for Johnson [18], will find an "absolute" dimension when using mathematical models, logical number sequences, sets of permutations, etc., given that, when arriving to a certain point, the piece is inevitable, much like a big funnel that converges to a necessary rhythm. This is what we refer to and name in our present study funnel music.

> "The Rational Melodies were completely written out, yet there was a relentless logic in each one. After a few bars, the sequence had begun, the rules were clear, and the rest of the piece was inevitable [...] I did have to make a few subjective choices when I selected scales, and when I decided how long to let things go on, but basically I was just writing down interesting things that I happened to find". [18, p. 4]

Under what conditions is musical creation compatible with the teaching of mathematics? To what measure is it possible to balance the impact in the two disciplines (music and mathematics) without one being subject to the other? Is it possible to carry out an interdisciplinary experience that enriches the knowledge and interest in both disciplines?

Johnson [18] arrives to the conclusion that musical pleasure is not truncated if "creation" is substituted for "search", even when that creation is the result of an inevitable generation following mathematical patterns. "One could say that I had become merely a machine, but it was a very agreeable experience" (p. 5). Indeed, Johnson explicitly renounces musical control in some of his works and resorts to computer programming, concluding that human intervention is not always necessary from the musical point of view nor from the perspective of satisfaction, taste, and personal inclination.

> "[On the project Pascal's Triangle Modulo Seven], I gave up personal control even more than before, in the sense that I decided to allow my computer to play the music without me [...] And it was perhaps the success of these arrangements that convinced me that human performance would not be necessary here". [18, p. 5]

How can we bring these creative experiences to schools and make them compatible with the established curriculum? How can we involve students in a *muthsics* project when in Secondary Education there exists a disciplinary organization, which overrides certain proposals? How can we involve teachers without advanced studies in mathematics or in music and those with monolithic training in one of the disciplines? Under what conditions is it possible to propose these projects in a controlled and evaluable manner for schools?

The Onto-Semiotic Approach of mathematical knowledge and mathematical instruction (OSA) [8] contributes with theoretical tools to address these questions. On the one hand, the OSA establishes an ontology of objects: language, situations, definitions, propositions, procedures and arguments. On the other hand, according to the agents that move them and the meaning that is assigned to them, the concrete appearance of these objects and the reference to ideal entities and their contextual and relational functions with other mathematical objects, the OSA establish five dual dimensions: (1) personal/institutional; (2) ostensive/non-ostensive (or sensible/ideal); (3) intensive/extensive (or exemplar/type; particular/general); (4) unitary/systemic; (5) expression/content. "These dual dimensions demonstrate how the primary entities must not be understood in an isolated manner, but according to their function and their relation in a contextualized mathematical activity" [23, p. 142].

(1) *Language* (terms, expressions, notations, graphics, etc.), which includes natural language, mathematical language and, in our case, musical language, where students must learn the names of the terms (time span, pulses, notes, rests, rhythm, piece, musical variations, timelines) and receive a succinct musical alphabetization. The duality expression/content plays an important role here given that one of the foreseen difficulties was that of relating mathematical and musical content, and their identification in diverse expressions.
(2) *Situations* (problems, extra or intra-mathematical applications, exercises, etc.). Here the crucial extra-mathematical application refers to music. There is also the intra-mathematical aspect that allows progress through the activities and, of course, the interdisciplinary aspect in general. Furthermore, the institutional compartmentalization of the different disciplines imposes specific pedagogical intervention, which should take into account the

unitary/systemic duality that avoids atomization of personal learning.

(3) *Definitions* (number, point, straight line, mean, function, etc.), not as a "measure" of the object, but as a contextualized description. In our case the interpretation of mathematical definitions in musical terms, devoid of formal language, demands the dualities ostensive/non-ostensive and expression/content. This is because the mathematical definitions are translated to musical terminology and these dualities specify the differences between the material (and the senses) on the one hand, and the idealization on the other hand.

(4) *Propositions, properties or attributes*, which are often given as statements and that allow the establishment of relations between the notions. Our interest, above all, consists of determining the mathematical–musical relations that articulate the progress in both disciplines and permit a systemic view (duality unitary/systemic).

(5) *Procedures or subjects' actions* when solving mathematical tasks (operations, algorithms, techniques, procedures). These tasks are related to the musical component and, for this reason, the intention is to generalize to contexts that originally were not considered (intensive/extensive).

(6) *Arguments* used to validate and explain the propositions or to contrast (justify or refute) the subjects' actions. Given the low level of the students' musical training, the reasoning is empirical and intuitive, focused upon personal cognitive development more than on the acquisition of previously fixed institutional content. However, given that the personal progress is subject to intentional didactical situations planned for group progress, we look for a balance between the personal and institutional dimensions; understood, of course, as a shared educational project.

Finally, the study process should be evaluated. The didactic suitability [9, 10] describes the workings and the control of the didactic system in function of the dimensions: epistemic-ecological, cognitive-affective and institutional-mediational.

- Epistemic-ecological suitability: adaptation of the proposed activities, which can be carried out with the institutional meaning used as a reference.
- Cognitive-affective suitability: adaptation of the institutional meaning that will be implemented so as to find beforehand, within the students' capacity, the personal meaning, as well as the search for some emotional identification that can enhance the activity to be developed.
- Institutional-mediational suitability: pertains to the interventions and interactions of the students (future teachers) in their work in pairs for the evolution of the study process, depending upon the material resources and the availability in time.

Finally, given that the mathematical knowledge has a very concrete context, it will be necessary to evaluate the capacity that students have to use mathematical language to solve or interpret situations in a musical context, that is, if the progress in that activity implies a flexible adaptation of the personal meaning.

> "[Flexible mathematical thinking is defined] as the action carried by a subject that allows the routine transition among the different models associated with a mathematical object, recognizing the specific limitations of each one of them; furthermore, flexible mathematical thinking lets the subject establish solid links between the models and one or more mathematical contexts, allowing him to establish an efficient control of the activity and capacitating the subject to assume mathematical responsibility of the results he produces". [30, p. 72]

All the above motivates situations in which mathematics and music are articulated and can be, on the one hand, presented in an intelligible way to the teachers and, on the other, respond to the demands of the curriculum (or of innovation) in the schools. Montiel and Wilhelmi [22] establish that "it is necessary to carry out studies that really inform about the conditions that allow the reproduction of situations which will guarantee that the designated institutional meaning (mathematical and musical) will be acquired" (p. 9). The following experiment is an attempt to respond to this necessity.

10.4. Experimentation

10.4.1. *Context and sample*

Candidates for secondary school (12–20 years old) teaching in Spain, both in the mandatory cycle (12–16 years old) as well as in the pre-university (17–18 years old) or in the vocational training programs,[a] should pursue a Master's degree in Teaching at the Secondary Level [20], which lasts one year and consists of 60 ECTS.[b] This Masters is a professional requisite, that is, it is not possible to teach at the secondary level without this degree.

The structure of this Masters takes into account a general module, common to all the specializations, with an emphasis on educational psychology and sociology in a pedagogical context, as well as a specific disciplinary didactic module (Mathematics, Biology and Geology, Physics, Chemistry, Language Arts, Foreign Languages, etc.) The general module is usually composed of approximately 15 ECTS (25%) and the specific didactical area of 45 ECTS (75%), which include educational practicum in the classes corresponding to the curricular content and a monographic work in the didactical area (the End of Master work).

The applicants to the Master's program must have a Bachelor's degree. The students who opt for the specialization in Mathematics come from different backgrounds: Bachelor's degrees in Engineering, Physics, Mathematics or, less commonly, in Architecture or Economics, and these last solicitants must present specific subject exam.

---

[a]The two technical diplomas are given at the high school level (17–18 years old) and the associates' degree level (19–20 years old).

[b]ECTS is a learner-centered system for credit accumulation and transfer, based on the principle of transparency of the learning, teaching and assessment processes. ECTS credits express the volume of learning based on the defined learning outcomes and their associated workload. 60 ECTS credits are allocated to the learning outcomes and associated workload of a full-time academic year. In most cases, workload ranges from 1500 to 1800 hours for an academic year, which means that one credit corresponds to 25 to 30 hours of work (ECTS Users' Guide, http://ec.europa.eu/education/ects/users-guide/).

The specialization sessions are usually carried out in small groups, with a maximum of 15 or 20 students, although this varies according to the university. We used two courses in our experiment with students specializing in the Master's in Mathematics: 13 students all together; 6 and 7 per course, respectively. The majority were engineers (8); two had studied architecture, one had studied economics at the undergraduate level, one physics, and one mathematics. The distribution by sex was: 8 women and 5 men (Table 10.3).

10.4.2. *Instruments, premises and objectives*

Before carrying out the activities the students answered a brief survey about their musical training (Fig. 10.3).

The survey offers a specific idea with respect to the musical training (questions 1, 2 and 3) and with respect to habits and taste (questions 4, 5 and 6). Musical education in Spain at the primary level (6–12 years old) has occupied a limited space in the curriculum. As a general rule it includes a minimal alphabetization in musical language, listening to musical works, and the interpretation

Table 10.3. Student distribution by training and sex.

School year	Total	W	M	Engin	Archi	Maths	Phys	Eco
1st	6	4	2	4	1	–	–	1
2nd	7	4	3	4	1	1	1	–

Key: W: Women; M: Men; Engin: Engineering; Archi: Architecture; Maths: Mathematics; Phys: Physics; Eco: Economics.

1. Have you received musical training at school? (Yes/No)
2. If you have received musical training at school, have you played an instrument? (Yes/No) Which one?
3. Do you have musical training outside of school? (Yes/No) Explain?
4. Do you listen to music? (Every day/Frequently/Sporadically/Almost never)
5. What type of music do you listen to?
6. When you listen to music do you like to hum along or keep the rhythm with your feet, hands or body?

Fig. 10.3. Initial survey.

of simple children's and popular pieces, generally on the recorder. In spite of the no-mandatory nature of artistic training (including musical training) in the curriculum [3], the majority of regional administrations have proposed strategies to maintain its presence, within their sphere of competency.

Thus the premise is that all students receive some musical training at school, but presently they are only consumers. It is assumed that the students have solid scientific-technical training, but little musical training and, in this area, they are inexpert (*muthsics for clueless*). The objective is to assess the musical intuition of subjects without the prejudices inherent to previous technical or academic training in music.

After the brief survey a sequence of activities was initiated and distributed in two sessions of 1 hour 45 minutes each, which alternated individual answers to proposed tasks with the collective discussion of their musical and mathematical content, as well as their relation to the school curriculum and the present tendencies concerning Secondary Education students and how they can acquire the knowledge and the skills mandated in the general program requirements. The sequence of activities of session 1, with the amount of time dedicated to each activity, the "discipline" (mathematics, music, or *muthsics*), and the organization of the study process (independent learning, dialogic teaching, plenary class, participant interaction), is presented in Table 10.4.

Activities 1 and 2 have two different intentions: on the one hand, according to the affective dimension, we want the students to feel confident and, for this reason, the tasks are related to their area of expertise. On the other hand, and according to the ecological dimension, we should emphasize the difference between their technical knowledge (calculation of the GCD through arithmetic procedures) and the content (the GCD as the possibility of common groupings of two quantities) which condition the management of the study processes and the implementation of the curriculum.

The musical terms, necessary for a common intelligible discourse for all participants, are introduced in activity 3: time span, pulses, notes, rests, rhythm, piece, musical variations, timelines. These terms

Table 10.4. Session 1: Sequence of activities.

Activity	Time (min)	Focus discipline	Organization
S1.1. The greatest common divisor (GCD) can be obtained by forming groups. Show this procedure, calculating as simply as possible, the GCD(16, 12)	5	Maths	Independent learning
S1.2. Euclid's lemma and Euclid's algorithm for calculating the greatest common divisor of two natural numbers. They also analyze the relation between graphical calculation of the GCD and the standard numerical calculation (factoring prime numbers)	20	Maths	Dialogic teaching
S1.3. Familiarization with musical terms: time span, pulses, notes, rests, rhythm, piece, musical variations, timelines	30	Music	Plenary class
S1.4. Examples with clapping or striking the table using different timelines with different lengths in terms of number of pulses or notes/rests	35	Music	Participant interaction
S1.5. The time period is divided in 12 pulses. It represents a rhythm as "even" as possible, with 4 notes (•) and 8 rests (—) (see Fig 10.4)	40	Music	Independent learning
S1.6. The time period is divided in 12 pulses. It represents a rhythm as "even" as possible, with 5 notes (•) and 7 rests (—)	45	Music	Independent learning
S1.7. Representative flamenco rhythms with 12 pulses: fandango (4 notes and 8 rests) and soleá, bulería, seguiriya and guajira (5 notes and 7 rests)	55	Music	Participant interaction

(*Continued*)

Table 10.4. (*Continued*)

Activity	Time (min)	Focus discipline	Organization
S1.8. The time period is divided in 12 pulses. It represents a rhythm as "even" as possible, with 8 notes (•) and 4 rests (—). Once you have found a rhythm, try to show one that preserves regularity ("evenness")	65	*Muthsics*	Independent learning
S1.9. What methods have been used to obtain the rhythms?	75	*Muthsics*	Participant interaction
S1.10. If we want to play 7 notes and apply the principle of maximal evenness in a time period of 12 pulses, a resulting rhythm could be: •—•—••—•—•—• Is it possible to find other rhythms?	85	*Muthsics*	Independent learning
S1.11. Technique for the determination of Euclidean rhythms through the grouping technique of pulses (1) and rests (0)	100	*Muthsics*	Dialogic teaching

are exemplified in activity 4 with a dynamic of clapping or striking the table; the different timelines have different lengths in terms of number of pulses or notes/rests (Fig 10.4).

This dynamic seeks both the understanding of the musical content (epistemic dimension), and the lack of inhibition that will contribute to more creative dynamics that improve the clause of the *didactic contract* [11] according to which all classroom activities can be reflected in the summative evaluation (interactive dimension).

In activities 5 and 6 the students produced rhythms of 12 pulses (4 notes and 8 rests, or 5 notes and 7 rests, respectively). They were

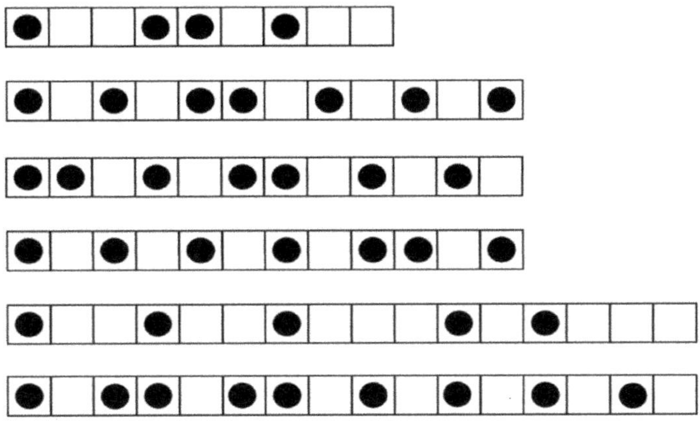

Fig. 10.4. Timelines with different lengths in terms of number of pulses or notes/rests.

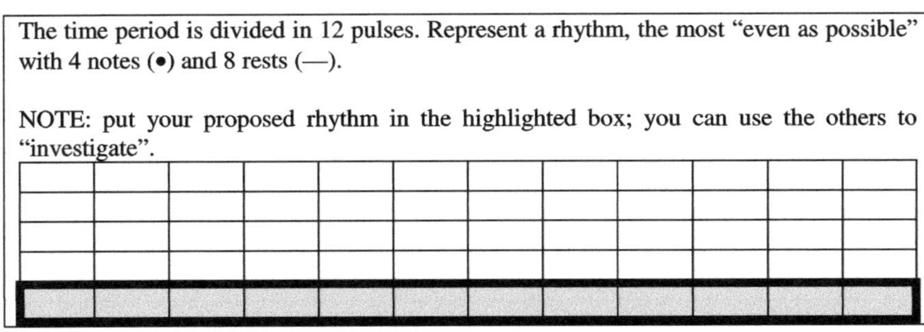

Fig. 10.5. Search for rhythms.

given a grid to facilitate an empirical search (Fig. 10.5). The idea was to anticipate flamenco rhythms that would be described and clapped in the following activity 7 (*fandango, soleá, bulería, seguiriya* and *guajira*). These rhythms exemplify the fact that the answers given by the students to activities 5 and 6 cannot be classified according to criteria of “correctness” but of “taste”.

In activity 8 the students, “on the march”, were to apply the notion of “evenness”. It was assumed that they would use musical or technical criteria, but that mathematical knowledge would not play a role in the activity, that is, they would not search for an algorithm based on the principles of maximal evenness and Euclid's algorithm.[c]

In activity 9, apart from sharing the results obtained, the idea is to establish the difficulties that arise when making analogies and generalizations to other contexts different from those of the original results. Hence, it is necessary to introduce the formal notion of "maximal evenness" that arises as the solution to a mathe-musical problem, but still without specifying the procedure that allows the calculation. Activity 10 is designed to execute this notion (Fig. 10.6).

Finally, in the plenary session, the technique for the calculating Euclidean rhythms by grouping pulses (1) and rests (0) is introduced, as a solution to a musical and social (to systematize and better comprehend the solutions given by classmates) necessity. To arrive, we begin with rhythms whose division is evident and eventually

The time period is divided in 12 pulses. Represent an "even" rhythm with 8 notes (•) and 4 rests (—). Once you have found the rhythm, try to give another one that preserves evenness.

NOTE: in the first highlighted box put your proposed rhythm; in the second highlighted one put, if it exists, another rhythm that preserves evenness. Use the other boxes to "investigate".

Fig. 10.6. The search for even rhythms, starting from a first one already found.

[c]The search for efficiency in carrying out a task is a crucial aspect in the learning process and progress from the earliest age. For example, children 4–5 years old, to "set the table", should arrive to the conclusion that counting the plates before taking them to the table is more efficient than taking them one by one, thereby establishing a guest-plate correspondence or, eventually, the idea of "multiplication as an abbreviated sum".

Table 10.5. Session 2: Sequence of activities.

Activity	Time (min.)	Focus subject	Organization
S2.1. Programming with Texas Instruments 81 (TI-81): manipulation of the calculator and identifying commands	5	Maths	Plenary class
S2.2 Editing simple programs, ones which the students consider relevant	20	Maths	Work out by pairs, with support from the teacher
S2.3. Common setting: difficulties and solutions	35	Maths	Dialogic teaching
S2.4. Program for calculating the GCD	55	Maths	Work out by pairs
S2.5. Program analysis of the efficiency of the two programs	70	Maths	Dialogic teaching
S2.5a. What do the permutations of the syllables of the words "ma-the-ma-tics "and "mu-sic" alphabetically ordered, without repetition, (only one "ma") sound like? S2.5b. Information about the nature of the music (title, artist, genre, tempo, description), aesthetic assessment of the result, and appropriateness for inclusion in Secondary Education	105	*Muthsics*	• Work out by pairs, with support from the teacher • Work out by pairs (homework), to finish the activity

propose a task that requires deeper analysis: "in a 12-pulse time span, form a 12-note rhythm, form a 4-note rhythm, form a 6-note rhythm, etc. How to do an 8-note rhythm in a fixed 12-pulse time span?"

In the second session, the activity is less dense (Table 10.5). The number of activities is reduced given that they will consist of, essentially, two programming activities: first, the calculation of the greatest common multiple with the programmable calculator Texas Instruments 81; the second consists in obtaining a "musical" piece automatically by generation of all possible permutations of the syllables of the words "ma-the-ma-tics "and "mu-sic" ordered alphabetically without repetition (only one "ma").

Programming is a "natural" solution to curriculum demands with respect to the use of technology, as mentioned in Section 10.2 (ecological dimension). In the case of musical programming, the importance of this solution increases, as it responds to the interdisciplinary aspect as well, and to the creation of reusable materials in Secondary Education that will allow the establishment of curriculum exploiting the relation between mathematics and music (interactive dimension).

Situation 5, which supposes "musical creation", is carried out in three steps, all with free software that is available in the vast majority of computers:

(1) Calculation of all permutation ordered alphabetically of the syllables: "ma", "mu", "the", "tics" and "sic".
(2) Reproduction of the permutations in Google Translate and the downloading of audios with the complement Flashgot from Mozilla Firefox, which produces audios with a maximum of 17s.
(3) Concatenation of the audios with some program, to obtain a unique track that reproduces the 120 permutations (the 600 syllables).

All the permutations can be obtained "by hand". This is not very efficient. Excel can be used to arrange and order the presentation in the computer, which is necessary for the reproduction with Google Translate. In the context of the Masters degree it is also possible to produce the sequence with the software R (https://www.r-project.org/). In Fig. 10.7 the way of obtaining all the permutations is indicated, with two possible orderings as a 120×5 matrix or as a unidimensional vector.

Six audios were generated. The audios were classified in two groups; within each group, the difference is the tempo. Group 1 is the result of the alphabetic ordering of the syllables of the words "ma-the-(ma)-tics" and "mu-sic", with only one "ma", and interpreting the result as a sequence of syllables structured in a 120×5 matrix. The tempo changes as the syllables appear between

```
permutations <- function(n){
 if(n==1){
 return(matrix(1))
 } else {
 a <- permutations(n-1)
 b <- nrow(a)
 P <- matrix(nrow=n*b,ncol=n)
 for(i in 1:n){
 P[(i-1)*b+1:b,] <- cbind(i,a+(a>=i))
 }
 return(P)  }}
muthsics<-c("ma","mu","the","tics","sic")
A<-matrix(muthsics[permutations(5)],ncol=5)
A # permutations ordered as a 120x5 matrix
x<-as.vector(A)
x # permutations ordered as a vector
```

Fig. 10.7. Obtaining of the permutations of the syllables “ma”, “mu”, “the”, “tics” and “sic” with R.

quotation marks, without quotation marks, or with the elimination of spaces (that is, as one 600 character word), each time with more acceleration. Group 2 is also the result of ordering the same syllables but in a vector with 600 components, resulting from the ordering of the columns of the 120×5 matrix. In this case three tracks are produced, with tempo in crescendo.

10.5. Results and Discussion

The preliminary survey about musical training, and habits and taste (Fig. 10.3) corroborate that the students' musical training is very limited. All students, except one, had some musical training at the school level and played the recorder; in two cases the students also had played regional popular music, with simple wind or percussion instruments. Four students received instruction at a music school or individual instrumental classes as an extracurricular activity during one or two years when children.

However, the majority of the students listen to music every day, or frequently. Only two students said they listen to music sporadically or almost never. However, they do not have defined taste, given that they use expressions such as “I listen to different types of music”, "whatever I hear on the radio", "pop-rock"... Although they do identify the types of music that they do not like ("I listen to all music except techno or latin-pop") or that they are not accustomed to listening to ("all types, except classical music that, although I like it, I almost never listen to it"). Finally, those that listen to music on a regular basis admit that they usually follow the music with gestures (feet or hands) or sounds (humming or whistling).

10.5.1. *First session*

The students carried out the activities of sessions 1 and 2; hence, the experiment never came to a standstill. In the first activity of session 1 the objective was to determine the GCD(16,12) by graphical methods, and 11 of the 14 students actually did so (Fig. 10.8a). The other three worked exclusively with the familiar arithmetic method of factoring and ignored the instruction. There were also two students who combined the graphing method with arithmetic calculations; one of them just to check his work, and the other relied on the arithmetic calculation and used the graphing method as an "explanation" (Fig. 10.8b).

The fact that five students used the conventional arithmetic method to calculate the GCD, either as the only algorithm or accompanied by graphical methods, is an indicator of how difficult it is to adjust the procedures to restrictions that modify the familiar context in which they are usually carried out. That is why, in activity 2, the Euclidean algorithm is explained, together with the graphical procedure of calculating the greatest common divisor by successive groupings. This regulatory moment guarantees that the whole class shares the same knowledge, but does not avoid the difficulty of translating this knowledge into a method of determining maximally even rhythms in the activities that follow.

As will be seen, there is a semiotic conflict in the generalization of the mathematical procedure to the musical context.

Activities 3 and 4 are of a different nature:

- *Epistemological.* To familiarize the students with the musical terms (time span, pulses, notes, rests, rhythm, piece, musical variations, timelines).

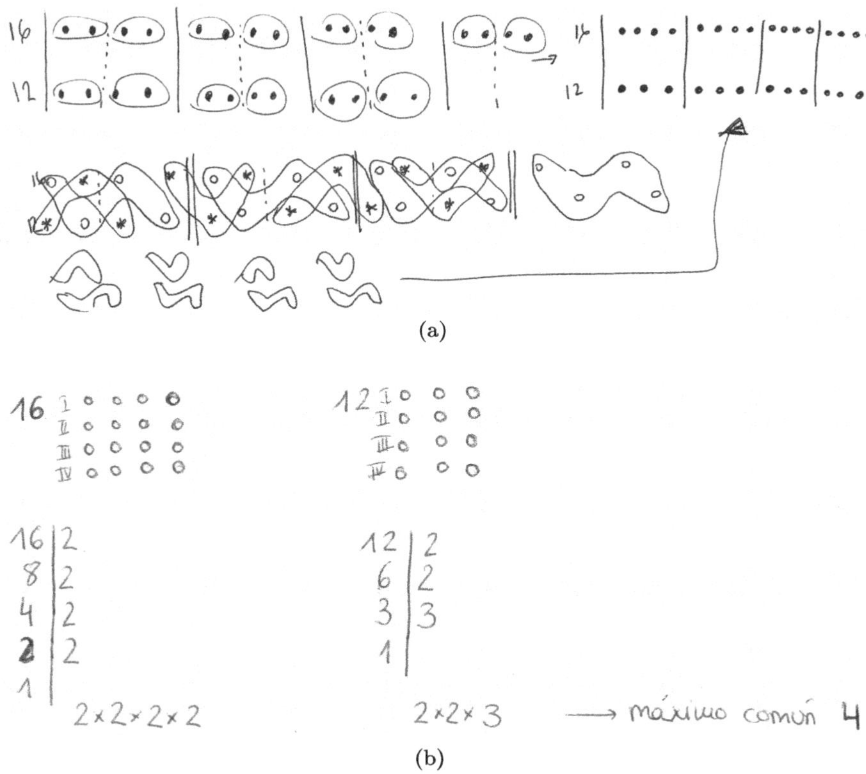

Fig. 10.8. Calculation of the GCD(16,12) using graphical methods.

- *Interactional.* To be able to share a language, intelligible for everyone, that allows communication and shared production of results.
- *Cognitive.* To generate the conditions for autonomous work during the following activities.
- *Affective.* Activity 4, in which the students play timelines of different lengths by clapping or tapping on the table, contributes to disinhibit the participants and prepare them for a creative activity that is not limited to the pedagogical norm in which the activities are designed to form part of the cumulative sum leading to the final grade.

Thus, activities 3 and 4 set the stage for the implementation of activities 5 and 6, in which the students work on their own.

In activity 5, in which the students should determine a rhythm as "even as possible" with 4 notes (•) and 8 rests (—), only 6 of 14 students proposed an "even" rhythm of 4 groupings formed by 2 rests and 1 note, indeed a Euclidean rhythm. The others proposed different rhythms by following geometric criteria of spatial distribution of the notes and rests. In all the cases, the rhythms are assumed as "circular" in the sense that they should be played periodically, from left to right and, once the timeline ends, the rhythm should be repeated.

The proposed rhythms are formed by a longitudinal characteristic (the repetition of a pattern) or by symmetry with respect to the center (6 pulses "to the left" and 6 pulses "to the right"). In Table 10.6 all the proposed rhythms are shown, together with the

Table 10.6. Rhythms proposed by the students, as "even as possible" (4 notes, •; 8 rest, —).

CAT	CUF	Rhythm	N°	G	Total
A	L	[• — —][• — —][• — —][• — —]	5	C	6
		[— — •][— — •][— — •][— — •]	1		
C	CS	[— • — — — •][• — — — • —]	2	C&P	3
		[• — — — • —][— • — — — •]	1		
B	CS	[— — • • — —][— — • • — —]	1	C	2
	L	[• • — — — —][• • — — — —]	1		
D	SE	[— — — •] — — • • [• — — —]	1	U	1
E	LRP	[— • — •] — — • • [— • — •]	1	Not	2
		— — — • [— — • •][— — • •]	1		

Key: CAT: Category; CUF: Characteristic used in forming; L: Longitudinal; CS: Central Symmetry; SE: Symmetry at the extremes; LRP: Longitudinal, with a maximum of repeated patterns; G: Grouping; C: Circular; P: Permutation; U: Unique; Not: Does not respond to the proposed rhythm.

indication of the characteristic used in forming them, grouped in five categories.

The proposals for these rhythms (Table 10.6) were the result of several attempts that neither in the written work, nor in the oral presentations that followed, included procedures such as Euclidean division or the calculations of the GCD. Indeed, all the rhythms were obtained by trial and error (Fig. 10.9). The difficulty of proceeding with flexible mathematical thinking is manifest, as it is this feature that would have allowed the adaptation of this recently emphasized mathematical knowledge to new contexts.

In activity 6, where the students should determine a rhythm as "even as possible" with 5 notes (•) and 7 rests (—), the positioning of the rhythm is more complicated, given that 7 is not divisible by 5 and, consequently, distributing the notes by trial and error is a poor option. The distribution technique that produces "maximal evenness" follows from the graphical calculation of the GCD and gives the rhythm in which there are no two notes that follow one after the other, that is, the notes are separated by one or two rests (Fig. 10.10).

Only one student proposed this rhythm by positioning the notes "sufficiently spread out", with a pattern of longitude 5 (two times) in

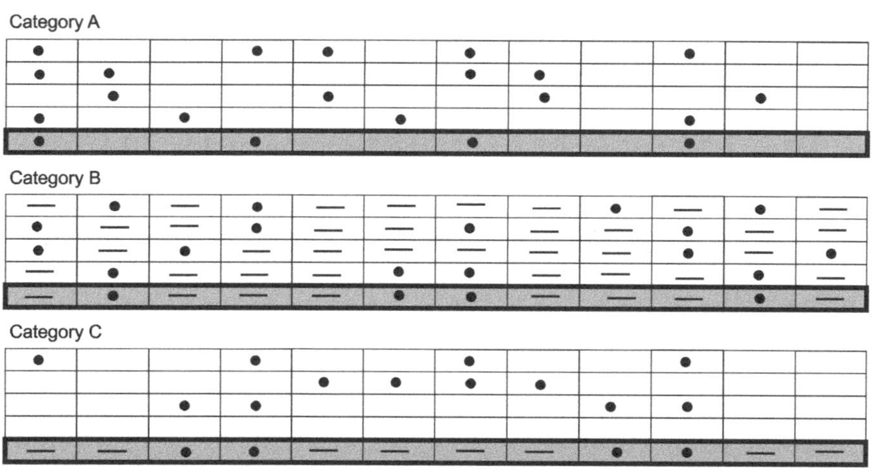

Fig. 10.9. Determining the "maximally even" rhythms (4 notes, •; 8 rests, —).

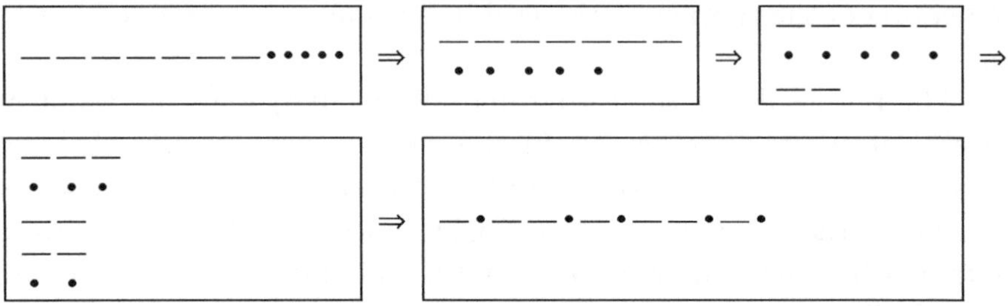

Fig. 10.10. Determining the "maximally even" rhythm (5 notes, •; 7 rests, —).

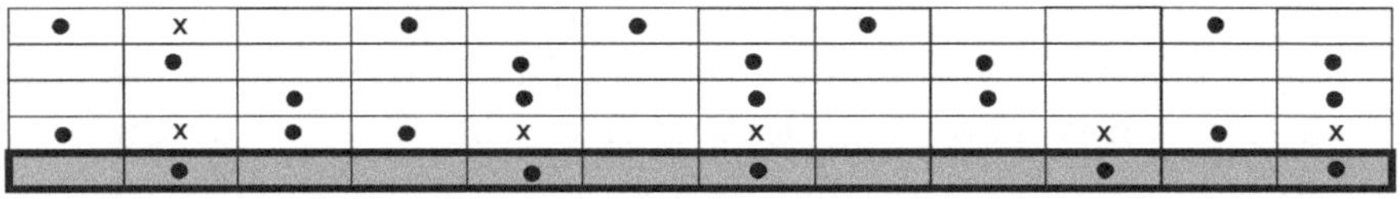

Fig. 10.11. The "maximally even" rhythm (5 notes, •; 7 rests, —) given by a student.

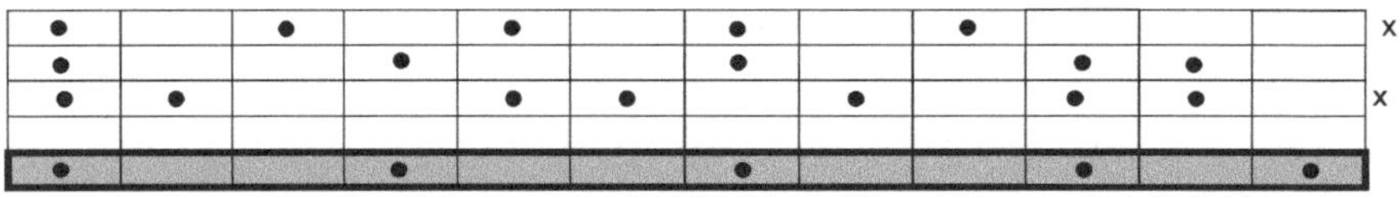

Fig. 10.12. "Even" rhythm (5 notes, •; 7 rests, —) given by a student.

the center and with the two remaining pulses placed in the extremes. Thus, this student's obtaining of the "maximally even" rhythm did not follow from the application of the algorithm in Fig. 10.11.

The rest of the rhythms produced by the students show two or three notes in a row, either in the timeline pattern (12 of the 14 students), or in the rhythm as a cyclic repetition of the timeline (Fig. 10.12).

The criteria used by the students for determining the rhythms are varied:

- Central pseudo-symmetry (CPS). The search for a distribution that preserves, as much as possible, a central symmetry around a particular position or a grouping of positions.

- Repetition of a maximal pattern (RPM). The "maximal" repetition of patterns in groupings of a specific number of pulses.
- Mixed (M). The combination of the previous two criteria, CPS and RPM.

In Table 10.7 all the rhythms presented by the students are given, indicating the characteristic of how they were formed.

The difficulty in obtaining a timeline that satisfies the students is the key for understanding the sequence that follows. The presentation of representative flamenco rhythms with 12 pulses in activity 7, such as the *fandango* (4 notes and 8 rests), and *soleá, bulería, seguiriya* and *guajira* (5 notes and 7 rests), contrasts the rhythms given by

Table 10.7. Rhythms proposed by the students as "maximally even" as possible (5 notes, •; 7 rests, —).

CHAR	N	Rhythm	Total
RPM	1	[• — —] [• — —] [• • —] [• — —]	6
	2	[• — —] [• — —] [• — —] [• — •]	
	3	[• — •] [• — •] [— • —] — — —	
	4	— [• — •] [• — •] [— • —] — —	
	5	[• — —] [• — —] [• • • — — —]	
	6	[• • • — — —] [— • • — — —]	
CPS	7	— • • — — [•] — — • • — —	6
	8	— • — — — • [•] • — — — •	
	9	• — — — • • — [—] — • • —	
	10	— • — — [• •] — — • — • —	
	11	— — — • — [• •] — • • — —	
	12	— • [— —] [• • —] [• • —] [— —]	
M	13	— [• — — • —] [• — — • —] •	2
	14	— [• — • — —] • [• — • — —]	

Key: CHAR: Characteristic of how the rhythms are formed; RPM: Repetition of the maximal pattern; CPS: Central pseudo-symmetry (the center of the structure is highlighted); M: Mixed.

the students, who judge them in terms of "evenness". That is, a "good" sequence is perceived as a sequence as evenly distributed as possible, coming to the agreement that the rhythms that have three rests in a row (rhythms 3, 4, 5, 6, 8, 9 and 11 in Table 10.7) should be dismissed; however they could not determine which of the 7 that were left would be preferable, taking into account the "evenness" characteristic. The following activities are aimed at generating the need for the technique indicated in Fig. 10.10.

In situation 8, where they must represent an "even" rhythm with 8 notes (•) and 4 rests (—), the students contributed 28 timelines. Half of them (14 out of 28) are obtained by a repetition of the pattern that contains two notes and a rest (•• — / — •• / • — •) or combinations of these three patterns. This type of timeline is produced by 9 of the 14 students. On the other hand, 5 of 28 patterns are repetitions or combinations of the two patterns that contain four notes and two rests (• • •• — — / — — • • ••). In Fig. 10.13 the answer of a student who showed these two patterns is given, as well as the justification of why the first was preferred as "even".

The justification of the proposed "even" rhythms is not anecdotal. Several students make notes in the margins or the back of their notepaper that refer to the symmetry ("making groups, by symmetry, because they are in pairs") or groupings by divisibility

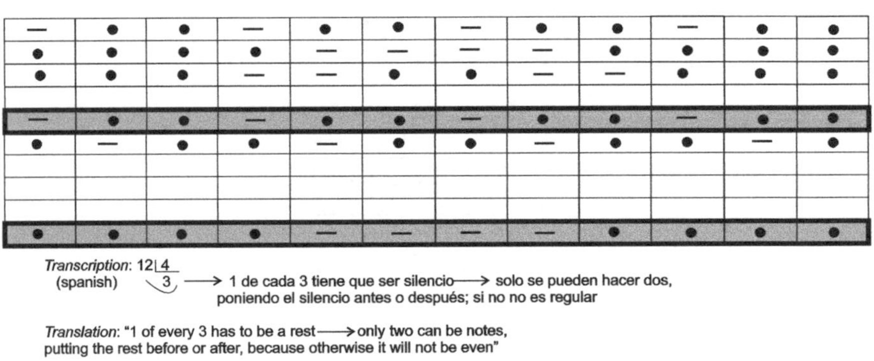

Fig. 10.13. "Even" rhythm (8 notes, •; 4 rests, —) with the justification given by the student.

Transcription: 4 silencios a distribuir de forma regular en 12 tiempos
(spanish) $\frac{12}{4} = 3 \longrightarrow$ cada 3 pulsos 1 silencio

x	x	—	3 opciones
x	—	x	
—	x	x	

Translation: "4 rests to distribute evenly in 12 pulses. 12/4 = 3⟶ every 3 pulses a rest" (3 options)

Transcription: Si tenemos un periodo de tiempo de 12 pulsos al tener 4 silencios al dividir esos 12 pulsos entre 4
(spanish) nos dice que habrá 3 posibilidades.
Agrupando los tonos de 2 en 2, de 4 en 4 y en 8 como los mostrados antes.

Translation: If we have a time period of 12 pulses, then as we have 4 rests when we divide these 12 pulses by 4 it tells us that there will be 3 possibilities. By grouping the tones 2 in 2, 4 in 4, and in 8, as the ones showed before.

Transcription: 8 notas:
(spanish) - Grupos de 2 en 2, en medio un silencio.
- Grupos de 4 en 4, en medio 2 silencios.
- Grupo de 8, después 4 silencios.

Translation: 8 notes:
- Groups of 2 in 2, in the middle a rest.
- Groups of 4 in 4, in the middle 2 rests.
- Groups of 8, then 4 rests.

Fig. 10.14. Justifications about determining "even" rhythms (8 notes, •; 4 rests, —).

(Fig. 10.14). The mathematics is then revealed as an instrument that generalizes and expresses "type" characteristics (the duality example/type). This specificity is necessary in iterated processes or in those that require shared and understandable answers. This essential fact in mathematics arises from an activity. That is, the teacher asks: "The majority of you have contributed a rhythm that supposes the repetition of three patterns [writing on the board: •• — / — •• / • — •]. What methods have been employed in obtaining these rhythms? The debate introduced in activity 9 and the practices carried out in activity 10, give way to the introduction of the technique that closes the session.

The result for the students in these final sessions (activities 9, 10 and 11) is triple:

- They obtain a technique to determine rhythms as evenly distributed as possible (activity 11).
- They come to appreciate traditional musical styles that follow the "maximal evenness" principle in a timeline of 7 notes and 5

rests (activity 10). Concretely, in the musical style called *gamamla*, where a double bell (the *gankogui*, from Ghana) is played.

They realize that mathematics can model musical patterns and that this leads to different types of music (circular permutations) in a much more efficient manner than the trial and error method. Likewise, they see that "known" mathematical techniques (calculation of the GCD) in a specific context (arithmetic, by factorization) has not been easily extrapolated to an extra mathematical context. This supposes a very deep learning experience in terms of what "learning mathematics" and "using mathematics" means.

10.5.2. *Second session*

In this session, the activity is centered on the use of programming and certain technical resources to address interdisciplinary activities. As in the first session, in this second session we began with the mathematical knowledge, in this case through programming with the Texas Instruments 81 (TI-81) calculator. The instructor showed some of the possibilities of the TI-81 (activity 1); the students edited some simple programs and shared them (activities 2 and 3); the students edited a program for determining the GCD (activity 4); the students analyzed the programs previously edited by the instructor (Fig. 10.15)[d] and, in each case, they were compared with the student edits (activity 5).

The analysis of activity 5 is centered on the velocity of the programs GCD1 and GCD2. Very quickly the students declared that the second one is "slower" or "worse" than the first. Hence, the difference between the programs GCD1 and GCD2 is the computational cost understood as the "time needed to carry out a task". To exemplify the situation, the instructor proposed calculating

[d]In the session there was a discussion about the possibility and importance of "completing" the GCD1 and GCD2 programs for obtaining the intermediate values of the Euclidean algorithm (the remainders of the successive divisions) and relevant information about the relation between the numbers (is one a multiple of another? Or, reciprocally, is one is a divisor of another? Are they relatively prime?). The discussion is not presented in this chapter.

```
Prgm1: GCD1
: Disp "A"
: Input A
: Disp "B"
: Input B
: Lbl 1
: Int (A/B)->C
: A-B*C->R
: If (R=0)
: Goto 2
: B->A
: R->B
: Goto 1
: Lbl 2
: Disp "GCB(A, B)="
: Disp B
: End
```

```
Prgm2: GCD2
: Disp "A"
: Input A
: Disp "B"
: Input B
: Lbl 1
: 0->N
: Lbl 2
: N+1->N
: If (A-B*N=0)
: Goto 3
: If (A-B*N>0)
: Goto 2
: A-B*(N-1)->R
: B->A
: R->B
: Goto 1
: Lbl 3
: Disp "GCB(A, B)="
: Disp B
: End
```

Fig. 10.15. Programs for obtaining the GCD.

the GCD of A = 5846 and B = 679. The Euclidean algorithm produced the following sequence of remainders: 414, 265, 149, 116, 33, 17, 16 and 1. Thus, the greatest common divisor of A and B is 1 — $\text{GCD}(A, B) = 1$ —, that is, A and B are relatively prime. Are GCD1 and GCD2 equally efficient? To respond to this question the time that the algorithms took to carry out the task was controlled. Given that the TI-81 does not have an internal way of keeping time they used a chronometer. Determining the time it took to carry out the task depended not only on the algorithm and, of course, A and B, but also on the subject's velocity of reaction. The same student controlled the programs' velocity during 20 trials, obtaining the following values (in hundredths of seconds):

- GCD1: 57, 67, 66, 64, 64, 67, 61, 60, 60, 64, 65, 67, 67, 65, 63, 64, 67, 62, 58, 61.
- GCD2: 132, 117, 129, 126, 117, 130, 121, 114, 115, 124, 126, 125, 127, 125, 127, 117, 120, 119, 115, 123.

The results confirmed that the programs are not equally efficient. To justify this, the students determined the confidence intervals and carried out hypothesis tests for the means with a significance level of $\alpha = 0.05$, using the free software R (https://www.r-project.org/). The results allowed the rejection of the null hypothesis (the equality of the means) and, consequently, it was accepted that the GCD2 program has a greater computational cost that the GCD1 program. Hence, the first is preferred over the second due to its efficiency (Fig. 10.16).

The activity is evaluated according to suitability in the different dimensions, always thinking about its implementation with secondary students:

- *Epistemic-ecological suitability.* The evaluation is high. Arithmetic procedures are related to automation and statistical methods of data analysis (contrasting means) as well as establishing mathematical connections. These techniques and activities comply with

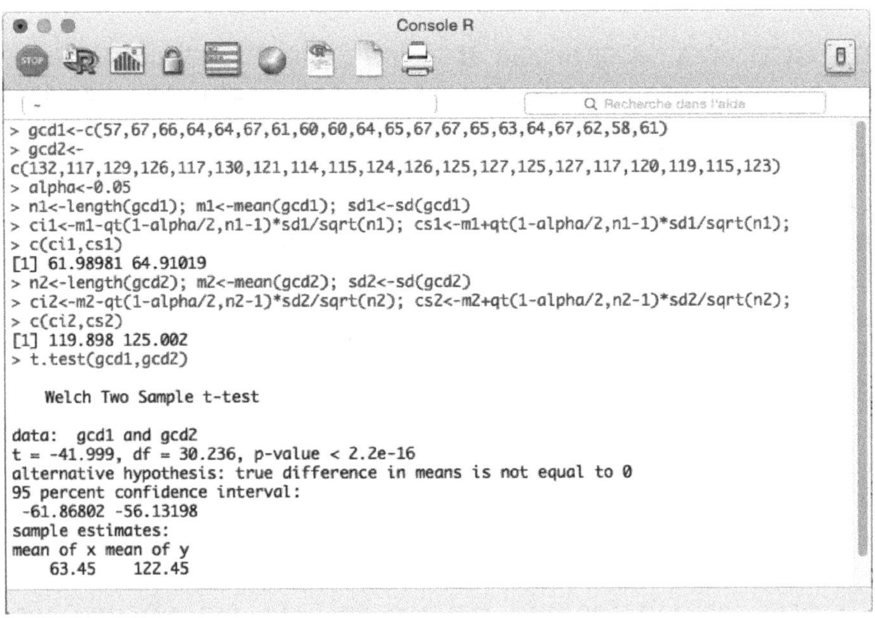

Fig. 10.16. Efficiency and computational cost of the programs GCD1 and GCD2.

the curricular expectations related to the use of software and the search for mathematical connections.

- *Cognitive suitability.* The evaluation is high. The activity contributes to the students' flexible mathematical thinking.
- *Affective suitability.* The evaluation is low. The activity supposes a rupture with the work initiated in session 1, about the relation between music and mathematics, given that it is centered on programming and mathematics.
- *Institutional-mediational suitability.* The evaluation is medium-low. The instructors' intervention allows for the adjustment of the time dedicated to the activity, as well as adjusting it to the requirements of the curriculum. However, the actual TI-81 might not be available in all the schools (it is not free) and the use of the software R is conditioned by the students' age and educational context.

For this reason, we proposed an activity that contributes to the affective suitability by means of free computational tools. Hence, the rest of the session is focused upon obtaining a musical piece produced automatically by generating all possible permutations of the syllables of the words "ma-the-ma-tics" and "mu-sic" ordered alphabetically, without repetition (only one "ma").

The first step was to discuss how to obtain the 120 permutations of the syllables, which the instructor has obtained automatically, by showing the program edited with the software R (Fig. 10.6). Then, the permutations are reproduced in Google Translate and the audios are downloaded with the complement Flashgot of Mozilla Firefox, with duration of 17 second. They must be concatenated to form a single track that reproduces the 120 permutations, that is, the 600 syllables.

Six audios were generated. The audios are classified in two groups and, within each group, the difference is the tempo, *in crescendo*, according to whether the syllables are in quotation marks, without quotation marks, or whether the spaces have been eliminated (that is, as a single word). Group 1 is the result of ordering all the permutations of the "ma", "mu", "the", "tics" and "sic", in alphabetical order and interpreting the result as a sequence of syllables structured as a 120×5 matrix. Group 2 is also the result of ordering the same syllables, but considering a vector with 600 components that use the order of the columns of the previous matrix. Group 2 is denominated *funnel music*, because, from the repetition of the syllables ("ma" 24 times; then "mu" 24 times; 24 times "the"; etc.), follows a sequence in which the syllables are repeated 6 times, then 2 times and, finally, 1×1, creating phonetic sounds that evoke "mathematics" and "music" intertwined.[e]

The discussion of the product is assessed positively from the affective viewpoint. This is seen through the comments that reflect surprise and proposals of how to better the result, such as: (a) the proposal of a sequence with different velocities (200 syllables with quotation marks and spaces; 200 syllables only with spaces; 200 syllables as one word); (b) to use the free software to edit different rhythms (which would be voices), to create a "chorus" effect; (c) to obtain the sequence with other automatic voices and other pitches (d) to carry out an *a cappella* interpretation.

10.6. Synthesis, Conclusions and Suggestions

The connection between mathematics and music is undeniable. The experience described in this chapter was carried out so that both disciplines would complement each other, without the subordination of one to the other. *Muthsics* is not a mere metaphor or play on

[e]The sequences of syllables structured as a 120×5 matrix or as a 600-vector with components that use the order of the columns of the previous matrix are available at the appendices I and II. The soundtracks in allegro tempo are available at: (a) *Funnel music*, as a 600-vector: https://youtu.be/qxPv8UDEcnA. (b) *Ordered permutation*, as a 120×5 matrix: https://youtu.be/wjaXlWGEGjw In tracks, the tempo changes as the syllables appear between quotation marks (61 PPM, slow), without quotation marks (107 PPM, andante moderato), or with the elimination of spaces, that is, as one 600-character word, (133 PPM, allegro), each time with more acceleration. Here, it is established that each syllable is an eighth note. The pulsations per minute (PPM) are calculated by dividing the number of syllables (600), and the duration of the piece and the result, by two (the duration of an eighth note is equivalent to half a quarter note).

words; it is a proposal for specific teaching and learning situations around mathematics and music, that will allow students to learn new concepts in both areas by starting from their previous formal knowledge. These situations should be suitable according to the epistemic-ecological, cognitive-affective, and instructional-mediational perspectives.

The situations should allow the integration of the creative experience with the demands of the curriculum, even bettering the usual delivery of the disciplines. It is also essential that teachers without advanced training in mathematics or music, and whose focus is just one of the areas, are able to propose *muthsics* projects that can be controlled and evaluated. The proposed experience is a partial answer to this challenge. It has allowed the connection between Euclidean division and calculating the GCD, with musical rhythms and repetitions of timelines (circular permutations).

However, it is not easy to promote these situations. The students with predominantly scientific-technical training have preconceived notions about the function, context, and language associated with mathematics. For this reason, it is difficult for them to translate their knowledge to a non-formal context, be it graphical or musical. It becomes manifest that the mathematical knowledge that emerged in a specific context is not necessarily extrapolated to another context in a flexible manner. If the students had been asked if they knew how to divide and to determine the GCD of two natural numbers the answer would have been unanimous and unequivocal: "yes, of course!"

The onto-semiotic approach allows us to affirm that the knowledge involved in a notion implies distinct objects (language, situations, definitions, propositions, procedures and arguments) and dualities (personal/institutional, ostensive/non-ostensive, intensive/extensive, unitary/systemic and expression/content). Hence, if from a mathematical viewpoint the definition is the "measure" of a notion, from the cognitive perspective a definition is only an object associated to the notion, with restricted application and validity. Thus, it is important to propose activities whose resolution can test the acquired knowledge in diverse contexts that demand flexible mathematical thinking.

Johnson [18] describes the difference between "search" and "creation" in music. We integrated technology to "find" compositions called funnel music, named as such because of the perception that behind the circular and repetitive beginning, where the syllables "ma", "mu", "the", "tics" and "sic" are repeated 24 times in a row, there follows a mixture arising from a structured pattern and whose union is the harmonic result of mathematics and music. As Johnson [18] affirms, musical pleasure — or at least curiosity — is not stifled by the substitution of "creation" by "search", not even when this is the result of an inevitable generation following mathematical patterns.

However, this search has been limited and adjusted to time requisites. Other searches can be made in a quest for better sonority, such as: (a) looking for compositions with the permutation of vowels, syllables used in other languages, different rhythms or combinations of rhythms; (b) generating compositions with other patterns or with mathematical patterns; (c) generating compositions by using audio software, for example, Audacity (https://www.audacityteam.org/), that it is free and open source.

In any case, all projects should recognize an essential starting point: the educational organization in schools is structured according to discipline and, consequently, the musical training of secondary mathematics teachers is usually limited, as is the mathematical training of music teachers. Hence, the proposal of feasible situations in which *muthsics* can thrive should take into account this specialization in the curriculum, as well as the teacher's training. Interesting projects might have to be sacrificed if there is not a general consensus and support for their development.

Bibliography

[1] American Mathematical Society, *Mathematics Subject Classification 2010 (MSC2010).* (American Mathematical Society, Providence, RI, 2009).

[2] A. An, D. Tillman, R. Boren and J. Wang, Fostering elementary students' mathematics disposition through music-mathematics integrated lessons, *Int. J. Math. Teaching–Learning* **15**(3) (2014) 1–18.

[3] O. Belletich, M. R. Wilhelmi and R. Angel-Alvarado, La educación musical en la formación básica en España. El problema de la dispersión curricular, *Perspectiva Educacional* **55**(2) (2016) 158–170, http://www.perspectivaeducacional.cl/index.php/peducacional/article/view/454.

[4] E. Demaine, F. Gómez, H. Meijer, D. Rappaport, P. Taslakian, G. T. Toussaint, T. Winograd and D. R. Wood, The distance geometry of music, *Comput. Geom. Theory Appl.* **42** (2009) 429–454.

[5] W. Fenton, Teaching permutations through rhythm patterns, *J. Math. Arts* **3**(3) (2009) 143–146.

[6] R. Filo and M. Yarkoni, A. Geomart — Geometry reflected through art, in *Proc. First Int. Symp. Mathematics and its Connections to the Arts and Sciences*, eds. A. Beckmann, C. Michelsen and B. Sriraman, 19–21 May 2005, Schwäbisch Gmünd, Germany (Euro Verlag Franzbecker, Berlin, 2005).

[7] V. Freiman and N. Lirette-Pitre, Innovative approach of building connections between science and math didactics in preservice teacher education using wiki-technology, in *Proc. First Int. Symp. of Mathematics and its Connections to the Arts and Sciences*, eds. A. Beckmann, C. Michelsen and B. Sriraman, 19–21 May 2005, Schwäbisch Gmünd, Germany (Euro Verlag Franzbecker, Berlin, 2005).

[8] J. D. Godino, C. Batanero and V. Font, The onto-semiotic approach to research in mathematics education, *ZDM, Int. J. Math. Educ.* **39**(1–2) (2007) 127–135.

[9] J. D. Godino, D. Bencomo, V. Font and M. R. Wilhelmi, Análisis y valoración de la idoneidad didáctica de procesos de estudio de las matemáticas, *Paradigma* **XXVII**(2) (2006) 221–252, http://revistas.upel.edu.ve/index.php/paradigma/issue/view/275.

[10] J. D. Godino, M. R. Wilhelmi and D. Bencomo, Suitability criteria of a mathematical instruction process. A teaching experience of the function notion, *Mediterranean J. Res. Math. Educ.* **4**(2) (2005) 1–26, http://www.ugr.es/~jgodino/articulos_ingles/suitability_criteria_functions.pdf.

[11] J. D. Godino, V. Font, M. R. Wilhelmi and C. de Castro, Aproximación a la dimensión normativa en didáctica de las matemáticas desde un enfoque ontosemiótico, *Enseñanza de las Ciencias* **27**(1) (2009) 59–76, https://ddd.uab.cat/pub/edlc/02124521v27n1/02124521v27n1p59.pdf.

[12] F. Gómez, Matherhythm — Follow up material (Euclidean rhythms), (2012), http://webpgomez.com/index.php?option=com_content&view=article&id=402:matherhythm-follow-up-material-eng&catid=54:contrasteatro&Itemid=239.

[13] J. Haack, Clapping music. A combinatorial problem, *The College Math. J.* **22**(3) (1991) 224–227.

[14] R. Hall, Acoustics labs for a general education math and music course, *J. Mathe. Music* **8**(2) (2014) 125–130.

[15] W. Hisschemoller, http://www.hisschemoller.com/blog/2011/euclidean-rhythms/ Retrieved on July 7, 2015.

[16] I. Izmirli, Directional pitch spaces, in *Proc. 3rd Int. Symp. Mathematics and Its Connections to the Arts and Sciences, Mocton* (2009).

[17] T. Johnson, *Foundations of Diatonic Theory: A Mathematically Based Approach to Music Fundamentals* (The Scarecrow Press, Lanham, MD, 2008).

[18] T. Johnson, I want to find the music, not to compose it, (2009), http://www.editions75.com/Articles/I%20WANT%20TO%20FIND%20THE%20MUSIC.pdf.

[19] J. Kovachi, Musica speculativa for the twenty-first century: integrating mathematics and music in the liberal arts classroom, *J. Math. Music* **8**(2) (2014) 117–123.

[20] Ministerio de Educación, Ciencia y Deporte (MECD), Orden ECI/3858/2007, de 27 de diciembre, por la que se establecen los requisitos para la verificación de los títulos universitarios oficiales que habiliten para el ejercicio de las profesiones de Profesor de Educación Secundaria Obligatoria y Bachillerato, Formación Profesional y Enseñanzas de Idiomas. Boletín Oficial del Estado 312, de 29/12/2007, 53751–53753, (2007), https://www.boe.es/boe/dias/2007/12/29/pdfs/A53751-53753.pdf.

[21] M. Montiel and F. Gómez, Music in the pedagogy of mathematics, *J. Math. Music* **8**(2) (2014) 117–123.

[22] M. Montiel and M. R. Wilhelmi, Funciones semióticas para el análisis de procesos de estudio integrados de matemáticas y música en la universidad, in *Actas del Segundo Congreso International Virtual sobre el Enfoque Ontosemiótico del Conocimiento y la Instrucción Matemáticos*, eds. J. M. Contreras, P. Arteaga, G. R. Cañadas, M. M. Gea, B. Giacomone and M. M. López-Martín http://enfoqueontosemiotico.ugr.es/civeos/montiel_wilhelmi.pdf.

[23] M. Montiel, M. R. Wilhelmi, D. Vidakovic and I. Elstak, Using the onto-semiotic approach to identify and analyze mathematical meaning when transiting between different coordinate systems in a multivariate context, *Educ. Studies Math.* **72**(2) (2009) 139–160, https://doi.org/10.1007/s10649-009-9184-2.

[24] National Council of Teachers of Mathematics (NCTM), *Executive Summary: Principles and Standards for School Mathematics.* (Author, Reston, VA, 2017), http://www.nctm.org/Standards-and-Positions/Principles-and-Standards/.

[25] S. Nikitina and V. Boix Mansilla, Three strategies for interdisciplinary math and science teaching: A case of the illinois Mathematics and Science Academy, GoodWork®Project, Project Zero, Harvard Graduate School of Education (2003).

[26] T. Pfaff, A. Erkan, J. Hamilton and M. Rogers, Multidisciplinary engagement of calculus students in climate issues, *Sci. Educ. Civic Engagement*, (2011), https://seceij.net/seceij/winter11/calculus_studen.html.

[27] S. Reich, *Clapping Music for two performers*, (1972) [Retrieved 2017/12/01: http://earreader.nl/wp-content/uploads/2016/01/SteveReich-ClappingMusic.pdf.

[28] G. Toussaint, The Euclidean algorithm generates traditional musical rhythms, in *Proc. BRIDGES: Mathematical Connections in Art, Music, and Science*, Banff, Alberta, Canada, July 31 to August 3, 2005, (2005) pp. 47–56.

[29] G. Toussaint, *The Geometry of Musical Rhythm* (Chapman & Hall/CRC, London, 2013).

[30] M. R. Wilhelmi, J. D. Godino and E. Lacasta, Epistemic configurations associated to the notion of equality in real numbers, *Quaderni di Ricerca in Didattica (Math.)* **21** (2011) 53–82, http://math.unipa.it/~grim/Wilhelmi_Q21.pdf.

Appendix I. The permutations of the syllables of the words "ma-the-ma-tics "and "mu-sic", ordered alphabetically without repetition (only one "ma") and according to the 120 X 5 matrix. How does it sound?

ma mu the tics sic ma mu the sic tics ma mu tics the sic ma mu tics sic the ma mu sic the tics ma mu sic tics the ma the mu tics sic ma the mu sic tics ma the tics mu sic ma the tics sic mu ma the sic mu tics ma the sic tics mu ma tics mu the sic ma tics mu sic the ma tics the mu sic ma tics the sic mu ma tics sic mu the ma tics sic the mu ma sic mu the tics ma sic mu tics the ma sic the mu tics ma sic the tics mu ma sic tics mu the ma sic tics the mu mu ma the tics sic mu ma the sic tics mu ma tics the sic mu ma tics sic the mu ma sic the tics mu ma sic tics the mu the ma tics sic mu the ma sic tics mu the tics ma sic mu the tics sic ma mu the sic ma tics mu the sic tics ma mu tics ma the sic mu tics ma sic the mu tics the ma sic mu tics the sic ma mu tics sic ma the mu tics sic the ma mu sic ma the tics mu sic ma tics the mu sic the ma tics mu sic the tics ma mu sic tics ma the mu sic tics the ma the ma mu tics sic the ma mu sic tics the ma tics mu sic the ma tics sic mu the ma sic mu tics the ma sic tics mu the mu ma tics sic the mu ma sic tics the mu tics ma sic the mu tics sic ma the mu sic ma tics the mu sic tics ma the tics ma mu sic the tics ma sic mu the tics mu ma sic the tics mu sic ma the tics sic ma mu the tics sic mu ma the sic ma mu tics the sic ma tics mu the sic mu ma tics the sic mu tics ma the sic tics ma mu the sic tics mu ma tics ma mu the sic tics ma mu sic the tics ma the mu sic tics ma the sic mu tics ma sic mu the tics ma sic the mu tics mu ma the sic tics mu ma sic the tics mu the ma sic tics mu the sic ma tics mu sic ma the tics mu sic the ma tics the ma mu sic tics the ma sic mu tics the mu ma sic tics the mu sic ma tics the sic ma mu tics the sic mu ma tics sic ma mu the tics sic ma the mu tics sic mu ma the tics sic mu the ma tics sic the ma mu tics sic the mu ma sic ma mu the tics sic ma mu tics the sic ma the mu tics sic ma the tics mu sic ma tics mu the sic ma tics the mu sic mu ma the tics sic mu ma tics the sic mu the ma tics sic mu the tics ma sic mu tics ma the sic mu tics the ma sic the ma mu tics sic the ma tics mu sic the mu ma tics sic the mu tics ma sic the tics ma mu sic the tics mu ma sic tics ma mu the sic tics ma the mu sic tics mu ma the sic tics mu the ma sic tics the ma mu sic tics the mu ma.

Appendix II. The permutations of the syllables of the words "ma-the-ma-tics "and "mu-sic", ordered alphabetically without repetition (only one "ma") as a one dimensional continuum,. How does it sound?

ma ma ma ma ma ma ma ma ma ma ma ma ma ma ma ma ma ma ma ma ma ma ma ma mu mu mu mu mu mu mu mu mu mu mu mu mu mu mu mu mu mu mu mu mu mu mu mu the the the the the the the the the the the the the the the the the the the the the the the the tics tics tics tics tics tics tics tics tics tics tics tics tics tics tics tics tics tics tics tics tics tics tics tics sic sic sic sic sic sic sic sic sic sic sic sic sic sic sic sic sic sic sic sic sic sic sic sic mu mu mu mu mu mu the the the the the the tics tics tics tics tics tics sic sic sic sic sic sic ma ma ma ma ma ma the the the the the the tics tics tics tics tics tics sic sic sic sic sic sic ma ma ma ma ma ma mu mu mu mu mu mu tics tics tics tics tics tics sic sic sic sic sic sic ma ma ma ma ma ma mu mu mu mu mu mu the the the the the the sic sic sic sic sic sic ma ma ma ma ma ma mu mu mu mu mu mu the the the the the the tics tics tics tics tics tics the the tics tics sic sic mu mu tics tics sic sic mu mu the the sic sic mu mu the the tics tics the the tics tics sic sic ma ma tics tics sic sic ma ma the the sic sic ma ma the the tics tics mu mu tics tics sic sic ma ma tics tics sic sic ma ma mu mu sic sic ma ma mu mu tics tics mu mu the the sic sic ma ma the the sic sic ma ma mu mu sic sic ma ma mu mu the the mu mu the the tics tics ma ma the the tics tics ma ma mu mu tics tics ma ma mu mu the the tics sic the sic the tics tics sic mu sic mu tics the sic mu sic mu the the tics mu tics mu the tics sic the sic the tics tics sic ma sic ma tics the sic ma sic ma the the tics ma tics ma the tics sic mu sic mu tics tics sic ma sic ma tics mu sic ma sic ma mu mu tics ma tics ma mu the sic mu sic mu the the sic ma sic ma the mu sic ma sic ma mu mu the ma the ma mu the tics mu tics mu the the tics ma tics ma the mu tics ma tics ma mu mu the ma the ma mu sic tics sic the tics the sic tics sic mu tics mu sic the sic mu the mu tics the tics mu the mu sic tics sic the tics the sic tics sic ma tics ma sic the sic ma the ma tics the tics ma the ma sic tics sic mu tics mu sic tics sic ma tics ma sic mu sic ma mu ma tics mu tics ma mu ma sic the sic mu the mu sic the sic ma the ma sic mu sic ma mu ma the mu the ma mu ma tics the tics mu the mu tics the tics ma the ma tics mu tics ma mu ma the mu the ma mu ma.

Section IV

Chapter 11

Can Mathematical Theory of Music Be Easily Learnt and Also Be Fun?

Maria Mannone

School of Music, University of Minnesota,
2106 4th St., Minneapolis, MN 55455, USA
manno012@umn.edu

11.1. Introduction: Motivations

11.1.1. *Question* 1

Why should I make the effort in understanding mathematics and music? This is the first question that a potential student may frequently ask, while the teacher starts a strategy to teach mathematics and music.

The beginner must be aware that he or she is going to deal with effort-demanding topics. However, each one of these topics, and, above all, their connections can provide not only cognitive benefits but also considerable pleasure.

In fact, the search for pleasant elements is a strong motivational principle, which manifests itself in several ways: curiosity, exploratory and manipulatory attitudes, attraction toward games, attitude toward the collection of information and motivation toward learning and acquiring competence in a field, as well as cognitional motivations.

Culture, in the broadest sense, and study itself constitute ways of accessing higher pleasure of intellectual type. Art is by definition connected with aesthetic pleasure. It is, in fact, a powerful lever to gain "control of the world" by following rules or scopes that are not dictated by survival or essential needs, but consciously elaborated.

11.1.2. *Question* 2

Rational thinking about art is also connected with aesthetic pleasure. A possible second question would be: *Why do we like something?*

Philosophers and sociologists have always discussed this topic. Here, we can just give some simple hints about a plurality of reasons, which are often antinomic; we like something because:

- it corresponds to something that is already within us;
- it surprises us for its novelty;
- it seems interesting for its complexity;
- we are able to understand its meaning;
- it communicates a message to us, even in an encrypted form;
- it fascinates us with its mystery.

This is only a short and quite elementary list, to support the initial assumption: aesthetic pleasure is not unrelated to rational thinking. *We like something because we are able to get it inside our world.*

11.1.3. *Question* 3

Another question by future students is often this one: proceeding in the learning process, and becoming "experts", will we be able to get more pleasure from this or that particular piece of artwork?

We will certainly be able to understand it better, because we will be able to understand its codes, and thus, its meaning and its message. If we extend our knowledge, we extend the borders of the reality that our conscience can dominate, and we gain some pleasure from that.

Somebody may still criticize on the grounds that, in some way, art is useless, because it does not have a direct force, it does not produces essential goods such as food, accommodation, tools or defending devices. However, art can, and must, transmit ideas and provoke emotions. It can also sensitize people, it can stimulate personal and social/collective engagement. Art is an immediate and pure form of knowledge. It is a "perception of mysteries of irrational through rational media" [17].

In several people's opinions mathematics is useless and even dangerous: it provokes discomfort, difficulty, and feelings of inability and inadequacy. Even being the most sublime of rational activities, mathematics is perceived by many as cold, dry, too-abstract and mind-demanding, as well as detached from daily life. In a specific study recently conducted, negative stereotypes have been found not only among elementary-school students, but also among their prospective math teachers: among them math seems to be associated to images of wild, aggressive animals, or even to monsters [14, 15].

For all these reasons, music and mathematics can be perceived as twice as useless!

With the elementary common sense of the "primum non nocere" (*First, do not harm*),[a] it is easy to observe that studies about mathematics and music, separated or joined, first of all do not use guinea pigs, neither human or animal, do not imply physical or psychological tortures, do not require raw materials or non-renewable resources, do not pollute and do not produce radioactive waste. Math and music are not related to rebellions, racism, religion wars, and nobody was hurt or killed because of them. This is already a good starting point. Maybe, inspiring a smile on the students, we can defuse the initial impact they may have with math and music, favorably predisposing them to learn.

11.1.4. *Question* 4 (*similar to question* 1)

Why should the student approach the effort-demanding study of mathematics and music? Mathematics and music are, first of all, two of the most ancient disciplines, common to each era and civilization. Math and music are not only important in themselves, they are the key to accessing a more general interdisciplinary thinking. It means that they help overcome barriers and obstacles, to build

[a]Latin sentence about bioethics for healthcare students, connected with a concept in the Greek *Hippocratic Oath: "... To abstain of doing harm."*

bridges between fields and connect different ways of thinking, highlighting common ideas and strengthening some main points. Interdisciplinary studies open the mind, reduce cultural differences, promote collaboration, generate availability to listening, opposing self-referential behaviors.

11.1.5. *Question* 5

But *how, and why, may the student find pleasure from the mathematical theory of music?*

It should be clear that mathematics does not destroy the mystery and the beauty of art, in particular, of music. Music is attractive under several points of view, and the attraction toward the mystery is one of the motors of science and scientific investigation.

The aesthetic content is also present in mathematics and in hard sciences, but often this is evident only to people that already have mastery of the specific formalisms. The use of external metaphors and of musical references contributes to the understanding *and thus* to the appreciation of mathematical topics. *Vice versa*, the mastery of mathematics can improve the comprehension, *and so* the appreciation, of musical phenomena. Last but not the least, theoretical ideas can act as a stimulus for artistic creativity, and art can stimulate scientific thinking.

Is that all? Of course, it is not. There is a scientific technique also within art: let us think of the laws of harmony, the acoustics of musical instruments, the discipline in orchestral playing, and the precision of composers' scores. But there is also a strong passion inside scientific work: let us think of the "eureka" effect, the insightful ideas, which can start a revolution on a process and start new fields of research.

11.2. Challenges and Objectives

Objectives and challenges do intersect themselves in the sense that the achievement of an objective necessarily implies overcoming a challenge. Here, we have to deconstruct negative stereotypes that students may have about mathematics and music, to promote their opening up, maybe completely new, toward creativity and the intertwinement of disciplines.

11.2.1. *Challenges*

11.2.1.1. *First: Get fear and hate away from math*

It may be a good rule to ask students to enucleate, orally or (anonymously) by writing, the elements they consider as complicated and difficult, even if they date far back to a long time ago. Often, there are not any cognitive deficiencies, but psychological obstacles that may be resolved through examples related to the students' world. However, other times it might be necessary to review the progressive steps in math learning (reviewing the flow diagram, we may say) to solve or bypass the critical point. After such a critical point, in fact, any other idea may be lost within the unexplored territory that, in ancient maps, was denoted with the expression "hic sunt leones", *Here, there are lions.*

11.2.1.2. *Second: Get fear away from technical sides of music*

All that concerns the notational side of music can be learnt with a reasonable dedication and in a lapse of time no too prolonged. The repeated exercise allows us to automatize those processes that may seem boring, and that often obstruct the continuation of music studies. For example, a clear explanation of the importance of music theory can motivate a lazy student to work on an exercise that he or she had thought as useless, but did just not fully understand.

11.2.2. *Objectives*

The main objective, as already mentioned, is that each student first understands *why* the interdisciplinary math–music studies are important. The second objective is guiding the student to develop his or her own ability to make new applications of math/music concepts starting from simple proposed examples. The student should also develop the ability to rationally approach music, and he/she should maturate a creative approach to mathematics. Our examples involve simple mathematical and basilar musical concepts: this is meant to show that interactions between mathematics and music do not only deal with high-structure and exotic cases, but also the daily practice of performers and composers.

11.2.2.1. *Understanding the creativity within scientific activity*

According to a common prejudice, scientific activity is essentially mechanical, tight on narrow tracks made by rules, laws, principles and binding methods. Scientific activity, however, is not less creative than artistic activity. In both there is the process of ideation, creation of new connections or fusion of already known elements and processes; there also is observation and discovery. The scientist is, first of all, a discoverer that is not satisfied with the already existing and known. The scientist is researching not only to discover and find: he or she researches to define new synthesis, easier connections, innovative methods. He or she observes, examines, puts into relation, and creates what was not there before. The names of Pythagoras and Leonardo da Vinci, as well as a collection of important names in more recent times, may easily exemplify the creative aspects of scientific activity. We will not make a case, but will mention, that both Pythagoras and Leonardo da Vinci were two leading personalities both in science and in art.

11.2.2.2. *Understanding the rationality within artistic activity*

The artist is not always and only impetus and madness, genius and disorderliness, insight and feelings. However, even in these cases, the result of the artistic production can be analyzed in light of rationality, and the results of such an analysis can bring new blood to the artistic creation itself.

Moreover, each art has its rules and its codes, techniques, procedures and materials. Painters know the laws of perspective and properties of colors; sculptors distinguish the characteristics of different kinds of marbles and they know how to appropriately use techniques for bronze fusion. In the same way, composers know musical acoustics laws, and both potentialities and limitations of instruments and human voice [20].

11.2.3. *How to creatively and independently manipulate ideas*

11.2.3.1. *Teaching the language of mathematical theory of music*

Often, music students lack advanced math knowledge, or *vice versa*. For this reason, the teacher has to, first of all, face up to the possible (and frequent) absence of a double background in the most part of students. Mathematics or music deal with specific and universal languages and symbols, which however must be learnt through study and application, also in their joint use. During the work with mathematics and music, the main problem is given by the language.

11.2.4. *In mathematics*

"Why we should care about equations that have zero as the final result? Zero means *nothing*, and thus it does not make sense to take care about nothing. Equations giving zero are useless."

That was a hard question asked by a student who, by the way, had a strong background in the humanities. The difficulty was successfully overcome when the student understood that, if you have twenty dollars, you spend them and you have zero, this is not exactly the same thing as if you never had those twenty dollars. The same result can be obtained from different processes. The equation not only gives us a result, but it also explains the process to obtain it. Once the conceptual importance of the mathematical process was clarified, the student understood the role of equations to modeling reality.

11.2.5. *In mathematics and music*

Intuitively, while dealing with math *and* music, we deal with a double formalism. And the teacher has to make efforts to avoid jargon, especially with younger students. To say nothing about the stereotypes: "Does the coolness of mathematics kill the artistic inspiration?"

11.3. Techniques to Overcome Challenges: Case Studies

Each mind is different, thus teaching styles should be flexible. A pedagogical approach that is also *creative* may be more effective. In this sense, we may refer to *creative pedagogy* [1].

We will illustrate two simple case studies, where math and music help each other, and they enhance students' intuitive understanding of abstract ideas. The reader will find (open and creative) exercises at the end of each section.

Creative strategies

Why games and fun strategies are important? Let us see the following scheme:

- Game;
- Interest;
- Motivation to make the effort in learning;
- Approach to the abstract formalism;
- Need of simple and/or tangible models;
- (A new) Game.

11.3.1. *CubeHarmonic*

Here we have a simple game to help students approach combinatorics, group theory, music theory, mathematical music theory, aleatoric music, voice leading, composition, and musical creativity.

During my studies in 2013 at IRCAM and Université Pierre et Marie Curie, in Paris, I saw, among the other classes, some elements of combinatorics applied to music. One day the Rubik's cube came to my mind, as I had never been able to solve it. Why don't we... use that cube to make music? The Rubik's cube was invented by a professor to help his students to understand concepts of group theory. The main element was the understanding of the transformations. Professor Ernö Rubik was not (initially) thinking of a way to solve the cube, that later became one of the most sold toys in the world. People started solving the cube and yielding competitions

Fig. 11.1. The *CubeHarmonic* in version $4 \times 4 \times 4$.

of speed-solving. The cube is today also the object of theoretical studies, from mathematicians, of course, and also engineers, and artists [4, 28].

I called this game *CubeHarmonic*; see Fig. 11.1. It is currently under development as a physical device, with and without the use of software.[b] My idea of a musical version of the game is described in "Cool Math for Hot Music" [16, 23], under the name of *CubeHarmonic*, in the section about group theory and permutations. The original idea is the opposite of solving: it is about mixing. On each face, we have a harmonic sequence, some from classical music, another from ancient music (Landini cadence), and others from jazz. Each little piece contains a note; three (or four, in the case of $4 \times 4 \times 4$ cube) vertical notes give a chord, a sequence of three (or four) notes give a chord sequence (with 4-part harmony); in particular, a cadence for the chosen notes. By mixing the cube we mix the sequences and the chords.[c] Some effects will be more interesting, some others will not. Every musical transformation

[b]I developed a simple prototype using sound modules on each facet of the cube, and another prototype is currently under development in collaboration with the ICD (Interactive Content Design) group of Prof. Yoshifumi Kitamura at the Tohoku University in Sendai, Japan [13].

[c]Some prototypes of the cube, currently under development, use $2 \times 2 \times 2$ and $3 \times 3 \times 3$ cubes, with a single chord per face — and some doublings.

has a correspondence in a mathematical transformation, and *vice versa*. The game can be used by composers to find new chords and new melodies (it is sufficient to play melodically the notes). The game can also be used by mathematicians: a fun exercise would be finding the transformation after a sequence of operations, and comparing the final sound result with a given solution. If it sounds familiar the solution is correct. A mathematician can also try to formalize the necessary transformation that lead to interesting and enjoyable musical combinations, given some initial sequences. The game can also be used by children and high school students to experiment with some elementary voice leading, movements and transformations. And a game may constitute a *more fun way* to introduce abstract concepts, a step preceding the formalism. The *CubeHarmonic* can also be used to accompany the study that is already started. It may constitute a tangible way to explain abstract ideas, both in music, and in mathematics. What are the problems solved by the *CubeHarmonic*? First of all, the formalism. Both mathematical combinatorics and musical theory of chords and cadence involve a certain degree of delving into the formalism, and the problem of students' background here is relevant: math students may be confused by the musical part, and *vice versa*.

Moreover, the *CubeHarmonic* can be put inside the long tradition of musical combinatorics, for which we may refer to Riepel studies, the dice game by Mozart, slot-machine musical transformations, and in most recent times, Riemann studies on the tonnetz, attempts to apply combinatorics to the tonnetz, and aleatoric music [5, 19, 26, 32]. Finally, we should note that music can also be used to solve the cube in the Rubik's classical version: if we have the same sound corresponding to each color, also a blind person can enjoy the game.

11.3.1.1. *Cube: Exercise* 1

Build your own *CubeHarmonic*, writing the names of the notes of chord sequences of your choice on a Rubik's cube. Try to mix and enjoy the combinations you obtain. Can you draw "experimentally" some relations between the mathematical transformations, and the obtained chords and melodies?

11.3.1.2. *Cube: Exercise* 2

With the same experimental device of the Exercise 1, try to do the opposite: think about relations between chords and transformations, and try to prove them with the experiment.

11.3.2. *Pangolin*

Let us see now a compositional strategy that combines mathematics, music, and visual art. It can be thought as a game that achieves a first approximation to category theory [7, 8], as well as networks [11, 12], algorithms, pseudocodes, informatics, visual and musical transformations mediated by mathematics, interdisciplinary thinking, and general "skeleta" for different musical compositions.

The idea came from the image of the *pangolin*, see Fig. 11.2. The pangolin is one of the most trafficked endangered animals in the world due to its meat and armor. The armor is object of study of biologists and engineers [25, 31].

Here, the shape of the armor and the shape of the animal in his characteristic behavior of closing in a ball is object of artistic inspiration and scientific investigation.

Fig. 11.2. A pangolin. Drawing by Maria Mannone.

My idea started from the image of a pangolin closed in defensive position, see the bottom left of Fig. 11.3. How to "build" such a complex image with a sequence of simple steps, and how to make music from visuals? Let us start with a single scale of the armor. Via horizontal repetitions, we get a row of scales. Via vertical repetitions, we get a series of rows — that can be seen as rows and columns. Then, we shift the even rows. Then, we change the envelope to describe (in a simplified manner) the shape of the back of the animal, with an enlargement, followed by a restriction. Finally, we complete the image with a loop, see the left side of Fig. 11.3.

This simple sequence can be used, in a mathematical context, to describe a process of transformation: we have an initial object, that is transformed into other objects via a sequence of morphisms, the arrows. The composition of scales still gives scales (then the associative property is verified), and a 'no-change' on a scale still gives a scale (then the identity property is also verified). A similar sequence of instructions can be used to compose music, see the right side of Fig. 11.3. The musical rendition of a single scale (for example, a free interpretation of its upper contour as a melody) is repeated and transposed (vertical repetitions). Then, we shift the onset of the even voices, we change the loudness to render the change of envelope (an intuitive choice is a change in loudness, with a *crescendo* followed by a *diminuendo*), and finally, we have a loop, rendered, for example, by the repetition of some specific fragments. In the musical case, we have some objects (musical fragments) and arrows (morphisms between musical fragments). The (mathematical) composition of musical fragments still gives music, and the repetition of a musical fragment without any change still gives a musical fragment (verifying the identity). This scheme can be used to compose, to improvise, and to program: in fact, it can be seen as a pseudocode, easy to translate into a specific code syntax. From the point of view of category theory, we can connect visual and musical objects, via a sonification step by step. The sonification is represented by other arrows, and we get a commutative diagram with several elements. But we can also connect the visual *transformations* to the musical ones: it means, we can draw arrows between arrows. In this way, we can define a *functor*,

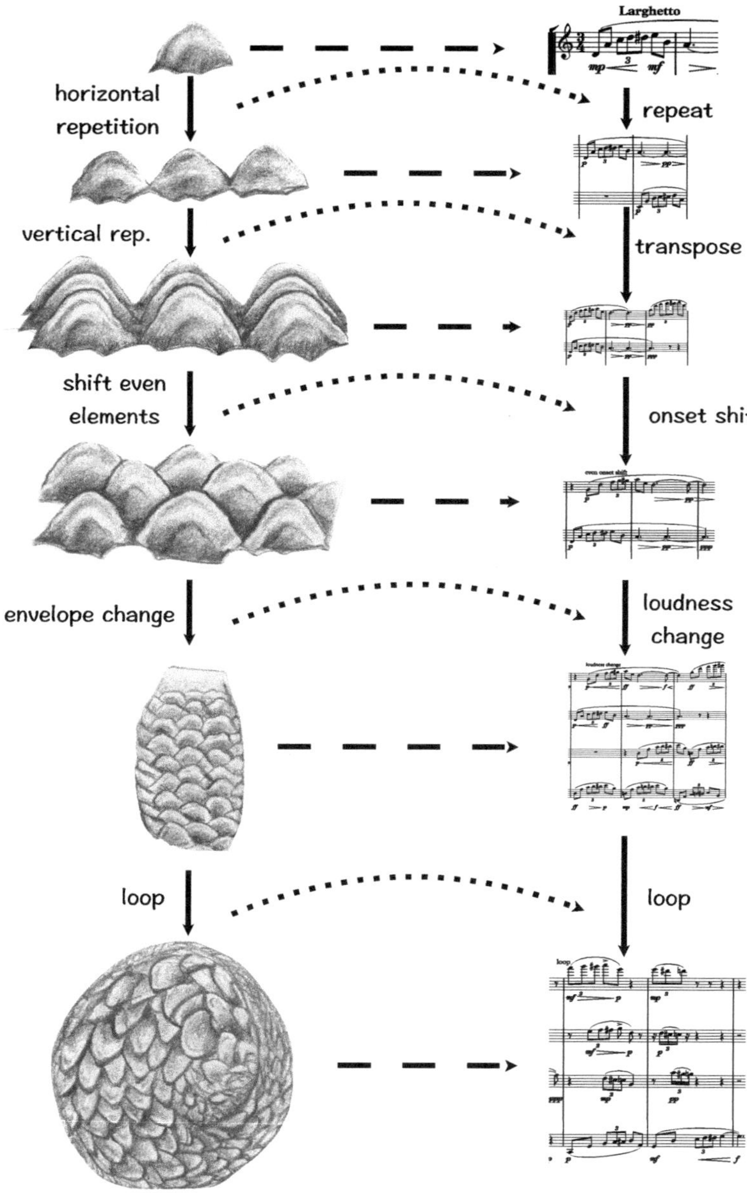

Fig. 11.3. Scheme for the musical rendition of the pangolin's armor. The functor, that we can call "sonification functor", brings objects from the category *images* into objects of the category *sounds* (dashed arrows), and it also brings morphisms from the first category into morphisms of the second category (dotted arrows).

the "sonification functor", that transfers objects of the category *image* into objects of the category *sounds*, and visual transformations into sound transformations. For example, the instruction "(visual) horizontal repetition" can be translated into "(musical) horizontal repetition", and so on. If we have another sonification functor, we can define *natural transformations* between the first and the second one. This pretty intuitive structure may constitute a tool to explain the first abstract concepts of category theory to the neophyte. At the same time, musical examples step by step help illustrate the ideas. For the math-proficient student, this scheme constitutes a help to understand musical transformations and compositional procedures. The scheme can also be used backward: how to break down, to simplify a complex shape, or a complex musical score, reducing it to some basic elements and a set of transformations acting on them.

Summarizing, we can use the *Pangolin Pseudocode* to solve problems related to: strategy for improvisation, strategy for composition, understanding of mathematical models, how to obtain a step sequence that can be transformed into a computer program, how to break complex visuals and problems into a sequence of simple steps. We can compose or improvise or compile computer programs starting from these structures. All the attempts will be different, *but* they will have something in common: the structure itself. The *musical pangolin*, in categorical terms, can be seen as the *colimit* of all these attempts.

On the mathematical side, the problems approached are: understanding the importance of mathematical category theory as a general model that can be not only investigated in its formal aspects, but also used as a conceptual paradigm to approach problems of different disciplines, and between disciplines [2, 3].

Finally, we can address interdisciplinary problems, such as the translation from image to sound and vice versa. This is the object of former studies about sonification [30]. I have been working with the musical rendition of tridimensional images, via a mapping of height, length, and width into pitch, loudness, and time — with an opportune choice of maximal and minimal values, and a choice of the level of discretization of the starting image [9]. Such a translation is more meaningful when you hear the piece and have an idea of the visual shape and vice versa. The most effective conversions verify what I called *gestural similarity* [10]. For example, a *staccato* in musical articulation is similar to a collection of points on canvas, because both, the staccato in music and the points in visual arts, are generated by a *similar gesture*. An analog argument works for *legato*, and so on. This topic can be investigated under the light not only of mathematical theory of musical gestures, but also with the help of cognitive sciences and neurosciences. In fact, studies about *crossmodal correspondences* highlight some universally shared effects, such as the *takete-maluma* experiment [18, 27], and the intuitive correspondence between, for example, an ascending melodic line and an upward movement in the tridimensional space, or a louder sound and a closer and bigger object [23, 24]. These visual-musical translations may also be thought in light of the theory of "indispensable attributes" for visual and auditory channels, with references to Gestalt [6]. In this way, we can create bridges between disciplines.

Developments of the model may involve the starting from the simple sequence described above, and the enrichment of the structure.

11.3.2.1. *Pangolin: Exercise* 1

The pangolin scheme can also be used to improvise. Watch and listen to an example of group improvised music with this structure, performed at the University of Minnesota: https://www.youtube.com/watch?v=TBfY3Tg9rUo. Have fun in improvising music upon a mathematical structure!

Here, also the initial melody was improvised, with the only constraint to have an "ascending & descending" short pitch sequence. It may not be a case that, for the pangolin armor, the "atomic" element is a *scale*, and for several musical structures, also a *scale*!

11.3.2.2. *Pangolin: Exercise* 2

Try to find another complex visual shape, and try to decompose it in simple parts. Then develop a method to "re-build" the initial, complex image via an algorithmic sequence of steps. In this way you will obtain a pseudocode, suitable both for programming, as well as for the skeleton of a musical composition.[d] And for music programming, of course!

11.4. Conclusion

We defined some motivational reasons to introduce students in the field of mathematical theory of music, and we presented two case studies with exercises. The ideal recipients of our analysis and creative approach would be students of the last two years of high school, and students at the beginning of their Bachelors degree. The ideal context would be seminars and laboratories, and the prerequisites would just be the school knowledge of music and mathematics.

These case studies can be a good starting point for math and music students: showing how to build an abstract model, general enough to be applied to different fields of music, and detailed enough to include essential elements. The equilibrium between simplification, generality, flexibility and details needs to be reached by performers, theorists, and it also helps mathematicians. Everything is finalized to improve art appreciation, creativity, as well as rational thinking. Similar strategies reveal their helpfulness in overcoming the immediate difficulty of the language, of the knowledge transmission, and of creative training in mathematical music theory, music theory, and mathematics itself. According to Patras [21, p. 129]:

"To keep mathematics alive, it is necessary that they can be easily communicated to beginners, in order for them to be able to make the change and to go further than their predecessors."[e]

And also:

"Those who are satisfied in transmitting to the public their results without communicating the capital of associated insights and eidetic

[d]In fact, a musical composition can arise from a mathematical composition of arrows.
[e]Translation by Maria Mannone.

references, do only half the job; in the same way, an artisan that keeps for himself or herself the job's secrets, would only have poor trainees. Communicating implicit strategies is the essential trait for a true mathematical education. It is also the condition to avoid the sclerotization of mathematics, or its fragmentation in neopythagorical schools, jealous of their specificity and their secrets."

These thoughts can be easily generalized to mathematical music theory, highlighting once more the importance of teaching techniques to help students in appreciating the beauty of science and art that work together [29], and in particular, to help them in *gaining pleasure from the study of the mathematical theory of music.*

Bibliography

[1] A. Aleinikov, Creative pedagogy, in *Encyclopedia of Creativity, Invention, Innovation, and Entrepreneurship* (Springer, New York, 2013), p. 327.
[2] C. Alunni, Diagrammes et catégories comme prolégomènes à la question: Qu'est-ce que s'orienter diagrammatiquement dans la pensée? in *Penser par le diagramme—de Gilles Deleuze à Gilles Châtelet*, ed. N. Bätt (Presse Universitaire de Vincennes, 2004).
[3] B. Coecke, Introducing categories to the practicing physicist, (2015), http://www.cs.ox.ac.uk/bob.coecke/Cats.pdf.
[4] A. Frey and D. Singmaster, *Handbook of the Cubik Math* (Onslow Publishers, 1982).
[5] J. Hook, Why are there twenty-nine tetrachords? A tutorial on combinatorics and enumeration in music theory, *Music Theory Online* **13**(4) (2007).
[6] M. Kubovy and M. Schutz, Audio–visual objects, *Rev. Philos. Psychology* **1**(1) (2010) 41–61.
[7] W. Lawvere and S. Schanuel, *Conceptual Mathematics: A First Introduction to Categories* (Cambridge University Press, 2011).
[8] S. Mac Lane, *Categories for the Working Mathematician* (Springer, 1978).
[9] M. Mannone, *Dalla Musica all'Immagine, dall'Immagine alla Musica — Relazioni matematiche fra composizione musicale e arte figurative (From Music to Images, from Images to Music — Mathematical Relations Between Musical Composition and Figurative Art)* (Compostampa, 2011).
[10] M. Mannone, Introduction to gestural similarity in music. An application of category theory to the orchestra, *J. Math. Music* (2018).
[11] M. Mannone, Networks of music and images, *Gli Spazi della Musica* **6**(2) (2017) 38–52.
[12] M. Mannone, Knots, music, and DNA, *J. Creative Music Sys.* **2**(2) (2018) 1–23.

[13] M. Mannone, E. Kitamura, J. Huang, R. Sugawara and Y. Kitamura. CubeHarmonic: A new interface from a magnetic 3D motion tracking system to music performance, *NIME Conference Proceedings* (2018).
[14] Z. Markovits, Beliefs hold by pre-school prospective teachers toward mathematics and its teaching, *Procedia Soc. Behav. Sci.* **11** (2011) 117–121.
[15] Z. Markovits and H. Forgasz, "Mathematics is like a lion": Elementary students' beliefs about mathematics, *Educ. Stud. Math.* **96** (2017) 49–64.
[16] G. Mazzola, M. Mannone and Y. Pang, *Cool Math for Hot Music* (Springer, 2016).
[17] V. Nabokov, *Strong Opinions* (Mc-Graw Hill, 1973).
[18] L. Nobile, Words in the mirror: Analysing the sensorimotor interface between phonetics and semantics in Italian, in *Iconicity in Language and Literature 10: Semblance and Signification*, eds. P. Michelucci, O. Fischer and C. Ljungberg (John Benjamins, Amsterdam/Philadelphia, 2013), pp. 101–131.
[19] C. Nolan, On musical space and combinatorics: Historical and conceptual perspectives in music theory, in *Proceedings of Bridges 2000: Mathematics, Music, Art, Architecture, Education, Culture*, ed. R. Sarhangi (Winfield, Kansas, 2000), pp. 201–208.
[20] P. Odifreddi, *Penna, pennello e bacchetta: le tre invidie del matematico* (Editori Laterza, 2005).
[21] F. Patras, *Il pensiero matematico contemporaneo* (Bollati Boringhieri, 2001).
[22] R. Polfreman and B. Oliver, Rubik's Cube, Music's Cube, in *NIME Conference Proceedings* (2017); M. Staff. How to play a Rubik's Cube like a piano (2015). https://ed.ted.com/lessons/group-theory-101-how-to-play-a-rubik-s-cube-like-a-piano-michael-staff.
[23] S. Roffler and R. Butler, Factors that influence the localization of sound in the vertical plane, *J. Acous. Soc. Amer.* **43** (1968) 1255–1259.
[24] C. Spence, Crossmodal correspondences: A tutorial review, *Atten. Percep. Psychophy.* **73** (2011) 971–995.
[25] T. Stankowich and L. Campbell, Living in the danger zone: Exposure to predators and the evolution of spines and body armor in mammals, *Evolution* **70**(7) (2016) 1501–1511.
[26] D. Tymoczko, The generalized Tonnetz, *J. Music Theory* **56**(1) (2012).
[27] D. Uznadze, Ein experimenteller Beitrag zum Problem der psychologischen Grundlagen der Namengebung (An experimental contribution to the problem of the psychological foundations of naming), *Psycho. Forsch.* **5**(1–2) (1924) 24–43.
[28] J. Weed, Sub-optimal multi-phase path planning: A method for solving Rubik's revenge preprint (2016), arXiv:1601.05744.
[29] F. Wilczek, *A Beautiful Question* (Penguin Books, 2016).
[30] I. Xenakis, *Formalized Music* (Pendragon, rev. edn. New York, 2001).
[31] W. Yang, I. Chen, B. Gludovatz, E. Zimmermann, R. Ritchie and M. Meyers, Natural flexible dermal armor, *Adv. Mater.* **25** (2013) 31–48.
[32] J. Zweig, Ars combinatoria, *Art J.* **56**(3) (2014) 20–29.

Index

E

F

G

H

I

J

L

M

N

O

P

T

U

V

W

X

Y

Z